TO PIEDMONT COMMUNITY LIBRARY.

BEST WISHES TO YOU NOW AND

ALWAYS

Peter Vachon

Journey For Freedom

The events described in this story are true. However, the names of the individuals involved have been changed to protect their privacy.

Library of Congress Cataloging-in-Publication Data
Copyright © 2010 by Peter Vodenka

Journey For Freedom: Defection From Communist Czechoslovakia

1. NON-FICTION, East Europe, Czechoslovakia, Czech Republic, Yugoslavia, Austria, Hungary, Defection, Immigration to America, Communism, STB, Political Prisoners, Political Persecutions, Forced Labor Camps, Russian Invasion to Czechoslovakia 1968, Family, Refugee Camp, Religion, Willys Jeep

2. HISTORY, Cold War, Communism, World War II, Czechoslovakia, Czech Republic, Eastern Europe, Family, Refugee, Legal Immigration, Communist Oppression, Red Terror, Secret Police, STB, Political Prisoners, Russian Invasion 1968, Harley Davidson, Willys Jeep, UNNRA, Uranium Mines, Government Health Care, European Castles

International Standard Book Number (ISBN) 978-1-61658-816-8

DISTRIBUTED EXCLUSIVELY WORLDWIDE BY:
Journey For Freedom
PO Box 1571
Rapid City, SD 57709-1571
www.journeyforfreedom.com

The publisher and distributor of this book, Journey For Freedom, PO Box 1571, Rapid City, SD 57709-1571 USA, wish to make clear that this book was published in the United States of America for consumption by Americans who, through tradition and under the protection of the US Constitution and the Bill of Rights, are guaranteed certain absolute rights to freedom of speech and the press, and all the benefits that such rights imply.

Edited by Deborah Stewart

Front page designed by Patty Vodenka-Reed and Peter Vodenka
*Cover picture for sale with or without writing. Please contact us for details.

Appendix A – "Escape" Copyright© by Patty Vodenka 1998 and Patty Vodenka-Reed 2010.

Acknowledgements

First and foremost, I would like to thank Debbie Stewart, who has been my friend, editor, and assistant throughout this project, for her tremendous morale support and the many hours she put into it. Her help, persistence, and dedication helped me stay focused and motivated. Her words, "The people in America need to hear your story," became part of my life, echoing through my mind, sometimes even in my sleep. Thank you Debbie for believing in this book before it was written, and even before I believed in it myself.

I would also like to thank the following people for their encouragement and input: Ray and Josephine Cowdery, Ray and Paula Meyer, Jeffrey Burnoski, Kevin Stewart and his children, and others who are not named.

A special thanks to my cousin, Jindruška Racková, her husband, Peter, and their daughters, Hana and Kamila. Their support, guidance, and ideas helped us tremendously in the very beginning of our new life. Their drive, courage, excitement, and accomplishments enabled me to piece together the last missing fragments of information necessary for our journey for freedom. Without them, the events of our defection could have had a totally different outcome.

Thanks to my wife Lída (Lilly) for believing in my dream, and to my children Patty and Peter for their encouragement and motivation along the path of life.

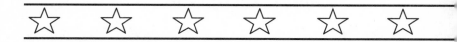

PETER VODENKA

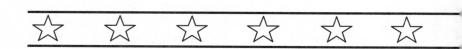

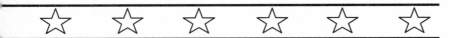

JOURNEY FOR FREEDOM

Defection from Communist Czechoslovakia

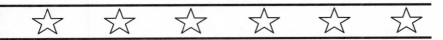

Day One   ====================
Day Two   ·····················
Day Three ◆◆◆◆◆◆◆◆◆◆◆◆◆◆◆◆◆◆◆◆◆◆
Day Four ─────────────────

0   80   160   320   Kilometers
├────────┼───────┼──────────────┤
0   50   100   200   Miles

In the west today, we see a free world that has achieved a level of prosperity and well-being, unprecedented in all human history. In the Communist world we see failure, technological backwardness, declining standards of health, even a need of the most basic kind - - too little food. After these four decades, there stands before the entire world, one great and unmistakable conclusion: freedom leads to prosperity - freedom replaces the hatred among the nations with comity and peace - freedom is the victor.

> *Ronald Regan June 12, 1987,*
> *In front of the Berlin wall.*

Contents

Dedication

I would like to dedicate this book in memory of my father, Stanislav Vodenka, the man who taught me right from wrong. If it wasn't for his influence in my life, our *journey for freedom* would have never happened. I did not get a chance to tell him how much I respected, admired, and appreciated him. I also never told him that I loved him, as it is not common in my country... Without his influence, I would never have found the strength, courage, and resources to accomplish what my family has done.

I miss you dad!

This book is also dedicated to my grandchildren, who are the main reason for writing it. I hope it will help them understand their roots, where their ancestors came from, who they were, the lives they lived, what their thoughts were, what their motivation was, and to understand the struggle they went through to live in a free country.

When I became an adult, I realized how little I knew about three of my grandparents, who passed away when I was a little boy. I knew only my dad's mother. When my brother and I asked her about our grandfather's life and his role in World War II, she always shrugged it off saying those were bad memories that she did not want to talk about. It was not until 50 years later, when government archives were open after the fall of Communism, that we learned what our grandfather had done and that he was an underground resistance hero.

My grandchildren are the first generation in my family born in America. This book should help them realize who their ancestors were and also help them see the beauty of Czech cities, villages, historical structures, and countryside, while helping them understand what their grandparents and parents accomplished, sacrificed, and risked for their freedom.

Only a few people have experienced that one single defining moment in their life, which changes everything forever! The instant when their whole life comes to one single point, when everything - including time - seems to stop. The outcome of that moment will change that person's life. Some of those fortunate or unfortunate, who were there, did not realize it until later - sometimes much later.

When that single moment came in my life, I knew it right then and there, as it validated everything I had worked and prepared for.

Author

To you my reader:

The first thing I would like to do is to thank you for holding this book in your hands right now. I hope that reading it will be a special and pleasant experience, and will help you to understand the difference between your homeland, America, and the rest of the world.

Secondly, I feel that it is important to explain myself. English is my second language, and while learning it, I realized it is a rather dry language, with not a lot of imagination. My native tongue on the other hand, is a lot more colorful and poetic, with many different ways to express feelings and emotions such as excitement, sadness, and such.

Therefore I have a favor to ask of you - as you read this book, please read it slowly, notice the location of commas, hyphens, exclamation points and so on. They are not necessarily grammatically correct for two reasons, one - I do not know English grammar that well, so I could not put them where they belong if my life depended on it, and two - I am trying to express the emotions and help you read this book the way my family lived, and experienced, the following story...

Thank you.

Peter Vodenka

Part I

Chapter One

IN THE LION'S DEN

He was running as fast as possible in total darkness. The rain was pouring down, but he was hardly aware of it. Every cell in his body was energized, and his senses were heightened to the max. His frightened two-year old son in his right arm began to cry.

"You cannot cry right now," he said in a gentle, stern voice. "Remember, we talked about this yesterday!" As if sensing the urgency, the boy immediately stopped crying.

Peter's mind began racing as he analyzed the dangers surrounding them. He tried to stay focused on his feet and a solid surface beneath them. The shadowy figure to the left with the powerful military flashlight was a soldier. He was running at a right angle in an attempt to cut them off. There were two more flickering spots of light on the track behind them and catching up quickly. Peter listened intently for sounds of his wife and four-year old daughter running behind him in the dark.

Suddenly, there was no ground under him and he was falling head first in the darkness of night, finally landing in the water. He scrambled to his feet and picked up his son, while feeling for the bag that was on his shoulder seconds ago. The strap had broken off, but the water was only knee deep and he retrieved the bag quickly.

He was scurrying up the steep hill on the other side as fast as he could, while calling to his wife, "Don't worry, the water is not deep, just get in."

He was half crawling and half running up the side of the soggy hill. He was prepared to yell, *hit the ground*, at the first sound of gunshots. Just a few more steps and they would be in the woods. He was sure the forest would be across the border where they would be safe!

The undergrowth was really thick, and he was pushing through it with his chest. Peter was blinded by the dark of the night, but the adrenaline rushing through his body forced him forward. He was breaking through branches and brush that seemed to be trying to hold him back. He glanced over his shoulder to see how close the lights were behind them. Shock surged through his body when he realized that the pursuers were in the woods.

With horror in his voice, he called to his wife whom he could not see, "They did not stop. *They are still chasing us!!* Throw everything away so we can move faster!" He dropped the bag in his left hand and pressed forward through the night.

Chapter Two

IN HIS THOUGHTS

It was a beautiful summer day with only an hour of daylight left. The sun was shining softly across the countryside, pleasantly painting it shades of yellow and orange. Peter and his horse were standing on a hill enjoying the peaceful, quiet evening atmosphere. The beauty surrounding them was breathtaking. White clouds were moving through the blue skies, forming shadows that floated across the land. The leaves were bright green and everything looked clean and fresh. The grass and fields were sprouting new life, and in the distance, he could see dark patches of pine forest lining the hills. The magnificent view brought tears to his eyes. He had always loved nature, but now - he felt like he was seeing everything for the first time. He tried to burn these images into his memory.

In only two weeks, his family would be leaving this place forever. He did not know what was in store for them, or what to expect. What would the future bring? He had always hoped and prayed for the best. His heart suddenly felt heavy. There were so many things he still had to take care of, and so many things to remember, before he could take his family into the unknown. The big day was approaching quickly, and he felt unprepared, even though he had been preparing for the last ten years. Ten years of praying! Ten years of wishing! Ten years of hoping! Ten years of planning and trying to devise an escape from their homeland to a foreign country - where they would be free from the overwhelming oppression of the Communist government. If the escape worked, there would be so much to gain. If it didn't work, there would be a high price to pay. His mind began to debate as many times before, whether the risks he was taking would be worth the gain.

If they were successful, a new life and a new beginning in a free country would be waiting for them, but what would happen if they failed? The wrath of their government would follow. The persecutions! Immediate imprisonment for both parents! Losing the children! Even if they *did* make it out of prison alive, the government would consider them traitors and unfit parents. All those consequences and more - would happen if they were captured. What if some of them were shot? What if they were killed trying to defect from the country in which they were born - the country where they had lived their entire lives? What would happen then? He shook his head trying to force those horrible thoughts out of his mind.

"Don't think about that," he told himself. He had gathered every piece of information and consumed all the available facts that should help them succeed. Peter knew that others had made it before them - however - there were also many who did not! Again he struggled to push those negative thoughts out of his mind.

*

He could not remember exactly when he had decided to defect from his homeland and travel to America. He knew in America the people were free. He was aware of the freedom of speech there! He was aware of the freedom of religion! He was aware of the freedom of political belief! His entire life had been spent living in a Communist country with none of those freedoms.

Peter and his friend, Marek, used to talk about defecting. Over the years they had many different crazy ideas. They could tie themselves to the bottom of the train while it crossed the border to West Germany, or try to cross the border on foot in the middle of the night. Maybe they could use a car and break through the gate at the border crossing. Of course, those were the impetuous ideas of young minds, and they knew none of them would work. Capture and imprisonment were certain, even death was possible. Still, they continued to dream, hope, and wish for freedom.

His thoughts went back to many years ago when he was eighteen. Peter and Marek were walking through Václavské Náměstí (Wenceslas Square), the main square in Prague, the picturesque capital of Czechoslovakia. As they were walking down the sidewalk, a Porsche Carrera with a West German license plate pulled over and parked along the curb in front of the International Hotel. The hotel was an oasis for foreign visitors, but forbidden territory for Czech people. A young man stepped out from behind the wheel, closed the door, and disappeared inside the fancy hotel.

They stopped and peered into the windows of the car. They admired its shape, elegant curves, big wide tires, and the overall sheer perfection of the vehicle. They looked at the car and back at the man and immediately knew the difference. The car was so much bigger and nicer than the cars in Czechoslovakia. All the cars they were used to seeing had been made locally in Czechoslovakia or some other Eastern European countries such as Russia, East Germany, Yugoslavia or Poland. The difference between Eastern European cars and the car in front of them was incredible. It was elegant and beautiful, so much different from anything they were used to seeing.

However, it wasn't only the car that impressed Peter - it was the young man himself. He was dressed in fine West German clothes, which only added to his authority. One could not buy clothes like that in Czechoslovakia, but the biggest difference was the way the man presented himself - the way he moved, the way he looked, the way he walked! He radiated self-confidence and seemed perfectly sure of himself.

Peter could clearly sense the difference between the man and themselves. They were always somewhat hunched over. Not physically - not in their bodies - but in their minds. They were always intimidated and constantly looking over their shoulder, waiting for the next blow to come, unsure of who was listening or watching them. And suddenly - he felt it in his heart... This was it - the breaking point - the final straw! At that moment, he somehow knew he would defect. He did not know how or when, but he would do it. This was the deciding factor. He wanted to be just like the man he saw getting out of the Porsche - free, self-confident and sure of himself - able to walk with his head held high, not needing to watch over his shoulder all the time. No fear of the future or the unknown. Peter became very excited, almost euphoric, and wanted to share his feelings with his friend.

He looked over at him and said, "This is it - I am out of here!!"

But the look in Marek's eyes made Peter realize, he did not have the courage to defect. Peter felt a jolt of panic when he understood he would have to do it alone. He forced himself to believe doing it alone would be for the best. The chance of the Communists finding out about the defection would be decreased by not discussing his plans with anyone - the fewer people that knew, the better his odds would be.

From that moment on, Peter kept his dreams, plans, and ideas to himself.

*

The mare snorted and shook her head, jarring Peter back to reality. He was twenty-seven years old now, was married and the father of two children. He took one more look around the beautiful countryside, while he patted his horse on the neck.

"Okay girl, let's go home," he whispered in a gentle voice. Their ride back to the stables was quiet, peaceful, and very picturesque in the dusk. He guided her into the stall and removed the saddle. Carefully he lifted each of her hooves to clean them, checking for possible problems. He wiped the sweat from her back, and after giving her water and hay, he said, "I'm going home. I'll see you in the morning." She was looking at him with sad eyes, as if she knew he was preparing to leave. His own eyes started to fill with tears...

Chapter Three

NELLY GRAY

His horse was almost like a family dog. When Peter and his wife, Lída, would take the children out for a walk, she walked along with them - not on a lead line but free - running back and forth, following them wherever they went. In the winter when it was too cold for riding, Peter would take her for slow walks across the countryside. There were times when she would get preoccupied chewing on grass or a tree branch, and he would jump behind a tree or in the ditch to hide from her. This was one of his favorite games. When she realized he was gone, she would start whinnying and run around frantically until she found him, then snorted softly while nudging him happily with her muzzle. The thought brought a smile to his face. The kids loved her, and she was always very careful around them. When his daughter, Patty, was little and played outside on the ground, the mare would playfully stick her nose and face in her toys. She was always very curious and wanted to be involved with the family. Often, she would pick up the toys with her mouth.

After his son, Peter, was born and they took him for walks, the mare would gently lower her head into the stroller, as if fascinated by the baby smell. Her head was bigger than the whole baby, but he was always very excited to see her. She would rub him with her muzzle, and little Peter would cup both hands on her face and giggle, often poking her in the eye or pulling her ears. This never seemed to bother her. Sometimes she would gently pull a sock off his foot with her lips and chew on it. It always amazed everyone how careful she was with the children. Those were images that Peter would never forget.

Owning a horse was very unusual in Czechoslovakia. It took most of a paycheck to provide food and clothing just for the family. Since World War II, more and more tractors were being built and horses were becoming obsolete. There was really no need for them, except every corporate farm had one team of horses used only in areas too steep or too rugged for tractors. Horses were also being used in the forest by loggers. The horses pulled trees to the roadside where workers would load them onto trucks.

Every since he was a little boy, Peter always wanted a horse and dreamed of being a cowboy. He read many books about cowboys and the history of the American Wild West when he was growing up. He learned about the gunfighters and the horsemen. Personalities like Wild Bill Hickok, Buffalo Bill, General Custer, Bat Masterson, Wyatt Earp, Jessie James, and Billy the Kid fascinated him. His father played the guitar and sang nostalgic songs about the great open plains - songs about the Rocky Mountains and the Black Hills, the Great Lakes and valleys, Niagara Falls and the Red Woods. Those songs were filled with stories about cowboys and Indians, cattle, prairies, and campfires.

Since it was Peter's dream to become a cowboy, owning a horse was an essential part of his plan. He was born and raised in a small town approximately 15 miles south of Prague and lived in an apartment building. That made it impossible as there was no place to keep or provide for a horse.

As he grew older, Peter learned about the shortage of employees working on the government farms called JZD,[*] Jednotné Zemědělské Družstvo (Unified Cooperative Farm). Times were changing and younger people born in villages did not want this type of life. They wanted to have easier jobs and more spare time. They were migrating into towns to work in factories or office buildings, where they did not have to get up at 2:00 A.M. to milk the cows. They also didn't want to work

---

[*] JDZ was structured after Russian collective farms. Farmers were forced to surrender their land, farm buildings, livestock, equipment, and machinery, to the Communist government.

the afternoon shift until 10:00 at night or on the weekends.

As older people were retiring and younger people were moving away, the government farms were increasingly short of workers. Because of this, the government bureaucrats increased the pay, lowered income taxes, and loaned small sections of land to employees to raise food. Some villagers raised rabbits, chickens, ducks, and geese. Some of them even raised a pig or cow for their own use. If they worked for the government farms, they could use a small section of land to raise grains or grass for hay. In addition to their wages, they received a portion of the harvest in the fall. This meant that once a year they would get a couple bags of potatoes and some grains free. The government also started to build six-plex apartment buildings in villages for people that were not born there or didn't have homes. This was another way to attract people to farm work.

Peter saw this as an opportunity to have a horse and better wages than he was making as a plumber. He found a job on a government owned corporate farm in picturesque Southern Bohemia. Peter and his family moved to the small village of Litochovice, where they lived for about a year.

He was living the country life, milking cows, and working with cattle and pigs. However, it was not like his vision of life in America. Livestock was kept in the barns chained to the troughs, fed and milked in the same place. The animals needed to be taken care of twice a day which was demanding work, but the locals were used to this type of work as it was the only life and opportunity they had ever known.

*

While Peter worked on the farm and lived in Litochovice, his family traveled by bus to see their relatives since gasoline for the car was very expensive. The trip was difficult with small children, a stroller, carriage, and other essentials. Going home required switching buses four times and took four to five hours. This was hard on the children and very uncomfortable for all of them. After about a year, they decided to move closer to their hometown and their families.

They moved to another town in Southern Bohemia called Hrejkovice. Peter started working for another corporate farm and immediately began asking if there was a place to keep a horse. His employer showed him an old building where he could keep it. It was an ancient vacant building that had been used for horses or cattle before the Communists confiscated it. Now the building was owned by his employer, a government corporate farm. On one side of the building was a pile of artificial pig food, used for the barn next door. Peter didn't know what the food was made of, but he later learned it was ground up bones and animal body parts, mixed with chemicals and proteins. The smell was very strong and rancid, lingering throughout the entire building. He knew that horses did not like strong smells and were usually spooked by them.

People laughed and thought Peter was a little eccentric. Why would he want to have a horse? Horses were not common in Czechoslovakia. They were expensive and a lot of work to care for, but he was determined to have a horse and eventually found a young two-year old mare. The mare was born the same month and year as his daughter, which made his desire to own her even stronger.

After much preparation, the day finally came for Peter to get his horse. He purchased her and took her to the old building where she would be stabled. As he had suspected, she was petrified by the horrible smell of the pig food. She would not enter the building. Peter spent an entire hour trying to get her in the barn. She became more and more nervous and finally broke the leather strap he was holding her with and ran away. Peter was scared because the village was surrounded by forest, and if she ran in there he might not be able to find her. Eventually, she calmed down and let him catch her, but still refused to enter the building.

Peter felt helpless and soon had to leave to go to work. Fortunately, his brother who knew that Peter was getting the horse on that day, arrived. Peter asked him to hold the horse while he went to get a burlap bag. They put the bag on the horse's head so she could not see, turned her around and with one on each side, backed her into the building. Once inside, she calmed down some, but was still nervous. Peter was afraid that she might get injured so he decided to sleep in the barn. That night, he brought his sleeping bag and made a comfortable bed on top of the hay. He did not sleep much since the winter wind was blowing snow into the building, but it did not matter to him. His dream had come true. He was very happy to have his horse. He received grain from the government farm to feed her, but it was not enough. He taught himself to use a scythe to cut the grass in ditches, dry it, and use it for hay in the winters.

He knew he would have to give this beautiful mare the perfect American name. She had a name - a Czech name - but if he was going to live his American dream, she had to have an American one. His mind drifted back to when he was younger and his dad used to sing a song about a girl named Nelly Gray. Peter didn't know what it meant, but the sound of the name soothed him. He knew from reading books that most horses in America had two names, and Nelly Gray sounded good.

Then it was time to find some riding gear. He began asking everyone if they knew someone who had the right equipment. Eventually, he was told about an elderly couple who had an old military saddle in their attic. He approached them and asked if they would sell the saddle. They agreed and sold it to him for 200 Korunas (approximately 15 hours of work for Peter). He took the saddle apart and rebuilt it to look more like the saddles he had seen in the western movies. He lowered the stirrups and found a different bit. He found leather to make chaps and an old factory felt hat that he reshaped to resemble a cowboy hat. People in the village thought he was crazy and sarcastically called him 'cowboy', but it didn't bother him. He was used to being considered strange.

Nelly Gray had never been ridden before, and Peter did not know how to break a horse, but followed his instincts. Peter and Nelly Gray were learning together and from each other. After studying the western style of riding that he had seen in western movies such as The Electric Horseman, Professionals, Magnificent Seven, MacKenna's Gold, and others, he began teaching Nelly Gray to ride that way. They formed a strong connection and a very special bond. Soon, he could ride her bareback with no bridle and bit. She would respond to his thoughts and turn, trot, gallop, or stop as he wished. While they were walking through the countryside, he could just raise his arm or call her name and she would immediately run to him.

One day in early spring while they were galloping on a sloped meadow, they hit a frozen patch. Her legs shot out from under her, causing her to fall on her side, throwing Peter from the saddle. He landed on his stomach and due to the high speed kept sliding forward. He turned his head to see where she was, and to his surprise, her head was right next to his. They were sliding at exactly the same speed side by side, looking into each other's eyes. That struck Peter as being funny and he started laughing, remaining on the ground even after she had gotten up. Nelly Gray came to him nudging him with her nose, snorting softly as if asking if he was okay.

A different incident did not end as well. They were riding on a hot summer day and Peter took his tee-shirt off. As they were in a full gallop on a dirt road, the saddle strap broke. Peter fell on his back with his feet straight in the air, sliding that way for a while. He was hurt - he had pain in his chest and started coughing blood. He rolled onto his hands and knees, unable to get up for a while. Once again she came to him nudging him with her nose. Peter grabbed her neck and she helped him stand up. Luckily, he had a piece of rope in the saddle bag which he used to strap the saddle on her, since he was in too much pain to carry it! They slowly walked home.

Lída took Peter to the doctor. The X-ray showed nothing was wrong with his lungs, but the nurse had to use a sponge soaked with iodine to scrub mud made from a mixture of blood, dirt, and pebbles from his bleeding back. It felt like she was using a wire brush, while pressing with all her strength! It was a lengthy procedure, but it could have been worse.

Chapter Four

SECRET THOUGHTS

Peter walked in the dark to their apartment building, about 300 yards from where the horse was stabled. He put the riding gear in the basement storage room and walked up the steps to the first floor apartment. His wife had just put the kids to bed, so he went to the children's room to read them a good night story.

After eating dinner, Peter and Lída moved into the living room and lowered their voices. They needed to discuss the upcoming defection. They had to be very careful not to talk in the kitchen, because the apartments on all three floors were connected with one common exhaust vent pipe. The pipe ran through each apartment and out the roof, making private conversation difficult. Voices carried easily and could be heard through it. They could not take the risk of anyone overhearing their plans, which would mean disaster - no one could suspect anything.

"We can't do anything unusual that would raise suspicion from the neighbors or my employer," he said. "Everything has to look like we are leaving for a regular family vacation. Everyone knows we are going camping for two weeks at the Adriatic Sea. It has to appear just like that."

No one could know they were trying to defect. They did not tell their children anything either, because they were too young as Patty was four and Peter was two. They also didn't want the children to accidentally say something in front of their friends. There was no doubt, if those friends told their parents, someone would notify the police.

They would need as much cash as possible for the trip, but they could not do anything out of the ordinary. If they did something unusual like sell furniture or personal possessions, people would become suspicious. People in Czechoslovakia did not sell personal belongings because it was too hard to acquire them in the first place. It was common for young people to have furniture that was given to them by their parents. Once an apartment or house had furnishings, they lived with those things their entire life and passed them to the next generation. If they would have changed any of their daily routines, it would have raised doubts and people would gossip. During these times in Czechoslovakia, everyone was busy watching everybody else. People always had their noses in another person's business. As such, the villagers were all aware that Peter and his family were traveling to Yugoslavia for vacation.

Yugoslavia was also a Communist country, but the people there managed to keep a little more freedom than in other Eastern European countries. Marshall Tito, the World War II General who became the President of Yugoslavia, never succumbed to the Russians as much as rulers of other Communists countries. Marshall Tito did not let Russians completely control Yugoslavia and tell them what to do. Due to keeping some small freedoms, Yugoslavia's borders were not as closely watched as other Eastern European borders. The borders of Yugoslavia with Austria to the north and Italy to the west were easier to penetrate than other borders between the east and west. Those other borders were constructed of high voltage electrical fences, lines of guards in watch towers equipped with machine guns, and minefields. Some people in Communist countries figured this out, and began defecting through Yugoslavia to Austria or Italy.

*

Most people in Europe preferred to take long summer vacations. They would save all their vacation, taking two or three weeks off at a time. Since Yugoslavia was along the shore of the Adriatic Sea, many people spent their vacations there. Soon the Communist governments noticed an increase in people defecting through Yugoslavia to western countries and started adding more restrictions.

People from Eastern European countries could not travel to Western European countries because the government would not allow it. They could however, travel to other Eastern European countries, but even that was not simple. First, they had to have a passport. Before they could travel, they had to apply for the permit to go to their chosen destination in a designated time frame. Once they were permitted to go, the government issued a small piece of paper that was stapled inside the traveler's passport. That piece of paper stated, 'The named person with said birth date is allowed to travel to the specified destination in the designated time frame of four weeks.' That paper was not required to let foreigners *enter* the country, it was only required by the Czechoslovakian government to allow their citizens to *leave* Czechoslovakia for a short period of time.

Communists were also putting a lot more pressure on the Yugoslavian government to watch their borders closer to help prevent defections. One of the precautions they implemented was to deny an entire family permission to travel to Yugoslavia. Sometimes, the government would issue permits for a family, but they would leave one family member out. This was the way the Communists made sure people were not going to defect. Parents of course, would not defect leaving a child behind!

Communists also created a different color passport for Yugoslavia. Citizens in Czechoslovakia applying for a passport to travel received a green colored passport. Peter still had a green colored passport from when he traveled to Bulgaria with a youth group before he was married. His wife had traveled to

East Germany with her family in the past and was also in possession of a green passport. The passports were issued by the Czechoslovakian government, but the text was written in more than one language. If this passport did not have the above mentioned paper stapled to it, Czechs would not be allowed to leave their country. On a few occasions however, Yugoslavians *would allow* Czechs to cross the borders if they presented the green passports. The Czechoslovakian government wanted to stop that possibility, so they created grey passports which were used strictly for travel to Yugoslavia. A grey passport was not good for anywhere else. It was a meaningless piece of paper to be recognized only by the Yugoslavians. Yugoslavian border guards knew they were not allowed to let anyone with the grey colored Czechoslovakian passports travel into Austria or Italy.

Chapter Five

PREPARATIONS

Peter made the decision to defect in the summer of 1983. The first step was to apply for permits to travel to Yugoslavia. He picked up the paperwork and application forms in the county town of Písek, late in the winter on 1982. The deadline for the paperwork was February 15, 1983. If they missed the deadline, they would have to re-apply again the next year. The application had to be approved by the police, local government authorities, county government, the military, and from Peter's employer. That was how his employer and the people in the village found out they were planning to go to Yugoslavia for vacation.

All the paperwork was submitted and after a long waiting period, the papers arrived from the county. Peter was in the barn when the mail was delivered. Lída's hands were shaking as she opened the envelope and began to read the names. All four of them were listed. She was very happy and ran to the barn to tell Peter, arriving out of breath.

"We have all been approved," Lída announced with excitement, while gasping for air.

"Who is approved for what?" he asked, not understanding what she was talking about.

"All of us are approved to travel to Yugoslavia!" she said with a happy smile. That was the biggest and most critical part of the defection! If one person would have been left out, all hopes of defecting would disappear.

Peter and Lída knew the only things they could take with them had to fit in their small Russian Lada car. If they were successful and found a way to cross the border, it would take approximately two or three weeks before the government would seal their apartment. Peter had two weeks of vacation, so if they did not come back in that amount of time, it would probably take a few more days before his employer would become suspicious. His employer would then report to the police that Peter's family had not returned from their vacation, and the police would seal the apartment so no one could enter it as it would be classified a crime scene.

*

His family owned some personal things such as photos, family memorabilia, and books that were dear to them. They also had some items in their apartment that were not theirs. The clothes washer they used was given to them by Lída's parents. They had some furniture which was paid for, but there was an outstanding loan on the bedroom set. These things were very hard to come by in Czechoslovakia, since everything was very expensive.

Peter believed they should try crossing the Yugoslavian border as soon as possible, once their 'vacation' had started. He knew the sooner they defected, the more time there would be before the police showed up at their apartment to seal it. They wanted to make a phone call back to Czechoslovakia and let a family member know, after they had successfully defected. That would allow Peter and Lída's family enough time to go to the apartment, remove dishes, pictures, clothing, and things that were easy to carry. Peter knew all calls from foreign countries went through the central telephone station in Prague and were being recorded. Therefore, if he told his family that they had defected, the Státní Tajná Bespečnost, 'STB'[*] (National Secret Security - Communist government secret police) would hear about the defection and prevent their families from removing any possessions. Peter was trying to

---

[*] For more information about the STB see Appendix C in the back of the book.

figure out a way to let their families know about the defection without their government finding out.

There were many things that were very special and dear to both of them, but the more they thought about it, the more they realized they could not take anything unusual. Not only were they worried that the neighbors might see them loading items not essential for camping in the car, but they would also be crossing first the Czechoslovak-Hungarian border and then the Hungary-Yugoslavian border - all Communist countries. The family could not have anything in the car that might catch the border guard's attention, provoking them to search the car. However, they still needed to have enough gear and supplies for two weeks of camping. They did not know if they would make it across the border, but if they did not find the way in two weeks, they would have to return home as if coming back from a regular vacation.

Peter and Lída told their families they were going on vacation to Lake Balaton in Hungary, which was a well known tourist attraction and many people spent their summers there. They made the decision not to tell their families they were going to Yugoslavia, because they would be interrogated if Peter's plan of escape was successful. It was punishable by law to have knowledge of a defection and not report it. If the government suspected any family member knew about it and did not turn them in, they would be persecuted for assisting the crime. Avoiding the truth was the only way to protect the family from the danger of slipping during interrogations. If they did not know - they would not have to lie.

*

Peter's family owned a small cabin not far from the village of Hrejkovice. It was a basic one room wooden shack with no electricity or running water. The cabin was nestled on the cliffs overlooking the Vltava River and was very romantic and special to Peter. The top of the cliffs was 150 feet above the water and was crowned with pine trees. There were no roads leading there, only two tracks made by the family's car.

There were no other cabins around, and to Peter, this was the most beautiful place in the world. Summer vacations spent there were the best times of his life.

The river was used for taking baths, brushing teeth, and washing clothes. Every morning after Peter woke up, he would run down the little goat path to the river, brush his teeth and swim before going back up to eat breakfast. There was no electricity for the radios or TVs and no newspapers with Communist lies and propaganda, making it a perfect place to escape from it all. In the evenings they would light a campfire in front of the cabin, where Peter's dad played the guitar and sang nostalgic songs about far away exotic lands, long trails, and the American West.

There was a good possibility that the Communists didn't know about this place. Peter decided that it would be the safest place to hide the possessions they wanted to keep from falling into government hands, such as family photo albums, books, pictures, and some other small personal things dear to their hearts. Two weeks before they were supposed to leave for vacation, Peter began taking small things from the house to his car. This was usually done after dark. He was doing it in small increments, taking only things that would fit under his coat. That way if the neighbors happened to be looking out the window - and some always were - they would not see him carrying anything. He then moved these items to the cabin, hiding them under the bed.

*

Government regulations stated how much money people could carry across the border. Peter knew they would also need Hungarian and Yugoslavian currency. They had the permit to go to Yugoslavia, traveling through Hungary to get there. The main bank in the capital city of Prague was the only place that would exchange money. The family was allowed to exchange only enough cash to purchase gas and supplies while driving through Hungary. The Communists placed restrictions on the amount of money a family of four could possess for each day of vacation. Peter had to bring all their necessary documents, permits, stamps, and the approval letters from his employer, county, and city, to show they were approved for the money to be exchanged by the bank. Then, after two grueling hours in the bank, he had Hungarian and Yugoslavian money in his pocket.

The bank was also selling Yugoslavian gasoline stamps, which were needed to purchase gas. These stamps were needed since the government of Yugoslavia was rationing gasoline for their own citizens as well as visitors. People could not buy gas with money - they had to use gasoline stamps instead. Each stamp was worth ten liters (approximately 2½ gallons), with a limited maximum amount allowed to be purchased. Once the monthly quota of gas stamps was used, citizens would have to wait until the following month to purchase more.

They were planning to take more Czechoslovakian money

(Korunas) than they were allowed. Peter was the third owner of a 1943 Harley Davidson, which he decided to sell before they left for vacation. He sold it to a gentleman in Písek, a county town in Southern Bohemia, for 7,000 Korunas, which was the same amount he paid for it 10 years earlier. It was also the same amount that the other two owners had paid for the Harley.

Peter also decided it would be necessary to take personal documents, such as their marriage license, vaccination records, birth certificates, journeyman license, and some other personal and legal paperwork. Normally, people would not take these documents on vacation, as they were usually stored in a safe place at home. If these documents were found in the car, the authorities would immediately become suspicious and do a more detailed search of their belongings. He knew he would have to conceal the money and papers, but did not know where yet. However, there were still a few days left to figure out where to hide them.

Peter knew if they defected, they would never be able to return to their place of birth. Their government would mark them as political criminals and treat them as such. If they tried to come back, they would be arrested and sent to prison. It was rumored among the Czech population, that there was an automatic ten year sentence in a hard labor prison for political criminals. Prisons were broken down into three levels, which were classified as light, medium, and hard. The hard level housed the worst criminals - psychopaths and murders - but also priests, political criminals, and others who spoke out against the government. It was widely known through the country that if citizens became political criminals, their children would be taken away. The government believed a political criminal was not a fit parent, because he would not raise his children in the proper Socialist and Communist ideology!

*

The last few days before their 'vacation', Peter and Lída went back to their hometowns to say goodbye to family and friends. They had told everyone they were going on vacation to Lake Balaton and just stopped by to see them before they left. However, they knew they could be seeing their loved ones for the last time, but of course, could not let them know. Saying their goodbyes was very emotional and difficult.

When they went to Peter's dad's work for the last time, his father came out to the car to see the children. Peter was very close to his dad and this was the most difficult goodbye he had to say. It was not easy to stay composed and keep his emotions under control. When they got in the car and started driving away, his dad sat down on the small retaining wall in front of the building. He leaned forward and rested his elbows on his knees, a typical position for him. Peter drove to the back of the parking lot, turned around, and drove by him once more. They waved at each other. Peter had tears in his eyes, knowing that he may never see his dad again.

It was a beautiful sunny summer day - and it *would be* the last time he saw his father alive. Peter's dad passed away five years later in 1988, and since the Communist regime was still in complete control, Peter could not go back to Czechoslovakia for his funeral. His dad had lived the last 41 years of his life under Communist oppression, and hated watching what they did to the people and their country. Sadly, he died one year before the end of the Communist rule. Peter is still saddened by the fact that his dad did not live long enough, to see the miracle of the end of Communism in Czechoslovakia in November of 1989.

Chapter Six

FINAL DETAILS

The last few days before their departure were filled with feverish, hidden activity. Many things needed to be done and resolved. Extra money, personal documents, and the maps of Austria and America had to be hidden in the car. If their car was searched and the map of Austria was found, it would be a dead-give-away. They were not allowed to go to Austria. They were only approved to travel to Yugoslavia, so there was no reason for them to own a map of Austria, but Peter felt he had to have it. It was not easy to find a map of Austria since Communists outlawed all maps after World War II, and for some time, it was illegal to own any map, even a map of the country they lived in. Later, some maps became available, but not maps of Western European countries.

Peter had been thinking long and hard about where to conceal the compromising materials in the car, since there was a good possibility it would be searched. He thought about placing the documents in plastic to protect them, than insert them into the tire on the rim. After giving this some thought, he dismissed the idea, realizing it would be a difficult task to take the tire off its rim while traveling. He eventually decided to hide the paperwork in the trunk underneath the spare tire. If the car was searched the border guards would find it, but if they only looked through the inside of the car, they would not see it. Peter was hoping since they would be traveling with two small children, the guards would not do too much searching.

He was still pondering how to let their relatives know if

their defection was successful. Eventually, they decided to write a letter and leave it on the coffee table in the living room of their apartment. The note said, "We are not coming back. We defected and will live in America. Take anything you want from the apartment before the authorities seal it. We will miss you very much, but this is something we have to do!" While saying goodbye to their families, they had left the keys with them, "In case you need them," they said.

If they made it across the border into Austria, they planned to call home to tell their relatives to go into their apartment, knowing they would find the letter on the coffee table. Since everything was so expensive and hard to come by, they thought that their families could use their belongings instead of the Communists getting them for free.

Lída had some plants in the apartment and did not have the heart to let them die. Before leaving, she placed all of them in the bathtub. The front door to the apartment led into a small hallway, which had doors leading to the kitchen, bathroom, living room, and a bedroom. Each door had a separate lock and key. Peter made sure all the doors were locked, except the one leading into the bathroom.

Lída asked the neighbor lady to water the plants while they were on vacation.

"All the plants are in the bathtub. You do not need to go anywhere else in the apartment," she told her.

The lady assured her that she would take care of the plants. That almost proved to be a fatal mistake! Shortly after they left on vacation, the neighbor went into their apartment and started snooping around.

They had given her the key to the front door, but not to any of the inside doors. While the neighbor was in the apartment, she decided to try keys from her own apartment on the locked doors. Not surprisingly, they opened Peter and Lída's doors as well! Eventually, she ended up in the living room and found the letter Peter and Lída had written for their relatives. Now she had information that nobody else in the village possessed, and that made her feel very important! She began telling people in the village, her friends, and co-workers,

"Don't tell this to anyone, but Vodenka's defected."

The news of their defection was spreading throughout the village like wildfire and very soon everybody knew. The management of the company Peter was working for also found out. They called the authorities and reported them as defectors.

...the wheels of justice in the so-called 'people's democratic government' were put in motion...

Chapter Seven

LAST DAY AT HOME

Something had to be done with Nelly Gray. Peter had built a small corral in the forest close to their cabin. He asked his mom, Jarka, to take time off and take care of Nelly Gray at the cabin while they were on vacation. She agreed. Peter and Lída decided to spend their last night there, instead of the apartment. This would allow them to spend more time with his mom as they might never see her again!

Lída and the children drove the car to the cabin in the afternoon of the last day in their homeland. After they left, Peter went over all the last minute details one more time, making sure he had not forgotten or missed anything. He was still moving and preparing some things around the apartment, so the relatives could easily remove them. There was a nice crystal chandelier hanging in the living room. Peter took it down and laid it on the coffee table, so it could be easily carried away. He knew that when the relatives came to the apartment there would be only limited time to take as much as they could.

It was almost dark when Peter took his saddle and went to the stables to get Nelly Gray. The horseback ride to the cabin normally took over an hour. Peter knew the trail like the back of his hand, as he had ridden his horse there many times before. He knew all the unpaved service roads going through the forests and fields, and the two track trails made by service vehicles. Some were almost invisible and rarely used. He was also aware of the deer trails that wound through the trees.

It was twilight when he led his horse out of the stables, which was on the edge of the village just like their apartment. Peter crossed the county road in front of the apartment building they lived in. He guided Nelly Gray on the dirt path leading up the hill, through the fields, and into the dark line of the pine wood forest. Half way between the village and the woods stood a small steel cross. These types of crosses were often found in unexpected places, erected in the past by people as a symbol of thanks for a newborn child, in memory of a loved one, or as a sign of gratitude. Many of them were over a hundred-years old, some made of steel, others of stone. Peter halted Nelly Gray beside the cross and prayed to God. It wasn't the first time he had prayed here, asking God for help and guidance: "Please watch over my family, protect and keep us safe as we defect to start our new life in America!"

The trail went through the forests, fields and meadows, across the countryside he cherished and on the horse he loved. The feelings of being on the horse and riding like a cowboy were very special to him - after all - it was his lifelong dream. He knew this was his last time riding Nelly Gray to the cabin. It was a very emotional experience. All the countryside around him, every step his horse took - her every breath - was felt more intensely. His chest was heavy with emotions and his heart was aching. He had fulfilled his dream of owning a horse and riding her through the open country. This was no doubt the last time he would make this journey. Life was always in fast motion and he was always in a hurry, but not tonight - tonight he was going to take his time! Peter rode to the point where the trail entered the forest and stopped Nelly Gray. He turned her around to gaze back at the village, their home for the last two years. It was too dark to see it now, but he knew what it looked like - the white homes with red clay roofs surrounded by green fields - a creek winding gracefully through the center - and a small lake to the west. Emotions were rising inside of him, causing a hardening in his throat. For so many years, he had dreamed about leaving his country to start a new life, but now his heart was breaking! Why..? It wasn't the countryside or their families they were planning to leave behind, it was the oppressive Communist government they needed to escape.

He felt a warm evening breeze brushing gently across his face. He could feel the heat radiating from the fields where the sun had been shining earlier on the new crops. Peter took a few deep breaths through his nose, to inhale the light, pleasantly clean smell. He loved the changes in temperature and weather - each change brought new smells and different emotions.

He reluctantly turned Nelly Gray around, and drifted into the darkness of the woods. The forest was cooler with a pleasant smell of pine and sap. The air seemed somewhat cleaner and fresher than it was in the field. It was completely dark now, and the forest was pitch-black. As he gazed up into the trees, he could see the stars shining brightly in the sky. They were walking lazily through the timber, as he watched the moon rise higher into the skies, illuminating the trees. Peter was suddenly aware of the silver strips of moonlight casting shadows of trees, his horse, and himself across the forest floor. The frogs were loudly singing their love songs in the nearby swamp. As Peter and his horse approached, the frogs settled into silence as if watching their every move. Once they passed by, the frogs resumed their songs.

Peter loosened the reigns around Nelly Gray's neck. She knew these woods as well as he did and could function better than him in the darkness of the night. His thoughts flashed back to the first time he rode her in the dark. He was trying to control and guide her along the safest path, but soon realized, she could see better and move safer than he could. He had released control of the reigns and let her guide him home safely. She always knew their destination as if reading his mind. They had a strong bond. His heart suddenly felt heavy and his breathing became labored as he realized - this would be the last time!

Once again, he was aware of the changes in temperature and smell, as they approached the end of the forest. The green grass and blooming flowers covered the field in front of them. The trail leading through the fields to the village of Jickovice in the distance appeared silver and was shining in the moonlight.

The village was a small, quiet, and simple picturesque

Czech community, somewhat behind in time. Peter loved this place. It brought back pleasant memories of his childhood, growing up at their cabin, and the memories of carefree summers spent out of school. It had always been his dream to ride a horse through this village and for the last two years - he had been able to live that dream.

Nelly Gray carefully found her way to an old, narrow, winding road that led through the village. This road continued downhill to the first house. There was an old metal sign with the village name. Peter remembered how happy he was when he rode Nelly Gray through there for the first time. He snapped the sign with his reigns in excitement as he passed by. That startled Nelly Gray and she jumped sideways, almost throwing Peter out of the saddle. From then on, anytime they approached this sign, she would take large steps to the left to avoid going near it. As they strode by, the memory of this brought a boyish smile to his face.

The village was colorful with wooden boxes of flowers hanging outside the windows. There was only one street light in the center of the village and all the windows were dark. People were asleep since most of them in this region worked on farms and had to be up early to tend the animals. The entire village was lifeless and silent, except for the steady clomp of Nelly Gray's hooves on the road. The road had some sharp turns that came very close to the houses. Large mirrors were installed on the opposite corners of the road so drivers could see oncoming traffic. At the lowest point in the middle of the village was a large pond with a creek running through it, forcing the road to turn sharply to the left. When Peter was a young child, he was always afraid that the brakes on his dad's car would fail coming down the steep hill, and they would end up in the water. His stomach churned, which made him feel a little nauseated at the thought. He smiled thinking how relieved he always felt when it did not happen.

Once through the village, the road became narrower and led through the fields. This area was exceptionally beautiful. The road was lined with white birch trees, growing gracefully along both sides. Behind the wall of trees were huge open meadows with rolling hills, surrounded by a pine tree forest. The road abruptly disappeared into the Vltava River. On the other side of the river nestled on the cliffs, was the large medieval castle of Zvíkov.

The family cabin was ¾ of a mile down the river from the castle. Nelly Gray turned right and followed the path until they reached a settlement of four houses, the smallest village he had ever seen. Memories flooded his mind. When at the cabin, his mother would send Peter and his older brother to this village to buy milk and eggs. Peter always looked forward to those days. It was only a 20 minute walk, but it was through the forest and along the river. They always knew when the lady of the house was going to be milking the cow, and sometimes they would go early so they could watch her. She would milk the cow into a large metal can, and then pour the warm milk into their milk jug. They would cover the jug and carry it back to the cabin. Sometimes they would stop and take a drink of the fresh, warm milk along the way.

Now the village was silent and peaceful with the moon shining above. The path led downhill into a different part of the forest. They rode leisurely through the woods to the open clearing. The clearing was a small triangular shaped meadow with a narrow point wedged into the woods. This was where Peter built the small corral for his horse. A little brook running in the middle of the meadow disappeared into the trees, eventually ending in the river. This was another one of his favorite places. He took Nelly Gray into the corral and removed her saddle, wiped the sweat from her body, and fed her. He threw the saddle over his shoulder and walked the short distance to the cabin.

*

It was almost midnight now. He could see the candle light through the cabin window. A light breeze blew in as he opened the door, which made the candles flicker. The soft lights and shadows danced around the walls, across the pictures and carvings his dad had made. His mother and wife sighed with relief. He had finally made it. They had been expecting him two hours earlier. His mom was worried he had fallen off Nelly Gray, and his wife thought some of their neighbors had called the police and Peter had been arrested.

His mom quickly heated food on the wood cooking stove for him. After the meal, he wanted to take one last look at the river. He walked to the edge of the cliffs, where the natural rock formation created a bench. He sat down as he had done many times before. The bench was 150 feet above the water and he could see a long way across the river. The moon was sitting high above, creating a sparkling shining silver strip of light in the river, reaching the bottom of the cliff where he sat. The cliffs on either side of the river were crowned with the dark pine trees. The river was visible for about ¾ of a mile, and then disappeared around the bend where the old castle Zvíkov stood.

When Peter was a boy, he would take the wooden canoe and paddle to the castle on quiet peaceful evenings, after the tourists left and the doors were locked. It did not bother him to be there alone and locked doors did not stop him. He knew the castle well and knew where to scale the walls to get inside. It was a little spooky, but that made it so special. He spent a lot of time sitting, daydreaming, and exploring the historic structure. Sometimes he would lie down on his back with the huge walls surrounding him, looking up at the darkening sky, watching for the first stars to shine.

He knew there were dungeons below, and one time he discovered steps descending into the bowels of the castle. The room at the bottom was flooded, but he waded through the water. The ground under his feet rose slowly, until he came out the other side, and there - around the corner - was an opening to the underground tunnel. Peter cautiously made his way into the five-foot-high tunnel as far as he dared, but soon turned around and went back since he didn't have lights with him.

Once he was back at the cabin, he told his brother about his discovery. The next evening they took flashlights and ropes and paddled back to do some more exploring. The tunnel continued for approximately 150 yards and continued getting smaller until they had to get on their hands and knees. They crawled until the tunnel came to a dead end. This was an incredible discovery for twelve-year old Peter. He felt so proud of himself, as if he had discovered a treasure.

*

Now he was an adult, sitting on the cliffs overlooking the river. His heart was full of sadness knowing this would be his last time here. In the morning, he would have to say goodbye to this place and would drive to a foreign country. He didn't know where they were going, what it would look like, or what was waiting for them! However, he knew he would do his best to make it happen. Hopefully, they would find the way across the border to be free. Once again, he prayed for God's protection and a happy ending to their *Journey for Freedom.*

...would he have changed his mind if he could have seen into the future? If he had known that four nights later would be anything but peaceful and quiet...? Had he known the memory of that very night would stick in his head for the rest of his life...? A night that would change their lives forever...!

The six-plex in Hrejkovice where Peter and his family lived prior to their defection in 1983. The two bottom windows on the left and 1/2 the balcony was the apartment they lived in. The two windows on the right side in the middle, was where the 'nosey neighbor' lived.

The metal cross in the field by the village of Hrejkovice where Peter asked God for protection.

Nelly Gray on the cabin steps, drinking from a bucket held by Lída.

Lída and Patty with Nelly Gray.

Left: Castle of Zvikov.

Below: The tunnel Peter discovered in the bowels of the castle Zvikov.

Peter with his dad at the cabin.

Peter, as a dad himself, with Lída and Patty at the same place as above.

Chapter Eight

ON THE WAY

The next morning Peter and Lída woke the children before dawn. The air was thick with humidity and fog surrounded the cabin. While Peter's mother was making breakfast, he ran down to the river with a bar of soap and toothbrush. This would be his last time in the river. After breakfast they had to say goodbye. He held his mom in his arms a little longer than he normally would. He leaned over and kissed her on the lips. This surprised her since Czechs were not openly affectionate, but she did not say anything. They did not kiss or hug, even their own family members, just shook hands. They never said 'I love you' - it was not spoken, but understood.

Before getting into the car, they walked over to Nelly Gray to say their goodbyes. This was very emotional for Peter because he felt as if he was losing his best friend or a family member. He struggled to keep his emotions under control for the children's sake.

They drove away through the small four-house village, onto the road with the white birch trees, then pulled over and stopped. Peter got out of the car to take one last look around the countryside. He felt a lump in his throat and tears were welling in his eyes. It was only last night - just seven short hours earlier - when Peter rode his horse through here, but it already felt as if it had happened a long time ago.

*

It was difficult to fit two weeks' worth of supplies and camping gear into their small car. Lída filled the spaces behind the front seats with supplies and placed the sleeping bags over them, forming a soft comfortable bed for the children to play, sit, and sleep on during the trip.

They traveled approximately five hours eastbound to the Slovakian section of Czechoslovakia, and through the city of Bratislava, located close to the Hungarian border where they needed to cross. They made good time and arrived at the border around 11:00 in the morning. It was nerve-wracking for Peter, as he was very worried about the incriminating documents in the car, which would give them away if the border guards would have searched them. He was also afraid that the border officials might find the excessive amount of money they had hidden, which was also illegal. Peter and Lída had thought hard about how to conceal the money. They finally came up with the idea to remove one tampon from its plastic applicator, roll the money into a very tight roll, and insert it into the applicator before placing it back into the Tampax box. They knew this would not work if they were searched in detail, but they were hoping the guards would not search them too closely because of the small children.

Both children were sleeping soundly when they arrived at the border. Once the car was stopped for the routine check, the children woke up. Fortunately, little Peter started to cry and the Czechoslovakian border guard quickly looked at their passports and waved them through. The Hungarian border guards also just waved them through after checking their passports. Everything had gone smoothly and they had entered Hungary without any problems. They had one border behind them and only two more to go!

Back in their hometown as a result of their nosey neighbor, the local police had already found out the family was planning to defect to America. They had called the border patrol to alert them of their license plate number and their names. The border guards had orders to arrest them. Peter and his wife didn't know when that happened, but fortunately, it was after they already crossed into Hungary!

Peter had nightmares about being arrested at the border for years to come. He saw Lída and himself being pulled out of the car, handcuffed, and separated from each other so they could not communicate. All of this taking place right in front of their frightened four-year old daughter and two-year old son. Peter could clearly see the fear in their faces as they were ripped from the loving grip of their parent's arms, while being thrown in a car with a burly, mean, STB agent who was screaming at them to be quiet. The children were clinging to each other for comfort while crying for their parents, not understanding what was happening, only to be permanently separated at the end of the trip and sent to different institutions.

*

They had planned to stay overnight at a campground on Lake Balaton in Hungary, which was a big lake by European standards and a popular vacation destination. The family arrived at the lake late afternoon, just 15 minutes before the departure of the last ferry taking cars across. The trip on the ferry was exciting for all of them. They had never seen or experienced this before, and the whole family enjoyed it. Once they reached the other side, they continued to travel south. It was almost evening now, so they began looking for a campground. They found one, checked in, set up camp, and Lída started cooking dinner. After dinner, the sun was about to set, so they walked to the shore and found a wooden dock reaching far into the lake. The family walked to the end of it to enjoy the beautiful sunset. The whole day had been sunny with clear blue skies and the evening was quiet and peaceful. They watched as the sun slowly disappeared into the water, turning the sky gold, which then changed into vibrant orange. They had left their cabin early in the morning as the sun was rising – and now they watched the same sun, setting over a foreign land. They stood there for a long time, watching the fading colors of the evening skies.

Now they were in a different country where people were speaking a strange language they could not understand. It felt as if days had passed since they left. They put the children to sleep in the tent and made a small campfire while talking in quiet, hushed voices. Peter and Lída didn't want to attract unnecessary attention because everybody around them was speaking only Hungarian. They were avoiding the subject of defection - somehow it felt awkward to speak about it and the country they left.

They were tired from traveling all day and let the fire die out quickly. Lída went to bed and Peter laid on his back in the grass, watching the sky as it turned from orange to purple, dark blue, and eventually black. Then stars appeared above him one-by-one, until there were millions of them shining and sparkling like diamonds sprinkled on black velvet. The big orange moon slowly began to rise over the horizon, the very same moon that less than twenty-four hours ago, had guided his way through the trees.

Peter started to question himself once again. Is this the right thing to do? To calm himself down, he thought it was really no big deal. They could simply decide not to defect and have a nice vacation at the Adriatic Sea, then return home two weeks later as if nothing had happened. But in his heart he knew - he must try to defect! They had come this far and if he gave up now, he would not forgive himself for the rest of his life. Once again, he asked God to protect his family, then crawled into his sleeping bag and drifted off to sleep.

*

The next day as they arrived at the Hungary-Yugoslavian border, similar worries and anxieties surfaced once again. The same precautions were taken as the day before. He hoped one of the children would start crying again since that worked so well yesterday. This time they did not, but the border was crossed problem free. Two borders down and only one more to go! The only difference was that the borders behind them were easy, because they were between Communists countries. The next border would be the dangerous one.

They continued south through the city of Zagreb, traveling in the direction of the city of Rijeka, located on the shore of the Adriatic Sea. The countryside began to change. Yugoslavia was very green with colorful exotic plants and trees which they had never seen before. The climate was also changing as Yugoslavia was a southern European country to the east of Italy and its climate and vegetation were more Mediterranean. The road led over a mountainous ridge with a lot of vast open grassy areas, speckled with white boulders and rocks. Peter recognized this countryside from the movies he had seen. The Italians and East Germans made some Western movies that were filmed in this region. This was the countryside he related to America. It was special and exciting to him and he felt it was a good sign. The weather was beautiful and the days were filled with sun and blue skies.

They reached the highest point on the road and began to descend down the Dinaric Alps. They entered the shallow parts of the canyon, which was getting deeper and deeper as the road led down. Some parts of the road were built in the side of the mountain. The cliffs were going straight up on one side and way down into the river on the other. The road was winding back and forth as they continued on. At the very bottom was a small steel bridge crossing the wild river, which they had seen earlier from above. Peter was driving as slow as he could so they could enjoy the beautiful view, while trying to compensate for the traffic behind them. The roads were narrow and there was no space for passing. The family was looking around, enjoying the beauty surrounding them.

Peter was trying not to stop too many times unless it was absolutely necessary, he was afraid their foreign license plates would draw unwanted attention. They had a little plastic potty for the children to use, but it was quite difficult to have the potty balancing on the soft surface of the blankets and sleeping bags without spilling.

Every so often they had to stop to get gas. Peter had a 20 liter gas can with him just in case they ran out, since the gas stations were few and far between. Not knowing the country, he had no idea which city or town had a gas station, which made it easy to run out. Peter had purchased gasoline stamps from the bank in Prague, but did not know how they worked. Every stamp was worth 10 liters of gas, but if he only pumped 8 liters, would he get a refund for the other 2 liters or would he simply lose the money? Unfortunately, because of the language barrier, he was unable to find out. It was a constant worry not to run out of gas and still be able to use the whole 10 or 20 liters filling the tank. Nothing was ever easy in Communist countries - even a simple task like filling the gas tank was complicated and a struggle!

They were descending down hills most of the time now, approaching the Adriatic Sea, and finally saw it in the distance. It was huge and appeared to be everywhere. The body of water looked as if it was going uphill, sparkling in the sunrays on the horizon. They pulled into the first campground they could find along the seashore. Peter could smell the salt in the air and hear the waves crashing on the shore. The water was crystal clear, but it had a dark, almost black tint.

They pitched their tent and Lída began cooking dinner. The kids were restless and running around after spending the entire day traveling in the car. Peter pulled out his map and started studying the roads leading to the Italian border to the west and the Austrian border to the north. He was reading the names of the border crossings. That night they went to bed early since they were tired, and he wanted to get up in time to see the sunrise over the sea.

*

The next morning he crawled out of the tent and walked to the seashore. His timing was perfect. A small sliver of the sun appeared over the horizon. Peter had read that the sunrise and sunset were most beautiful over the ocean. This was his first chance to see it, and he wasn't going to miss this opportunity. He sat down on one of the boulders to watch the spectacular show. The various shades and colors were incredible. The sea was calm and looked totally black while the skies above and behind were dark blue. The sun was creating changes in colors from light blue to green, orange, and then gold as it was rising. The sun was sending sparkles and rays, painting the sky and sea yellow, gold, orange, and red.

Suddenly, Peter noticed an ocean ship just to the left of the sun. From the distance it looked like the size of a child's toy floating on the horizon. The ship was in the exact center of the sun when it had risen half way. At that moment the sun looked almost red. It was huge! It was the biggest sun he had ever seen! The colors were like nothing he had ever seen before. As the sun was rising, the ship was slowly moving across it. 'What are the chances of being at the exact right place and time to see the sun and ship line up perfectly, to create this fantastic show?' he thought.

The air was fresh, clear, and had a salty smell. Everything was peaceful as soft waves washed gently on the shore. 'This is another good sign - I think we will make it,' he told himself. He stood there for quite a while watching the sun rise above the water, until it became too bright to look at. He walked back to the tent to see if anyone was awake yet. It was early in the morning and most people in the campground were still asleep. Peter woke up his wife and children, and started to prepare to get on the road again. While Lída made breakfast, he took the children to the sea to play. They were throwing pebbles into the water and were chasing small crabs.

It was impossible for Peter to relax. He felt there was something big in front of them. His mind was creating images of a large, dark, dangerous, cloud waiting for them. He had to find a way to break through and conquer it - the sooner the better - since it would not go away. He did not know where the place he was looking for was, nor did he know what it looked like.

They had to get back on the road to get to the border of the western country and find a way to cross it. Today would be a long day since they had to drive across Yugoslavia from the south to the north, if they were going to cross into Austria. They would have to travel north half way and then west, if they decided to try for Italy. At that time, he still did not know which way to go. They packed everything up and headed north.

*

They were traveling one of the major highways and after about four or five hours came to a large intersection. If they continued traveling north, they would eventually come to the Austrian border. If they turned west, they would come to the Italian border. He knew about this intersection from studying the map. He was hoping by the time they reached this point, he would have made up his mind - but he had not. He was not sure if they should try to escape to Italy or Austria. He asked his wife what she thought, but she also had no answer. He was torn - he was frustrated - he was worried and didn't know which way to go! All the way up to this moment, he was expecting to get a sign from above that would tell him the right way - but it had not happened.

They drove straight through the intersection and continued towards Austria for about one mile, but it did not feel right. His brain was working in overdrive. He thought maybe they should go to Italy instead, so he turned the car around and drove back. He turned right at the crossing in the direction of the Italian border, but he still was not convinced it was the right direction. He turned around again and repeated the process. All this time he was waiting and asking for a sign from above to tell him which way to take. He started to worry about attracting too much attention by driving through the same intersection over and over again. He was worried they might get pulled over by the police and have to explain what they were doing. And then - it happened! There was peace in his mind! There was peace in his heart! He knew which way to go. It was Austria - Austria was the right way. He didn't know how or where the answer came from, but it was there. His mind and heart were at ease. He felt as if a big weight had been lifted from his shoulders, everything had become clear. They would defect to Austria, and possibly even tonight.

They drove in the direction of a town called Maribor, in the northern part of Yugoslavia. It was close to the Austrian border. He had the name and address of a specific Yugoslavian man who was living there, that supposedly guided people through the mountains, across the border, and into Austria for money. The decision was made. They would find this man and pay him to guide them to freedom. Of course, there was a chance that this information was not correct. This man might not exist, or he might be a decoy or police informant. Peter knew they had to try something and this seemed to be their best option.

They needed all the money they could get their hands on and since the gasoline stamps were not going to do them any good in Austria, he decided that next time he was filling the car he would try to sell the stamps to the gas station attendant. That could be a risky proposition, but Peter felt they did not have a choice. At the next gas station, he went inside to talk to the clerk behind the desk. Peter had some of the stamps ready in his pocket. He decided to try to sell half of them, so it didn't look too suspicious. If it worked, he would do the same thing again next time. After Peter gave the clerk stamps for the gas he had pumped, he pulled out more stamps and Yugoslavian money from his other pocket. He gestured to the clerk as if he was giving him stamps with one hand and receiving money with the other. The clerk quickly looked around and nodded. He counted the stamps and handed Peter money in return. Peter had no idea if he was getting the right amount, but could not ask. He wanted to get out of there as fast as possible, since there were other people around.

Peter walked swiftly back to the car, but was followed by a female customer from the gas station. She caught up with him before he could get into the car and tried to start a conversation. She was speaking a different language, but he knew what she wanted. The lady was gesturing to buy gas stamps from him. Somehow he understood that she was offering more money, than what he was paid at the gas station. He was very worried about this new development since this woman could be an informant or a member of the secret police. He kept telling her in Czech that he didn't understand what she was talking about. She kept explaining, offering, showing him money and some stamps she had in her pocket, but he continued to act like he did not comprehend. The more she insisted, the more he shook his head saying he did not understand. Eventually, she gave up and walked away.

Chapter Nine

FIRST ATTEMPT

The family arrived in Maribor that evening. The first step was to find the house where the guide lived. Maribor was a larger city and it was unlikely they would find the right street by chance. Peter pulled over to the curb and showed people who were walking by the address written on a piece of paper. They started explaining and pointing in one direction. He could not understand a word they were saying, but they were waving forward and to the left. After thanking them, Peter returned to the car and drove straight for a while then turned left. Again he stopped and asked for directions. At one point, the pedestrians were pointing in the direction the family just came from, making Peter realize he had turned too early. This continued for some time.

Suddenly - the name of the street they were searching for appeared! It should be easy to find the right house now. There were no more apartment buildings as the street was in the suburbs. The houses were single family homes sitting above the street level, with approximately ten steps leading to the front door.

It started to rain and the temperature dropped. When he first saw the house he did not stop, but continued driving up the street, looking into parked cars for anybody who could be watching this house. Peter did not notice anyone, so he turned around and drove past the house in the opposite direction. Everything appeared to be okay, so he drove back and parked in front of the house.

Peter walked up the steps and rang the door bell. A young man in his early thirties answered the door. He wore casual clothes, had dark hair, and good clean facial features. He had a square jaw and kept solid eye contact. He appeared to be a strong man with courage, a person to be respected. Peter was pleasantly surprised by his firm handshake and immediately felt comfortable with this man. He tried to explain why he was there and asked the man for guidance through the mountains, across the border to Austria. But the man just kept shaking his head in confusion. Peter pulled out some money in a desperate attempt to make him understand, but that did not work either. Peter was prepared for this, and retrieved a piece of paper and pencil from his pocket, drawing a picture of Yugoslavia, Austria, and Italy. He drew a line through the mountains from Yugoslavia to Austria, with the starting point in the town of Maribor. The man continued acting as if he did not understand and kept looking in the direction of Peter's car. Peter looked back a few times to follow his gaze, but the only thing he could see was his own vehicle. The car windows were completely fogged up from the rain and body heat, so his family was not visible. Peter kept trying to explain himself but realized he was fighting a losing battle. After a while he finally gave up, walked back to the car, and drove away.

Sometime later it dawned on him. The man was looking in the car to see who was inside. He must have been afraid they were conspirators or someone who was trying to deceive him. Due to the foggy windows, he could not see Peter's wife and two small children. Peter now believes if the man could have seen the family inside the car, he probably would have taken them across the border. He had no idea how long or how difficult the trip would be, and maybe it would have been an impossible journey to make with two small children, hiking through the mountains at night.

*

The dark was setting in as they tried to find a campground on the outskirts of Maribor. The nightfall came earlier than usual, due to the cloud cover and rain. Soon they realized they were not going to find a campground that night and would have to sleep in the car. Peter noticed a dirt road leading towards the Dráva River. They followed it to an area densely covered with bushes, with car tracks running in all directions. At one time, his headlights caught a box truck backed deep into the brush and covered with branches. Peter and Lída figured this was secluded enough to stay hidden from police or others who might ask questions. She prepared a quick dinner before they settled in as comfortable as possible and tried to get some sleep. The children were content lying on the bed made on the back seat. It was quite the opposite for Peter and Lída, since the car was small and the seats did not recline.

They had a restless night sleeping off and on for a few hours. Peter woke up a few times hearing some activity in the dark around them. Once he heard an engine start and a vehicle drive away. He realized it must have been the truck that was parked in the bushes. Later he woke up to someone pounding on his car window. He opened his eyes and to his horror, saw two policemen shining their flashlights into their vehicle. They were asking questions that he could not understand. He tried to explain in Czech they were traveling and night came too early, saw this place, and decided to spend the night there. The policemen soon realized that communication was impossible, shook their heads, walked back to their car and drove away. It was a common occurrence to see Communists walk away from a situation that required too much effort or work on their part. What a relief!

The next morning as they were leaving, they could see there had been a lot of activity around them during the night. The truck was gone, but a different car was hidden in its place. There were a lot of fresh car tracks on the muddy road winding through this area which made Peter realize this may have been a place for illegal activities. That did not bother him very much, because they were actually more frightened of the police than criminals. Peter assumed when the police saw a family with children, they might have realized they were caught in their travels and pulled over to sleep.

**Day one: June 17, 1983, beginning the journey for freedom in
Czech.**

Day two: Lída and the children somewhere on the road in Hungary.

Day three: Lída and the children at the Adriatic Sea by the town of Rijeka in Yugoslavia.

Day four: Having a picnic in the hiding place on the eve of defection in Yugoslavia.

Chapter Ten

THE LONGEST DAY

The first plan had been to have a guide take them through the mountains, but that did not work. A decision had to be made what to do next. Peter had heard that the two mile section of land along the Yugoslav-Austrian border next to Hungary was not heavily guarded. That would be the place, where they would try to cross the border.

Many Western European cars with German and Austrian license plates were on the road leading to Austria. The family realized that people from Austria and Germany might be traveling to the Adriatic Sea for weekends. Western Europeans could travel anywhere they wanted, their government did not stop them. However, the Eastern European governments would not allow their citizens to travel across the western borders. At one point, the road wound back and forth, while climbing the Pohorje mountain range, which was part of the Central Eastern Alps. Peter could see from the map this was one of the major roads leading from the Adriatic Sea to Austria and continuing on to Germany. The family had to travel a section of this road for some time, before they would exit and continue east.

Peter was driving his small Russian made car as fast as possible. The car was only three-years old and not bad by Eastern European standards. He was constantly shifting gears and revving up the engine. There were no places to pass so he would hold up traffic behind him if he did not drive fast enough. The engine was screaming in the high RPM's, and the tires were squealing on the blacktop. The children sitting in the backseat were struggling to keep from flying around. To his amazement, cars were still passing them. There was no place to pass - no straight stretches in the road - he could not understand it as the gas pedal was all the way to the floor. Could these cars be so much more powerful? How could they be designed so much better to travel at this speed without the tires screeching? 'Of course,' he thought, 'those cars are a product of Capitalism and competition!' His car was a product of Communism with no such competition! More proof of government lies and propaganda. Luckily they were almost to their exit since everybody in the car was getting dizzy and nauseated.

They took the exit traveling east and finally had time to discuss their plans. Peter felt they should try to escape tonight - the longer they stuck around, the higher the risk of attracting unwanted attention. There was always a chance that the police would pull them over and start asking questions. They were far away from the road leading from Hungary to the Adriatic Sea and that alone could raise suspicions. They would try to cross the border on foot and decided that 2:00 in the morning would give them the best chance. The guards would be tired and not paying too much attention. The information he had gathered stated there would be a paved road leading to the right, before the Yugoslavian guard house. He planned on taking that road, but not too far as he didn't want to get lost and accidently wander into the Yugoslav-Hungarian border - that would be a disaster! They would have to leave the car and walk to their left, making a half circle avoiding the Yugoslavian and Austrian guardhouses, then return to the same road only in a different country. If they accomplished this, they would be free.

It was shortly after noon on Monday, June 20, 1983, and they still had a long way to travel. They were driving parallel to the Yugoslav-Austrian border, which was approximately 60 miles north. They stopped at another gas station to fill the tank. When Peter was paying with the gasoline stamps, he offered the rest to the clerk as he had done before. This time everything went as planned, without any incident. They now had all the money they could possibly get.

By mid afternoon, they came to the intersection and turned north before the town of Murska Sobota. According to their map, this was the road that would lead them to the Austrian border. It was after 4:00 in the afternoon and they were getting closer. The Yugoslavian government was under pressure from other Communist countries to make their borders more secure and harder to penetrate. One of the new precautions was to have police cars patrolling the roads leading to the Austrian border crossings. When the police saw a car with Eastern European license plates, they would turn it around and send them away. If the same car was caught repeatedly, the police would arrest the passengers, hand them over to their government, and the authorities would be informed that they were trying to defect.

According to the map, they were approximately 30 miles away from the border. It was time to search for a place to hide until nightfall. Peter followed some tracks he had noticed leading across the grass into a small wooded area, which turned out to be the perfect hiding place. There were thick trees and bushes all around them, with a small grassy opening in the middle. They had to wait nine hours until 1:00 in the morning, when they planned to leave their hiding place. The danger of being discovered and reported to the authorities still existed, but luckily that had not happened so far. It had rained lightly all day until now, but a heavy cloud cover indicated the rain was not over. Peter and his family sat down and ate a picnic dinner. They played with the kids to keep them quiet, so no one would hear them.

He was expecting the children to start crying when they were awakened at 2:00 A.M. That just could not happen tonight, but what do you tell a two and four-year old child? How do you explain what they were planning to do? How do you tell them not to cry when you wake them up in the middle of the night from a sound sleep, and drag them from their warm bed into the coldness of the night? And what words do you use to keep them from becoming even more frightened? Maybe they will not cry! What if talking to them would make it

worse? Using the wrong words could scare them even more.
He had to choose the right tone of voice and words. He did not
want to talk to them too early when they were playing or
restless, because they would not pay attention. If it was too
late, they would be too tired and falling asleep. He waited for
the right time and then sat them down.

"I need you to listen to me," he said, "we are going to put
you to sleep in the car again. Mom and I will be driving while
you are sleeping. Late at night we will wake you up, and then
we have to leave the car and walk in the dark. I need you to
remember this because we need to make sure you do not cry
when we wake you up. We all have to be very quiet. You will
be tired and sleepy, but you cannot make any sounds at all.
There could be some people there, and if they hear us, we can
get into trouble. So remember, when we wake you up, you
have to be very, very, quiet!"

Peter and his wife were trying to decide what to take with
them and what to leave behind. Back home when they were
planning the defection, they thought there might be a chance to
make it across the border with their car and all belongings they
had packed in it. They brought their best clothes and expensive
bedding, which was saved only for special occasions and had
never been used before. There were a few other items that were
meaningful and precious to them. Now they knew they would
have to leave the car and everything in it behind, since they
would be traveling on foot. Each adult would only have one
free hand as Peter would carry his son, and Lída would be
holding her daughter's hand.

The decision was made to take the handbag with the
shoulder strap, filled with extra clothes for the children and
extra shoes for themselves. Those were their best dress shoes.
If they succeeded, they would have to eventually meet with the
United States Consul for an interview, and would need good
clothes to represent themselves better. Peter would carry the
handbag as it was the heaviest. They also decided to bring one
sleeping bag that had its own case and handle, wrapping the top
of Peter's suit and his wife's dress in it. Lída would carry this
along with a small plastic bag that contained all of their legal

documents and also maps of Austria and America. Patty would carry a tiny red backpack filled with a few of her clothes and her favorite slippers, which were precious to her. The rest of their extra clothes would be carried on their bodies, because they planned to wear two sets of underwear and two sets of socks. Peter planned to have his suit pants on with his regular pants over them, two tee shirts, a shirt, and jacket. Lída would also dress in layers. They put the children to bed fully dressed, removing only their shoes.

They decided to leave their hiding place at 1:00, so they could be at the border by 2:00 A.M., but it was only 9:30 P.M. now. It was going to be the longest night of their lives. The fog was building up, first it was only a mist but slowly it became more dense and heavier. Peter and Lída were sitting in their car, most of the time in silence. Their minds were overflowing with emotions, worries, and anxiety. They tried to sleep - at least doze off - but it was impossible. Their hearts were beating fast and they were wide awake.

Peter's mind was preoccupied with all the scenarios that could possibly happen. He was the type of person who thought and prepared for the worst in crucial situations. If the worst did happen, he would be prepared and know how to deal with it, not getting caught off guard.

There was one subject he needed to discuss with Lída, but did not want to scare her even more than she was already. He thought long and hard how to address the issue. He did not want the words to come across the wrong way. The longer he thought about that, the more he realized, there was no right way to say what he need to, but it must be done. It could be a matter of life and death.

"We need to be prepared for everything," he said. "That way, if the worst happens, we will know what to do and not panic. If one of us gets hurt, breaks a leg, or gets shot, the other person needs to keep pushing on. If we all get caught - that will be the end! They will arrest us and hand us over to our own government. If either one of us makes it, there is a possibility that the rest of the family would be let go. If they don't, the one who is safe must apply through the International Red Cross or some other organization, to get the rest of the family out of Czechoslovakia. Therefore - if I go down and cannot continue on, you must keep going. I don't want you to come back to help me. You must make it - that would be our only chance! If something happens to you - I will have to keep going. It is not that I don't love you, and I am not just leaving you behind. Once again, if I make it, there is a great chance that I can get the two of you out. I am not trying to scare you, but I want to let you know that the possibility is there. Then if something bad happens, you know what you have to do."

Then they sat in silence again, but the atmosphere in the car was saturated with anxiety! They had left their home four short days ago - but it felt like weeks or months had passed.

He kept looking at his watch, putting it to his ear to hear if it was still ticking. It felt as if time was standing still. Many thoughts were going through his head. He was thinking about his family in the car with him. What was waiting for them? He was also thinking about the family back home. What was going to happen to them if the defection was successful? What would happen if they did not succeed? What would happen if they were shot, captured, or arrested? There was a good chance that the Communists would not even let their families back in Czech know what had happened to them, or at least, not for a while. All they would know is that Peter's family had not returned from their vacation and disappeared without a trace.

At 12:30, he decided they should get moving due to the heavy fog cover, which would slow them down a lot. It would take longer to reach the border, especially if they happened to get lost along the way. He didn't want to risk being too late and arrive when it was daylight.

"Let's do it," he said. They put on the extra clothes they had planned to wear. She placed the children's shoes under her feet, so she could find them easily in the dark. They situated the bags next to the children for quick access.

*

Peter started the car and drove out of the protective

woods, turning north onto the road. They could not drive very fast as the lights were reflecting on the fog and not on the road, but fortunately, there were a few areas where the fog was less dense, allowing him to drive faster. They did not know the way and did not want to get lost. Lída was holding the map on her lap, constantly checking the directions. Every intersection! Every exit! Every cross road! She was matching the names with the map, making sure they were still traveling in the right direction.

He was expecting a police car or two to be patrolling the roads. If a police car was coming from the opposite direction, they would not be able to read Peter's license plate in the dark with the lights on. They would have to drive close behind them in order to see it was an Eastern European license plate. There were a few cars coming from the opposite direction, but they did not see any traveling the same way as they were.

Once they started moving, the tension in the car eased up some. Their minds were occupied by driving, reading the map, and checking the directions, so they did not have time to think about what could happen. The road took a ninety-degree turn to the right, going east. From the map, they estimated there was about 15 miles to go before they had to exit north towards the border crossing. About 6 miles later, they turned on a road with a sign pointing to Österreich (Austria). Five minutes later the road turned left, then right again, to circle around a patch of tall trees, and there - like with a snap of the fingers - lit up by two streetlights - the Yugoslavian border crossing appeared... The border gate was blocking off the road. An armed guard was standing beside the gate watching them. It startled Peter and Lída and their hearts skipped a beat! They were not expecting it yet - they thought they still had another 10 miles to go.

Peter stopped the car, and for a second, did not know what to do. Then he put the car in reverse and backed up around the trees, taking them out of the guard's sight.

"We are already there," they looked at each other in shock. He found a place off the road to park the car. "Stay here and lock the door. I will go and see what's going on." With those words, he disappeared into the dark.

*

A light rain started again, just a drizzle, but it knocked the fog down. The fog disappeared, but the rain was getting heavier. It was very dark and he had to feel for the road with his feet since he could not see it. He listened intensely for oncoming traffic, ready to disappear from the road and hide. When he came around the turn, he could see the streetlights and building again. The lights were reflecting on the wet road in front of him. That was not good! He jumped into the ditch and crouched down while moving forward. He was not afraid that someone was going to see him, as he knew from experience that people in the light could not see into the darkness. As long as he stayed out of the circle of light, he would be invisible to them.

He squatted down in the tall wet grass and studied the situation in front of him. His heart was racing and adrenaline was rushing through his veins. He was being very quiet and careful. Using his right hand, he formed a shield over his eyes to avoid the 'deer in the headlight' glare. He opened his mouth widely, that improved his hearing and helped him take more oxygen in and out of his lungs with shorter, slower, breaths, making his breathing much quieter. There was a car parked in front of the building that bore the border guard markings. The lights in the building were on. The guard standing beside the gate had an automatic weapon hanging off his shoulder. Peter could hear people talking inside the building, indicating there were at least two more guards. The road behind the gate entered the forest with tall trees on both sides. In the distance, he could see another streetlight. That must be the Austrian guard house, he assumed.

At this time his mind became clear and calm. It felt good to be unseen and watching *them*! His whole life he felt as if he was the one being watched by the dark, invisible, forces around him. He felt like an American Indian on the prairies sneaking up on his prey or enemies, just like he used to read about in his books.

Peter had information there would be a narrow, blacktop,

road leading to the right. The road was there but it was not paved. It was a dirt road that had been muddied by the rain. He assumed the information was not accurate.

For years he had been searching for this place. He did not know where it was - or what it looked like - but now he was there. For years he had prepared for this moment - and now it was here. Every step he took in the past, every thought, every action, led him to this place. His whole life funneled to this point. It felt as if this was the only place in the entire universe, and now he knew - this was the right place! Nothing outside of this mattered and had ceased to exist. There was no turning back now - this was it! His whole life ended right here, right now, at this very moment. There was nothing else - only his family and himself. He did not know what the next hour would bring, but whatever it was - it would change their lives forever! Within one hour they could be in handcuffs, beginning the long dreadful way back to their homeland and a life in shackles... they could be on the ground bleeding from gunshot wounds... or they would be free!

A quote he once read flashed through his mind: *'All your journeys have brought you to this place! All your yesterdays have brought you to this day! All your tomorrows begin now!'*

....and he knew - what he had to do....

Part II

Chapter Eleven

THE BEGINNING

All this began many years ago, a long time before Peter was born. His Grandfather, Stanislav Vodenka, was listening to the radio in disbelief. He felt angry and helpless! The German occupational forces had marched into Prague. The date was March 15, 1939. The young country of Czechoslovakia ceased to exist only twenty years after it was created. Before World War I, the Czechs were part of the Austro-Hungarian Empire. After the end of World War I, on October 28, 1918, the new country of Czechoslovakia was created. It combined Bohemia, Moravia, Slovakia, and Ruthenia, into one state. Bohemia and Moravia were industrial and densely populated, while Slovakia and Ruthenia were agricultural with less inhabitants.

In September of 1938, the Nazi leader, Adolf Hitler, demanded that Czechoslovakia return a section of land around its western border, amounting to approximately 11,700 square miles to Germany. This area was known as the Sudetenland and was populated mostly by German citizens. The German government was required to surrender this area, following the events of World War I in 1918. During the Munich Conference on September 29, 1938, representatives for Germany, Italy, Great Britain, and France were meeting to resolve this 'so-called' Czech problem.[1] The Czechoslovakian government representatives were not invited. The President Eduard Beneš found out about this meeting with delay. He sent the Czech representatives in a hurry. When the Czechs arrived, they were told to wait outside. The destiny of their country was being decided behind closed doors without them.[2] After a meeting that lasted eight hours, the Czechs were informed about the decision. The Germans would take back the Sudetenland. Another part of Czechoslovakia would be given to Hungary and even more land ceded to Poland. The amount of land Czechoslovakians had to give up was nearly 14,700 square miles, including close to five million of its people and many rich natural resources and industries.

At that time, the Czechoslovakian army was one of the most modern and strongest in Europe. It was well equipped with cannons, tanks, and military war planes, as well as a chain of strong fortresses along the German border. England and France were paralyzed with fear[3] from the potential danger of military conflict between the Germans and Czechs. They were pushing Czechoslovakian President Beneš to pull the military away from their borders, and let the Germans take their section without confrontation. President Beneš caved in under the pressure. Columns upon columns of Czechoslovakian military were slowly leaving borders unprotected. Beneš resigned as President of Czechoslovakia on October 5th. He left for London where he formed the Czechoslovakian government in exile. On October 10, 1938, the German army occupied the Sudetenland. People in Prague took to the streets with tears in their eyes and started singing the National Anthem. Five months later, on March 15, 1939, the German occupational forces marched into the streets of Prague. Czechoslovakia ceased to exist! It became a Protectorate of Bohemia and Moravia.

---

[1] These countries were represented by Adolf Hitler, Benito Mussolini, Neville Chamberlain, and Edouard Daladier.

[2] The Munich Conference will be known in Czechoslovakia history as the 'about us - without us' conference.

[3] Cowdery & Vodenka, "Reinhard Heydrich Assassination," page 11

*

Peter's grandfather was born on March 11, 1895, in the town of Dolní Bousov. He was the oldest surviving son of thirteen children, nine of whom died in childhood. He went to grade school in Prague, and then entered trade school to be a machinist. Since 1918, he belonged to an organization called Sokol, an athletic organization that taught members to live a healthy, proper life, with strong patriotism for their country. Sokol fulfilled their patriotic role during World War I by forming the Czechoslovakian legions. Many important people and leaders like Tomáš Garrigue Masaryk, the first President of Czechoslovakia, President Eduard Beneš, and many others were members of Sokol. Some members of Sokol represented Czechoslovakia in the Olympic Games and the Athletic World Championships. Sokol was banned during World War II by the Germans and again in 1948 by the Communists.

Stanislav Vodenka was married and had two children, a boy and girl. He was striving for independence from the Austro-Hungarian Empire. Later, he was drafted into the Austrian Army. After World War I he moved his family to Slovakia, where he worked as a volunteer for the Czech military. In 1930 he moved his family to a suburb of Prague, built a house, and started working as a machinist for a railroad.

It was only natural for him to fight against the German occupants. Since the Czechoslovakian Army was disassembled before the occupation, the only way to do so was to go into the underground, where he formed and led an illegal ten member underground resistance cell.

The railroad maintenance depot where he worked was attached to the railroad station Praha Bubny. The cell's sabotage activities were geared mostly against German trains delivering supplies, weapons, soldiers, and provisions to the eastern front. His men were delaying the trains by slicing air hoses and brake lines. They were also dumping grit scraped from sand paper into the bearings and moving parts of the locomotives and box cars.

Stanislav's underground organization built a printing press

and began publishing an illegal newspaper called V BOJ (Into the Battle). The newspaper was distributed at night throughout the streets of Prague. It was assumed that Stanislav was in contact with the famous 'Three Kings', who were active in distributing the newspaper and executing many other illegal and sabotage activities. The 'Three Kings' were on the Gestapo's (German secret police during the Nazi regime) Most Wanted List with rewards on their heads. They were Colonel Josef Balabán, Colonel Josef Mašín, and Captain Václav Morávek. It was dangerous to be involved in these operations, since the Gestapo was constantly hunting for the underground resistance members.

Stanislav's home was also used as a safe house, and he was heavily involved in raising funds for families of arrested or executed resistance members. His cell was active for almost six years and there were a few close calls. At one time, one of the members from a different cell was arrested and broke down while being interrogated. He gave the Gestapo the address of a safe house, where documents containing information about different members and operations were buried under coal in the basement. The Gestapo arrested the people in the house. They dug through the pile of coal and found all the documents, except the one that included the names of Stanislav's cell members. A total number of twenty-seven other members from different underground organizations were being arrested, but Stanislav's group lucked out.

On May 27, 1942, at 10:35 A.M., SS Obergruppenfuehrer (Lieutenant-General) Reinhard Heydrich was assassinated in Prague by two Czechoslovakian paratroopers, Josef Gabčík and Jan Kubiš of operation Anthropoid.[4] They had been flown from England and were dropped off on the night of December 28, 1941. After the assassination, arrests and executions happened daily in and around Prague.

On March 9, 1943, Stanislav's family was startled by the Gestapo beating on the door of their house. They searched for incriminating proof of illegal activity and led Stanislav away.

---

[4] Cowdery & Vodenka, "Reinhard Heydrich Assassination", page 36.

Some of the previously arrested people, under pressure and torture, had released the names of members of Stanislav's underground organization.

His family did not know where he had been taken. At one time while being moved by train to Prague, Stanislav found paper to write a short note, using ashes and saliva, stating he was alive and being transferred to the Gestapo headquarters in Pečkův Palác. The note had his wife's name and address on it. As the train was passing through a suburb of Prague, he threw it out into the night. Someone found the note and took it to Peter's Grandmother.

A few times she went to Pečkův Palác to plead for his innocence and for his family. The Gestapo was baffled. How did she know he was there? After a few visits, they threatened to arrest her also, but that did not stop her from coming back. One day they informed her that he had been moved.

Stanislav Vodenka was a prisoner for twenty months in Pečkův Palác, Pankrác, Hoff, Munich, Dresden, Berlin, and Augsburg prisons, mostly in total isolation! He was tried for treason, but was released on October 25, 1944, because the Gestapo could not prove his crime. Two of his underground cell members were executed for resisting arrest with firearms, while the rest of them were released. When he returned home, his wife was very sick and weighed a measly 80 pounds. He was also undernourished, weak, and shaken, but immediately resumed his underground activities.

The end of the war was close. The American Army was pushing east across Germany, and the Russian Army was advancing west. Stanislav was named the Chairman of The Revolution Organization of Railroads in April 1945, by the underground members. On May 6, 1945, the American Army liberated the city of Plzeň (Pilsen) in Western Bohemia. The Russian Army was about five days from Prague. Euphoria was building among the citizens. The people in Prague revolted against the German Army. They started building barricades in the streets of Prague to prevent German tanks and cannons from moving freely. Stanislav and fifty-seven other railroad employees, including three women, held up a train filled with

German soldiers returning from the eastern front. The Czechs took the soldiers as prisoners and disarmed them, using their confiscated weapons to fight in the uprising. The battle lasted four days until the arrival of the Russian Army. May 5, 1945, marked the end of World War II in Czechoslovakia. Thanks to Stanislav's leadership skills and the National Revolution Committee, the production at the railroad depot was restored as early as May 9, to full capacity.

Stanislav was a member of the Czech National Socialist Party, which was in exile during World War II. On October 25, 1946, he became a member of an organization called United Political Prisoners of War. He was decorated on March 12, 1947, by reinstated President Beneš with a Czechoslovakian War Cross. On February 20, 1948, he was decorated once again, this time with a Memorial Badge for participation in the battle to free Czechoslovakia from 1939 to 1945. Later - after the Communist Party took total control of the government - he was asked to join them. He refused! Of course that was defiance, which Communists would not tolerate. During World War II, he proved his leadership and organizational abilities, which was something the Communists were afraid of - especially in people who were not their party members.

In 1948, he was put on leave from work and forced into retirement. In March of 1950, he was interrogated by the STB in Prague. Stanislav was then kicked out of The United Political Prisoners organization. The Communists stripped him of his decorations and asked him to return the medals. He refused stating, "If President Beneš asked me to return the medals, I would, but not to anybody else."

Stanislav Vodenka - the leader and founder of the underground resistance cell - the man who risked his life and family by fighting the enemy - the man who organized a group of people to uprise against the German Army in a four day battle in which 1,691 Czechs lost their lives - the man who led people to renew production and work hard to rebuild a damaged country - a decorated hero by the President of Czechoslovakia - was dismissed and stripped of all his merits like a little child, by his own government, the self proclaimed people's democracy, which he helped rebuild!

Stanislav Vodenka, grandfather.

Chapter Twelve

COMMUNISM

Immediately after World War II, six political parties that actively resisted the Nazis were in existence in Czechoslovakia. The parties included the Czech Communist Party, Czech Social Democratic Party, Czech Popular Party (Catholic Democrats), Czech National Socialist Party (of which Stanislav was a member), Slovak Communist Party, and the Slovak Democratic Party (also Catholic Democrats). Some of the other parties were banned due to the accusations of cooperating with the Nazis. Other conservative but still democratic parties, such as the Republican Party of Farmers and Peasants were prevented from resuming activity in the postwar period.

The Communist Party started manipulating people's mind by promoting class envy. They also organized and centralized a trade union movement. Of the 120 representatives of the Central Council of Trade Unions, 94 were Communists. The party worked hard to acquire mass membership. Between May, 1945, and May, 1946, the Communist Party membership grew from 20,000 people to over 1.1 million. They won 38% of the votes in the May, 1946, elections as they were moving on the wings of postwar pro-Russian euphoria.

Beneš continued as the President of the Republic and Jan Masaryk, son of the founding father, continued as the Foreign Minister. The Communist, Klement Gottwald, was elected as the new Prime minister, the same person who as early as 1929, a short 11 years after the new free country of Czechoslovakia was founded, announced during his speech to Parliament, "You are accusing us (the Communists) of traveling to Russia to learn from their Communist leadership! Yes, our highest revolutionist staff is in Moscow and is training us, and do you know what we are learning? Russian Bolsheviks are teaching us how to ring your patriotic necks."

Although the Communists were holding only a minority of portfolios, they gained control over such key institutions as the Department of Information, Department of Internal Trade, Department of Finance, and the Department of Interior[*], which included the police apparatus. Through these departments, the Communists suppressed the non-Communist opposition by placing their own party members in positions of power, which created a solid base for the takeover attempt. They were removing non-Communist members in the police department and army and replacing them with their trusted party members. The Department of Interior was watching the higher non-Communist politicians.

Near the end of 1947, Klement Gottwald was reprimanded by Stalin for taking too long to take control. Czechoslovakia was the last country where the Communist victory was not yet secured, he was told. Without any explanation, the Communist controlled police department started to arrest opposition leaders, using fake accusations of collaboration with the Nazis or spying for the West. During 1947, the Communist controlled secret police force was set up under the Department of Interior Affairs. They passed a law prohibiting newspapers to be privately owned. Only Trade Unions, political parties, or the government, could publish a newspaper. Eventually, all the newspapers became controlled by Communists.

Non-party members were experiencing the same situation in the national military. Thanks to the Communist controlled media, most of the population did not know about changes in the military and police. However, the methods the Communists used to gain power and the stagnant economy, began turning many people against them. A poll taken at the beginning of

---

[*] STB

1948 showed that Communist popularity was declining. Their hope for an election victory diminished. The Communists began to create militia organizations among the party members in factories and mining industries. The explanation for these non-legal organizations was that they were there to "protect the industry."

They also created the Organization of Federation of Czechoslovakian Youth. The approved individuals, most from pre-Communist youth organizations, could enlist in special training. This training consisted of creating explosives, how to derail and attack trains, learning how to slit the enemy's neck, how to kill with a kick to the temple, how to use a wire noose and etc... Their training booklet was appropriately named "Kill or Be Killed."[5]

Minister of Interior Nosek fired eight high ranking non-Communist police officers and replaced them with Communist Party members. The 12 non-Communist ministers resigned in protest to induce Beneš to call for early elections. On February 20, 1948, the National Socialist Party also resigned from the cabinet in protest. Czech and Slovak Catholic parties followed suit. President Beneš refused to accept the cabinet resignations, and did not call for an early election.

The next day, 7,000 armed Communist militia members marched into the streets of Prague. The militia in factories and other places mobilized, taking control. The Minister of Defense, Ludvík Svoboda (a secret member of the Communist Party), placed all high ranking military officers under house arrest. The police declared they would not obey President Beneš. A group of students tried to organize an opposition march, but were dispersed by gunshots. The armed members of the militia were guarding all important places by patrolling intersections, post offices, railroad stations, bus stations, court houses, and factories.

On the 24th of February, the Communists called for a general strike in an attempt to shut down the country. On the 25th of February, President Beneš capitulated, perhaps fearing

---

[5] Barbara Masin, "Gauntlet" page 57

Soviet intervention. He accepted the resignation of the dissident ministers and received a list of new cabinet members from Gottwald. March 10, 1948, Czechoslovakian Foreign Minister, Jan Masaryk, the only non-Communist minister left, was found dead on the concrete courtyard under the bathroom window of the Foreign Minister building in Prague. Signs of struggle in the room above made many people believe that he was thrown out of the window. The Communist takeover was completed only 10 years after the German army marched into the Sudetenland.

After they gained complete control of the government, the Communists confiscated all of the land, apartment buildings, factories, and businesses from private hands. People that knew how to run businesses and take care of the land were replaced by party members with no management skills. Crops in the fields were not being harvested and simply rotted away. Shortages of food and goods followed, while product quality decreased. Citizens of all ages, including school children, were asked to volunteer for work in the fields on weekends. Buses were provided to transport them to the fields on Saturday morning. Even though 'voluntary', people were afraid not to show up since their names were being checked off a list. Individuals not attending were considered dangerous and anti-Socialistic. The economy was quickly going into a slump, and Communists had to find someone to blame. According to them, Communism was the best system in the world.

Potatoes were the largest agricultural crop being grown in Czechoslovakia. The potato bugs over populated and destroyed most of the crop. The Communist controlled media claimed that American airplanes were flying over Czechoslovakia at night, dumping millions of potato bugs into the fields to destroy the crops, weaken the economy, create shortages of food, and disrupt lives. Communists called the potato bug an American Beetle, "it even has stripes just like an American flag," they claimed. Fear spread throughout the nation as many people believed the story. Hatred of America was on the rise, and people were made to believe the Russians were their protectors.

Prior to Communism, businesses were privately owned, sometimes for generations. Now the owners were being told to hand them over to the government. Many people that refused to surrender all of their land, farm animals, apartments, hotels, restaurants, factories, and other properties, simply disappeared. Others were arrested on phony charges, or sometimes in the middle of the night, shots were being fired through windows into their homes. Threats were made by anonymous letters promising harm to their children. Barns filled with livestock burned down and crops were burned in the field. Some water wells were being poisoned, making people and animals sick and even causing death.

The Communists had to create a scapegoat to cover their own atrocities. They started spreading rumors about so called 'Werewolves', who were supposed to be rogue groups of German soldiers under American leadership, who stayed behind after World War II. It had been said they were hiding in the mountains or deep forests, continuing with terrorist activities against civilians. Anytime someone disappeared, fires started, or animals were poisoned, 'Werewolves' were being blamed. Hatred towards the Germans was growing.

In the early years of 1950, there were still too many people among the population with Anti-Communist feelings. The party wanted to have a total grip. The 'unsafe' people needed to be taken care of, to cleanse the population of dangerous individuals and families. The STB came up with a 'great plan' to accomplish this. Deep in the forests of Western Bohemia, close to the West German border, the STB built a replica of an American station, including a display of the American flag and the U.S. President. A few trusted secret agents, who spoke English, were dressed in full American military uniforms. They created another network of agents to act as guides, taking people across the border for money. Guides would lead groups and individuals who would not accept Communism, to this phony American station. People were led to believe that they were across the border in the safety of West Germany, where Americans would begin processing them. Those brought in this way were told that this was the first step to becoming U.S. citizens. They were also asked if they knew of other relatives or friends, who were unhappy with life under Communism and would like to defect to America. The so called 'Americans', lead them to believe they would help them get out of the country. Those people would disappear, end up working in the Uranium mines as slave laborers, or end up in prison, while their relatives and friends whose names they had given, were arrested in their homes without knowing why.

One of the so-called guides decided to become a free agent. He led the people into deep secluded ravines, where he simply killed them with an automatic weapon and helped himself to their possessions. Eventually, he was discovered and was found living in a small wooden shack in the middle of the forest. Inside the shack was a cage housing a thirteen-year old girl, who was now insane! He had been raping and beating her as he pleased. The exact number of people he murdered, including women and small children, is not known, but it is estimated to be in the hundreds.

*

This type of cleansing was happening everywhere. Trials of prominent people were being publicized. People in the entertainment industry, opposing political parties, and people in government were accused of treason by collaborating with Nazis during World War II or spying for the western countries. They were being presented to the public as traitors or Nazi collaborators, therefore, enemies of the state.

Radio stations transmitting from West Germany, were reporting about the members of the United States government, including President Eisenhower, discussing liberation of the East European countries from the Russians and Communists. Hysteria in the Communist government reached a boiling point. The party started a massive witch hunt. Nobody, not even Communist members, were safe. Even groups of the founding fathers of Communism ended up in jail and on trial. It was unbelievable to see the hard core Communists who used to execute people in the past, standing trial themselves.

In the famous trial of Slánský,[*] 14 prominent Communists stood trial, 11 were executed, their bodies were cremated and their ashes were dumped on the road near Prague, and the remaining 3 were sentenced to life in prison."[6] After weeks of torture, the accused were asking the courts to be sentenced to death. Communists were also bringing letters from the citizens in factories, media, and even school children, asking for the executions of the people on trial.

Other dangerous enemies existing in the Communist eyes that needed to be brought to their knees were the religious denominations, especially Roman Catholics, who were widely spread in Czechoslovakia and had the most followers. On December 11, 1949, an alleged miracle happened in the small village of Čihošť in the Czech Republic. During a church service, a 19 inch tall cross located on the altar, moved from side to side and then turned west.[**] The Priest, Josef Toufar, was in front of the cross and did not see it happen. It wasn't until the next day that he learned about the incident from one of the 19 people in the congregation who had witnessed the movements of the cross. News about the "Čihošť Miracle" spread quickly, and many people and members of the Catholic clergy visited the church.

The STB immediately dispatched undercover agents to investigate. The cross moved again during Christmas mass and was witnessed by many people. Father Toufar was arrested on January 28, 1950, and became subject to inhumane torture by his tormentors, who were trying to make him admit that he manipulated the cross. It wasn't until February 23, 1950, when the tortured Priest finally signed a pre-written confession, stating that he staged the miracle, had sexual relationships with

---

[*]   Rudolf Slánský - The long time Communist and one of the founding fathers of Communism in Czechoslovakia, was a General Secretary and senior lieutenant to party leader, Klement Gottwald, at the time of his trial.
[6]   "Wikipedia"
[**]   Under Communist reign, "east" represented good and "west" represented evil (Russian and eastern European countries were EAST, while America and western European countries were WEST).

children, and that he was treated well during interrogations.

The next day Father Toufar collapsed and was rushed to one of Prague's leading hospitals on direct orders from the Department of Interior. The Communists had a keen interest to keep him alive so he could attend an orchestrated public trial. They planned for the Priest to publically admit to staging the 'miracle' in front of the entire nation.

The Father was drifting in-and-out of consciousness when he was delivered to the hospital. Blood and saliva were leaking from his mouth with his teeth knocked out. His body resembled a bloody bag of broken bones. The horrible beating he endured during the interrogation ruptured his stomach and intestines, causing a deadly infection to spread throughout his body. The doctors performed an emergency surgery, but there was no way possible to save the Priest's life.[*]

Father Josef Toufar died on February 25, 1950. His body was then dumped into a mass grave with 40 other victims of Communism. His family was not notified about his death until 1961. They had been informed that Father Toufar died from a bladder infection. While keeping his death a secret and without any remorse for killing a Priest, the Communists continued with propaganda accusing him of being an agent for the Vatican, a western spy, and a con-man who staged a miracle to manipulate people's minds.

Communists made a propaganda movie about the Čihošť miracle, showing Father Toufar manipulating the movement of the cross with hidden wires. This film was shown in the movie theatres nationwide, except in the area surrounding Čihošť. The village of Čihošť was removed from all the Czechoslovakian maps by the Communist government.

The STB executed many hard measures against religious denominations after the arrest of Father Toufar. Many other

---

[*] Father Toufar's case briefly came to public eyes in 1968, thanks to the short-lived freedom of speech. The nurse who was present when he was delivered to the hospital stated, "I was in a concentration camp and have seen crimes against humanity, but I never saw anything like that. There was not one spot on his body that was not bleeding or gaping open." The doctor who assisted during the Priest's surgery said, "We did everything humanly possible to save his life, but there was no chance. He was beaten to death by an indescribable, brutal, sadistic way. I would call it murder."

members of the clergy were also arrested. On April 13, 1950, eradication of all male clergy from more than 140 Czech and 70 Slovakian monasteries took place. The Monk's personal possessions, lands, and buildings were being confiscated. That incident became known as Bartolomějská noc[7] (Bartholomew's night) of April, 1950 in Czechoslovakia.

*

The citizens arrested for political 'crimes' had no right to defense lawyers and often ended up in prison for years without knowing what the charges were. The accused were often given a script by their tormentors to memorize. These scripts were to be recited in the courtroom during the trial. There were cases when the prisoner forgot the lines and fell out of sequence while answering questions from the judge, but that did not matter.

No one was safe. It was easy to resolve a dispute or rivalry by reporting somebody you had a grudge against to the Communists, accusing him of illegal anti-government activity. Cases involving prominent people were publicized, but due to the Communist controlled media, cases with regular people never came to the public eyes. Most of the time those people just disappeared. Some of them came back to their families two or three years later, talking about being in prison. Often times, families were not even notified of what happened to their loved ones. They did not know if their family member was still alive, dead, kidnapped, in jail, or in Russia.

If anyone would dare to question anything which involved Communism, they ended up in trouble. Questions about the skyrocketing suicide levels, the number of children born with defects, the high percentage of miscarriages in young mothers, the air pollution that was way above maximum allowable levels, the devastation of nature, large regions of forests which

---

[7] Bartholomew's night began in Paris on the night of August 24, 1572, lasting several weeks, with bloodshed geared at the members of the Protestant denomination. Modern estimates for the number of dead vary widely between 5,000 and 30,000 in total.

were dying from acid rains, the factories spewing waste into the rivers and poisoning them, or acids which were being pumped into the mines contaminating the underground water.[8]

In Communism, party membership was more valuable than education. Therefore, businesses were being run by party members who had no education or knowledge about the business. Their decisions, no matter how bad or stupid, were never challenged by anyone, due to the fear of the Communist party. Many of the policemen had nothing more than a grade school education and often times not even the full nine years.

It slowly evolved to the point that education was reserved only for the children whose parents were party members. If a teacher failed a student whose parents were high ranked on the Communist ladder, he would be talked to by a party official, and the student would be allowed to pass the exam or bars. The Chief Doctors in hospitals were chosen for their party membership and not for their merits. Therefore, there were cases when doctors who were supposed to remove a female's appendix, removed part of the female reproductive organs instead. The appendix would burst after surgery, causing the patient to die. These types of cases were not uncommon!

Most of the businesses and factories had more people than they needed. The ratio of management employees to workers was too high. A shortage of merchandise was everywhere. If damage caused by a party member became too obvious, the common Communist practice was to relocate them to a different business, usually with a higher position instead of punishing them.

Regular people could not criticize or point any of this out. There were informants spread throughout the population. These informants were also common citizens, such as neighbors or family members, who were recruited by the STB or volunteered for whatever reasons. They were living their everyday life and working a typical job like everyone else. They were supposed to eavesdrop and inform the government about their neighbors and sometimes even their own family

---

[8] Václav Hamr, "Listy" January 1982, article: Uran za každou cenu, page 65

members, especially those in groups that were being closely watched. Some informants were being paid, some did it for a better career or position at work, and some did it for their own beliefs. A good place to eavesdrop was in bars and restaurants, where people often got drunk and their tongues would loosen up, letting out their frustrations.

Regular citizens were not aware of the informants. All this information became public knowledge in 1968, with the short-lived freedom of speech and once again in 1989, after the Communists lost power during the Velvet Revolution.[9] Names of the STB members and informants were published in alphabetical order in 1990, after the fall of Communism. People found out that their co-workers, neighbors, friends, and sometimes family members, had been working for the STB.

Peter's dad's co-worker, a man who he shared an office with, also turned out to be one of those STB informants. People were finding they had been sharing their private dislike of the lack of freedoms and human rights in the Communist country with 'friends', who were government informants. Many times the conversation about Communism was being initiated by the informant himself, and then the report was placed into the victim's ever-growing personal file. The STB were experts at controlling people, manipulating their lives and minds, without their knowledge.

Every once in a while, they decided to teach an individual, family, or group a lesson. In 1968, a new style of music bands started. They were playing American music, mostly Bluegrass and Country Western. They played songs by Johnny Cash, Merle Haggard, Buck Owens, Hank Williams, and such. They also called themselves by American names like 'Greenhorns', 'Rangers', 'Mustangs', 'White Stars' and others... They wore cowboy hats, cowboy boots, and something similar to blue jeans. This was not popular with the Communists, because in their eyes it was too American.

These band members were watched closely and harassed by the STB, especially the leaders. Sometimes one of the

---

[9]   The non-violent revolution in Czechoslovakia in 1989, which saw the overthrow of the Communist government.

members was arrested on phony charges. The STB usually picked up the weakest member and sent him to prison for approximately six months, where he would be exposed to tremendous harassment by common criminals, some of whom were also classified STB informants. This happened to the fiddler in the band 'Taxmeni'.[10] When a person like that returned from prison, he was usually a changed man. He would relay the horrors of what took place there. The purpose of this was to keep the entire band in check and keep them from getting out of line. Many times, these people were forced to inform on other band members, by constant threats of being sent back to jail for a longer time, in a worse prison, etc... These people became classified as STB informants, but were not on the payroll.

A similar situation happened to one of Peter's dad's co-workers. The family was too outspoken against the Russian occupation and lack of human rights under the Communist government. One day, the son-in-law went for a Sunday walk with his newborn child in a stroller, along the Vltava River in Prague. He stopped at a hotdog stand and bought a beer. As he was drinking his beer, a drunk Russian military officer standing next to him, kept addressing him in Russian. The man was not paying any attention, pretending that he did not understand. The officer told him that he liked Czechs and Czechoslovakia.

"Czechs are the Russians *little brothers*," he said.

He was acting overly friendly, telling the man how cute his baby was, and putting his arm around him. He kept talking to him with a big smile. The man did not want to have anything to do with the soldier, so he told him in Czech that he did not understand. The Russian on the other hand, was gesturing that he did not speak Czech. Then the Russian wanted to propose a toast to the brotherhood between Russians and Czechs, to which the man responded, "Ty jsi ten poslední člověk s kterým bych si tady připil." (You are the last person in this whole country I would ever have a drink with.) He finished his drink and walked away. The police picked him up before he returned

---

[10] Jaroslav Čvančara, "Taxmeni", page 53

home.

His wife received a phone call from the police department to come and get her child. She kept asking what happened to her husband, but they would not tell her. She insisted on knowing what was going on, and was told she had better leave or they were going to arrest her too, then decide what they will do with their child. The family was sending letters and making phone calls, trying to find out what had happened, but they never received an answer. They did not know anything about his whereabouts or if he was dead or alive. He returned home 2½ years later. He had been in prison that entire time. There had been no trial, no court appearance, or accusations brought against him. They never told him why he had been arrested, and when he asked why he was in prison because he had done nothing wrong, they replied, "If you would have done something, you would be dead!"

Chapter Thirteen

PRISONERS OF COMMUNISM

After being arrested and his clothing was removed, each prisoner was photographed, fingerprinted, stripped of their personal possessions and identity, and then referred to by only a number assigned to them by the Communist institution. They were then addressed by that number and reported to their superiors by number only.

Teams of interrogators, each with their own methods of coercing information, were working around the clock on the prisoners. Beatings, along with physical and mental exertion, were common. Prisoners were forced to stand at attention and were not permitted to use the toilet or drink water for hours, sometimes days. The horrifying screams of torture and death, along with insane howling and incoherent chattering, were heard all hours of the day. Badly beaten prisoners were being dragged through the hallways, groaning in pain, as they could no longer walk on their own. [11]

Some interrogators preferred to set prisoners on a triangular shaped chair in the corner of the room, with his legs chained to the wall. [12] One interrogator's favorite method was beating a metal bucket placed on the prisoners head with a wooden stick. Another interrogator actually killed several people during his interrogations. One time he had beaten a confession out of three suspects, even though only one of them

---

[11] Barbara Masin, "Gauntlet", page 85
[12] Josef Frolík, "Špion Vypovídá", page 263

was guilty. They would not retract their confessions even after a new interrogator took over. Only after being tortured again, all three reversed their confession of guilt. Even though only one of them was guilty, the results were all the same. [13]

A different case was of an interrogator who chained a suspect to the wall and forgot about him due to his 'heavy work load', as he later explained. When he remembered, the suspect was already dead. His body was thrown from Barrandov Cliffs in the suburb of Prague. His death was alleged to be the work of the CIC[*] (Counter Intelligence Corps). [14]

An interrogation prison used in the city of Bratislava was equipped with a basement room finished with white tile flooring and walls splattered with red paint, resembling blood. A person wearing a hangman's hood and holding an axe was standing next to the execution stump in the middle of the room. Even the strongest individuals confessed to anything after being pushed into the room when the hangman called 'next'. [15]

Many kinds of psychological torture were also being used. Sometimes direct lies like, 'your wife has been arrested and the children are home alone', 'your child could have an accident', 'you do not want anything to happen to your loved ones do you' were being used to intimidate prisoners, while showing them pictures of badly beaten, bloody people. [16]

Sometimes politically 'unpopular people' received a visit at home, usually in the late evening hours. A team of four showed up, as in the case of one targeted man. His wife was not home at the time they came. The STB team locked his three children in one room, while putting him through hours of 'special treatment' in another. He was beaten up, burned with matches, chocked with a towel, threatened with arrest, and promised to have his teeth knocked out.

In another case, they waited for a middle-aged lady to be home alone. They beat her up enough to cause a concussion, cut off her hair, ripped her nightgown, violated her by touching

---

[13] Josef Frolík, "Špion Vypovídá", page 266
[*] CIC-Was the U.S. Army's intelligence gathering organization.
[14] Josef Frolík, "Špion Vypovídá", page 267
[15] Josef Frolík, "Špion Vypovídá", page 267
[16] Josef K., "Právo Lidu" #4/82, Cesta do Jámy Lvové

her all over, threatened her with death, cut her phone lines, and stole her tape recorder before they left.[17]

*

After Communists in Czechoslovakia lost power in 1989, committees to investigate prison environments were created. The following is their findings in the prison of Valdice, which is categorized as a level III prison.[*]

The prison complex was built hundreds of years ago as a Monastery. The combination of peeling stucco and the stench of disinfectants mixed with human waste was depressing to all who entered.

Small prison cells were overcrowded with prisoners who were forced to walk or stand from 6:00 in the morning to 10:00 at night. Sometimes they were required to walk even during the meals.

Prisoners who broke the rules, for example, the toothbrush was not laying down with the bristles up or for sitting down outside allowed hours, would end up in the 'hole'[**] for 30 days, or their privileges were revoked. The prisoners were allowed to receive up to a 1.5 kilogram (3.3 pound) package and receive visitors for one hour every eight to ten months. One of the punishments was to cut these privileges in half.

The worst punishment was to be transferred to section III, the so-called 'house-of-horrors', which was like a prison inside a prison. Prisoners were sent there for 30 days either in solitary confinement or crowded into a very small area with many prisoners together. Food portions were cut in half, from a daily

---

[17] Marie Benetková, "Právo Lidu" #4/82, Povolání Pravých Mužů

[*] Prisons in Czechoslovakia were separated into three levels, with level I being the lightest and level III for the hardest criminals sentenced to 20 years, 30 years, or life in prison. Those who committed murder, rape, sex offenders, along with alcoholics, political prisoners, handicapped, visually impaired, epileptics, etc...Some were repeat offenders, for example, a person stealing a bottle of liquor was sentenced to probation. The second time with the same offense , they spent time in a level I prison, but the third time they broke the law, they were sentenced to 20 or 30 years in a level III prison as a repeat offender, even for stealing just one can of food.

[**] A cell in the basement equipped with boards for the bed and one blanket.

monetary value of 7.30 Korunas (20 cents) to 3.50 Korunas (10 cents) per day, per prisoner. A tiny piece of meat was removed from their meal.

Only the strongest individuals survived the constant dark, damp, cold environment, and hunger. The committee found an unknown male human being lying on the saturated floor in a basement cell, filled with steam from a leaking radiator. He turned out to be a young man who was completely insane and did not know his name or where he was.

Guards were often drunk and would beat prisoners for fun.

"They beat me until I was bleeding heavily," said one of the inmates, "then made me lick my own blood off the floor."

One level called the 'level of death' in the 'house-of-horrors' was used for total isolation. Prisoners were living in complete solitary confinement, some for a number of years. Death was always present. Suicides were common and so were 'mystery deaths'. There was one doctor for 2,500 prisoners.

Prisoners not in solitary confinement were required to work in manufacturing buildings with obsolete machinery, no safety training or equipment, and were required to meet absurdly high quotas.

Half of the inmates small wages were deducted to cover their expenses for imprisonment. Additional money for child support, court expenses, not meeting their daily quotas (without consideration of their health conditions), daily penalty for being in solitary confinement, and damages caused by their crime were also deducted. The rest of the wage was deposited to their individual account. When released after years in prison, it was common for the prisoner to enter society with only a few dollars in his pocket. [18]

---

[18] Vladimír Mlynář, Lidové Noviny #3, 1/13/1990, article: Trestat zločin zločinem

Chapter Fourteen

OUTDOORSMAN

Peter's dad, who was also named Stanislav Vodenka, was a very gifted and spirited person. He was born on July 26, 1921, and like his father, was a member of Sokol. He was handsome, tall, muscular, intelligent, a true gentleman in all aspects of life, and highly respected by everybody who knew him. His many talents included drawing, painting, wood carving, and the ability to play many different musical instruments.

He married Peter's mom in 1946, shortly after the war. Jarka was nineteen and he was twenty-five. Their means of transportation was a Harley Davidson motorcycle. It was a U.S. military Harley that had broken down during the war and was thrown in the ditch by the U.S. Army. Peter's dad picked it up and fixed it. There was a big shortage of gasoline, and it was very expensive when available. Diesel fuel was a little more accessible, so Stanislav mounted a gas can to the Harley, which would then be filled with diesel. He split the gas line leading to the carburetor and installed a second shut off valve. When they traveled, he started the Harley with regular gasoline, and after awhile, switched to diesel when the engine was hot. It didn't run very smoothly, but it ran. The trick was to switch it back to gasoline about 15 minutes before the engine would be shut off. That allowed enough time for the gasoline to wash the diesel fuel from the carburetor and clean the spark plugs. The Harley would not start if the gas valve was not switched in time.

In 1947, their first son was born. Now they had a family

and needed something bigger than a motorcycle. Once again, Stanislav returned to the ditch and picked up a German military 'jeep', a KdF (Kraft durch Freude). It was wrecked and did not run, so he rebuilt the engine. He disposed of the open style body, and using the body of a civilian Opel car, he remodeled it to fit the frame of the KdF. The air-cooled engine was in the back of the vehicle like a Volkswagen Beetle, and in summers it would often overheat. The car was quite cold in the winter as there was no heater. However, it would be their family car for the next 17 years. At that time, they were one of a few families in Czechoslovakia that owned a car.

In those days it was not required to have a driver's license for motorcycles, but Peter's father had to have one for the car. He scheduled the examination and was told to provide his own vehicle. He did not have time to put the vehicle completely together, so when he arrived, there were no doors or seats. He put in a wooden box for himself and a small kitchen chair for the instructor to sit on.

"I had to take it easy on the gas and brakes," he used to say while laughing. "I did not want to make the instructor mad by causing him to tip over or fall out of the car."

Peter's dad loved the outdoors, and from an early age, he would go camping and spend as much time as he could in nature. The workweek consisted of six days back then. On Saturday afternoon, he packed up his backpack and guitar, and traveled out of town into the wilderness. He was living with his parents in a northern suburb of Prague, so he had to travel by bus and city tram through Prague to the train station on the south side. The train traveled through the picturesque valley along the Sázava River, to the town of Štechovice. From there he would follow the trail along the river to the base of the hill called Medník. It was a very beautiful place, popular with people like him who liked to camp overnight. They would set up campfires, play guitar, and sing songs until early morning hours, then sleep under open skies as there were no tents in those days. Stanislav was always welcome at any campfire. He was one of a few that could play guitar and sing songs. He sang nostalgic songs filled with stories about the wild American

West, open plains, cowboys and Indians, starry nights, cattle punching, desperados, the Northern Lights, and other things that stimulated people's imagination and helped them dream.

After he was married and his first son was born, he took his family into nature as often as possible. When the weather was nice, they spent most Sundays away from towns, streets, factories, and people - out in the forest, by the river where they could play, lay in the sun, and swim. Stanislav and his wife would save all their vacation throughout the year so they could take a big vacation during the summer, most of the time lasting two or three weeks. They bought their first two tents big enough to fit two people each. These tents had no floors so Peter's mom took heavy duty canvas rubber coated on one side, and sewed it on the bottom of the tents. They took camping gear and supplies to last three weeks while traveling into beautiful Southern Bohemia, searching for good camping places. Eventually, they found a beautiful secluded grassy place along the banks of the wild Vltava River, heavily wooded on both sides.

About one mile up the river was the beautiful medieval castle of Zvíkov. This place became their summer vacation spot for the next seven or eight years. They usually went on vacation from mid July to early August, but one year they had to move their vacation forward, since Jarka was expecting a baby at the end of August.

The next year they were back camping at the same place. Peter was only eleven-months old. All food had to be cooked on an open fire, since propane bottles were not yet known in Czechoslovakia. The diapers had to be washed in the river, and baths were also taken there. There was no civilization, no other people, and no Communism - only open blue skies and sun during the day and the moon and stars at night. It was like Heaven being in the woods on the banks of the untamed river, with its soothing sound cradling Peter to sleep. Every night they had a campfire, and Peter's dad sat by it with his guitar.

"There are two kinds of fire," he would tell his boys. "The utility fire is used for cooking and heating the house. That fire is useful and it's okay to start it with human products like matches and paper. However, there is also another kind of fire. It is the campfire which you sit by on quiet evenings, where you play songs, tell stories, and dream. That fire is sacred," he said. "You see - animals cannot start or use fire - only people can. Fire is a present from God to humans so they can stay warm and cook their food. The campfire is sacred and should be kept pure. You cannot degrade it by using artificial, human products. We don't use matches or paper to start this fire."

He taught them that Scotch pine trees usually had dead branches with twigs at the bottom that stayed dry most of the time, even in the rain. When it rained, the water ran off the branches above like an umbrella.

"It is okay to break these branches off because they are already dead. When you crush them, they burn as easy as paper. The white bark from Birch trees is another good source, it even burns wet. You place these items on the bottom with bigger sticks on top. Instead of using matches," his dad said, "start a small fire on the side and light one of the branches, and then transfer it to the campfire. You can also use a magnifying glass or prescription glasses with sunrays, to ignite the fire. Never throw any human products in the burning campfire. No paper! No garbage! No cigarette butts! No cans or glass! Never spit in the campfire - it is as disgraceful as walking into a church and spitting on the floor!"

A campfire is a place where songs are sung and stories are told. You feel its warmth on your face while listening to the crackling sounds of the burning wood, and watching the flames dance around in the dark. Late at night when you stop feeding the fire, it gets smaller and smaller until you watch the last red sparks glowing among the ashes. It makes you sad - because something special, something beautiful is ending. Then you crawl into your sleeping bag and drift into your dreams, while hearing the soothing sounds of the breeze in the tree tops, sounds of the wild river and night life in the forest.

The place where they used to camp was breathtaking. It was an open grassy area about 30 feet higher than the river bank. On the other side, crowned by pine trees, the cliffs stood 300 feet high above the river. The grassy place they used for camping was accessible by a narrow service road made of stone that followed the river. This road was constructed many years ago, during the time when the river was used as the main supply line for merchandise delivered to Prague, or as far as Germany. There was a steep bank behind the grassy area that was also covered with pine trees. Another narrow road leading to this place was too steep and rough to travel by car. That road led uphill, through the forest, and leveled out into the meadows and fields. It split into two small picturesque villages.

The two rivers, Vltava and Otava, joined approximately one mile up the river, with the castle of Zvíkov creating the peninsula between them. The castle was mostly in ruins, but it was open to visitors a few hours a day, during the summer. The tour guides were an older couple that had living quarters in one of the castle buildings. Peter's dad became good friends with them and some other local people. He loved to talk to them and listen to their stories about the days-gone-by. The main section of the castle was protected by a large wooden door. This door locked at 6:00 in the evening, but not for Peter's dad. Anytime he wanted to go there with the family, the gate keeper would open the door, let them in, and lock the door behind them. The keeper told them to pound on the door when they wanted out. Those were the best of times. It was very nice, but a little spooky being in that big old castle by themselves with the sun setting.

On each side of the castle was a ferry large enough to carry a vehicle. The ferries crossing the Vltava and Otava rivers were connected by a dirt road along the foothill of the castle. Peter's father became friends with the Ferrymen that lived in small houses by each river. The Ferrymen moved people across the river. This way of living was passed down to them through generations for centuries. This was their way of life and the only one they knew. They never had time off or vacations. There were large brass bells situated on each side of the river. If travelers came in need of crossing during the day or night, they would ring the bell until the Ferrier came to get them.

The beauty of the forests and wild rushing river with cliffs was incredible. The big old castle stood peacefully high above, surrounded by water on all three sides. It was overwhelmingly beautiful even for a small child. The river was crystal clear with a lot of white water rapids and calm sections. It wound through towns and villages, meadows, forests, and fields. There were many old castles along the banks of the river. It was amazing to see such a huge monumental structure reaching for the Heavens appear while coming around the river bend in a canoe.

Some people's idea of a vacation was to travel down the river in their canoes or kayaks, and camp along the way. It was always interesting to watch people float by. There were large rapids a short distance up the river from their family campsite. Sometimes there would be an empty canoe floating by upside down, with people in the river trying to retrieve it.

Every once in a while, a big raft constructed of tree trunks, with a group of five men would go by. These were very special sights to Peter. In the deep forests of Southern Bohemia, the trees were being harvested for lumber. The tree trunks were pulled to the river by horses, where men would construct rafts by tying them together. Approximately 15 trees were tied side-by-side to form one section. Five of these sections were linked together behind each other, to create a large raft with enough flexibility to move with the bends in the river. Three twenty-foot long paddles were sticking straight out from the front of the raft and two similar paddles were in the back. As the raft was being carried by water, men used the paddles to miss the boulders or steer the raft to compensate for the bends in the river. Sometimes it would take two weeks to reach their final destination of Prague or beyond. Every day before the sun set, men would tie the raft to the shore to anchor it for the night. In the center of the raft, a raised platform was built to keep their supplies dry and to cook their meals. They slept directly on the raft or on the river bank beside it.

Some restaurants located along the river, had a landing area designed especially for rafts to be anchored to. In those cases, the men could eat in the restaurants and have shelter for the night, if they timed it right. The timing depended on the water level and how fast the river was moving. As the rafts passed by the restaurants, the men would blow a horn and the restaurant owners would put beer and food in the basket. They held these baskets out on a long stick with a hook on the end. The men would take the food out and put money in the basket. After reaching their destination, they would take the train as far as they could, then walk alongside the river to return home.

Peter wished he was one of those men. He dreamed of being on the river at sunrise when the mist was lingering, or in the quiet evening when nature was settling down to sleep - to be able to travel through the rapids and lazy parts of the river - float through the forested areas where the air was cool - travel through beautiful Southern Bohemian villages - pass through the fields heated by the summer sun - to be in the deep canyon surrounded by tall cliffs with blue sky above, and listen to men telling stories when the moon and stars were shining brightly in the dark summer nights... *unfortunately, the beauty of this river would soon end...*

*

The government was building a large electrical water dam that would stop the river from flowing and raise the water level by 150 feet. The castle standing on the cliffs would soon have water to the footings of the walls. The high banks of the river allowed engineers to raise the water without spilling out and flooding the land.

Villages and remote settlements along the river would soon perish. The government started logging all the trees that would eventually end up below the water level. People in the villages would have to move, which created quite a big problem since there were no extra homes in Czechoslovakia. People could not easily buy a house or rent an apartment. Many times there were three generations living in the same house together. These were grandparents, parents, and children, all born in the same house. Some of the buildings that would soon be under water were demolished, especially tall buildings like churches, while others that would end up submerged deep under water were left alone.

There were a few buildings worth preserving that had historical value. One of them was a church and bell tower from a small village called Červená. The workers placed a pair of railroad tracks leading up the bank. The church was taken apart and moved up the track in pieces to be reassembled above the future water level. This project was beginning to run behind and suddenly there was no time to disassemble the tower, so they simply blew it up and rebuilt this historical structure from memory, using new material. This was the typical Communist mentality - nothing was ever sacred to them. Both of these buildings are still there today.

Two Ferrymen taking people across the river were going to lose their homes and way of life. One of them later described his experience when the water level raised enough to stop and close the rapids. He said it happened in the middle of the night while he was sleeping in his house, as he had done since he was born. Suddenly the silence woke him. For the first time in his life, there was no roar of the river. It caused chills to run up and down his spine. He felt as if the river died and something inside him died along with it! The other Ferrier simply refused to leave his home, planning to stay and die there. The water in his house was already three feet deep when his relatives came to drag him away, fighting and crying. He never fully recovered and spent the rest of his life as a broken man, and eventually died alone.

The main entrance to Zvíkov. Many years ago this entrance was protected by a draw bridge. The two small holes on each side of the round entrance were used for the chains. The two narrow openings above the door were used for shooting muskets to defend the castle.

Man-made log raft downstream from the Zvíkov Castle on the Vltava River. Notice the roof of the Ferrier's house on the left side.

Zvíkov Castle overlooking the Otava River. In the middle of the river is the Ferrier's raft hauling a car.

Stanislav Vodenka and Jarmila Křivánková on their wedding day, July 15, 1946.

Peter's dad, Stanislav, at work.

Peter's mom, Jarka, with Patty.

Chapter Fifteen

GIRL WITH BLONDE CURLY HAIR

Peter's mom, Jarmila (Jarka) Křivánková, was born on September 2, 1927, the youngest of seven children, four boys and three girls. Her father, Hugo Křivánek was a widower, who already had two sons when he married Jarka's mother, Marie. When Jarka was born, her oldest brother was married and had a four-year old child.

She grew up in a small town called Osek, located in the northwestern part of Bohemia, approximately ten miles from the Czechoslovakia-Germany border. Her dad was the chief of the railroad station, which was a prestigious government position. They lived in a designated house next to the station along the railroad tracks. She was 5' 3" tall with blonde curly hair, green eyes, and was considered to be very attractive.

After finishing grade school, she attended business school and graduated with honors. She met a tall, muscular, handsome man, with black hair and brown eyes, who was six-years older than her. They were married on July 15, 1946 and had two sons.

Jarka did not have an opportunity to utilize her business education and worked in an iron ore factory in Mníšek pod Brdy for most of her life, until she retired. She took samples from each iron pour and analyzed it for its chemical content and mechanical properties such as strength and hardness. It was a dangerous job. She lost a section of her middle finger just below the nail, which was torn off by one of the machines at work. Anytime Peter was hurt, his father told him to think about the pain his mother had endured from the accident. Peter still uses this mental picture today.

Peter liked to jump on her back for a piggyback ride. He recalls coming home from school one day and to his surprise, she was home already, sitting straight up in a chair, leaning slightly forward in an unnatural position. Peter's heart skipped a beat as he knew something had to be wrong.

The first words out of her mouth were, "Please don't jump on my back!"

She explained that she had an accident while scooping melted iron flowing from the blast furnace that had came in contact with a foreign substance, which caused the liquid to erupt into the air. Some of the pieces landed on her head and inside her collar, burning her badly, leaving permanent scars on her neck, back, and scalp.

Jarka was a very talented cook. It always amazed Peter how quickly she could prepare a meal, especially when they were camping and she had to mix the ingredients on her lap, and then cook them over an open fire. It seemed as if it only took her a few minutes to prepare an entire meal. All the food was made from scratch, even the noodles that she prepared and dried in the sun. They did not have meals that were precooked or from a can or jar.

He remembers her picking and canning fruits from the trees that created hedges along the country roads. She canned fruits such as apples, pears, plums and cherries. Jarka was steadfast and always had three meals a day prepared for her family. In the morning before Peter went to school, she was already at work but there was always bread and cocoa, or something similar, ready for him when he woke up. Dinner time, around 2:00 in the afternoon, was always their biggest meal. It usually included some type of soup and generally a meatless second course. For supper they would eat a smaller meal. Sunday dinners were special because they consisted of soups, meats like rabbit, duck, chicken, pork or beef, home canned fruits, and always some type of homemade baked goods.

Many of the underclothes and shirts Peter wore were

handmade by his mom. She was very good at both sewing by hand and using the large sewing machines, which was not electric, but ran by manual foot pedal. He remembers the dresses she made for herself.

After she retired from the factory job, she worked in a sanatorium outside the village of Nová Ves pod Pleší as a nursing assistant. She was always a hard worker and would still be working today if it were possible.

Chapter Sixteen

LIFE ALONG THE RIVER

Another interesting story is of the old chain bridge close to the town of Podolí. The new bridge was built beside the old one, but it was a lot bigger and higher. Many years ago when the old bridge was built, there were stone gates on each side of the river, with the platform suspended by chains in between. At the dedication ceremony, people from a nearby town filled a metal case with documents and letters about the town, a town history, who built the bridge, and other interesting facts. They also put money in the case, so future generations would know what it looked like at that time. Everything was documented in the town history book. The metal time capsule was cemented inside one of the gates. Years later, due to the water level changing, the bridge was taken apart to be moved to a different location. The metal case was retrieved and opened, and to everyone's surprise, the money was gone. No one ever figured out how or when the money was taken from the box.

*

A species of fish called Sumec (Wels Catfish) was living in some Czechoslovakian rivers. It is a predator that can grow very large and live many years, since it has no natural enemies. Sumec is a territorial fish that stays in the same area their entire life. A large one lived in the river by one of the Ferrier's house.

The fish was doing damage by eating the Ferrier's ducks

and even attacked his dog while swimming in the water, almost biting off his leg. The Ferrier and other people were trying to catch the fish for years, but were not successful. One day, somebody came up with the idea to take a live domestic duck and put it in a leather harness with large hooks attached to it. Then they tied the duck to shore with a rope and let it swim in the river. The fish took the bait and swallowed the duck, but the people could not pull it out of the water. A horse was brought in to pull the fish on shore. It weighed over 220 pounds and was almost 7 foot long. People were coming from all over to see this monster. Peter remembers seeing it laying on the hay wagon with its tail hanging off.

During the last summer when Peter's family went camping at their old place, the river was already rising and in a few areas, the water was spilling over the old stone road leading out. Peter's dad had to drive through water as they were leaving. That was the end of the beautiful old wild river. Luckily, the new water level created a different beauty and scenery.

The next year, his family needed to find a new place for camping. They were looking in the same area. One day, a small, nearly invisible road led them through the forest to a grass opening on the cliffs. The road ended at a small wooden cabin. It was locked up and no one was around. In one area, the cliff changed into a steep bank that led to the river, making it accessible. There was also a crystal clear brook running through the woods providing drinking water. They set up the tent and spent their vacation there.

The following year they returned to the same place again, but this time the owner of the cabin was there. He talked to Peter's dad and told him he was the engineer who designed and supervised the building of the electrical dam that closed the river. One day while surveying the land to see how high they could raise the water level, he stumbled upon this place. He fell in love with the area and built the cabin there. Everybody was laughing at him and thought he was crazy for building a cabin high on the cliffs, with no access to the river below, but he knew what would happen within the next few years.

Now, the government was going to send him to Egypt to build an electrical dam. He would be gone for six to eight years and was thinking about selling the cabin, since he would not be around to use it. That was how Peter's family ended up owning the cabin in this completely secluded place with no roads, surrounded by beautiful scenery. The cabin was very simple and basic with no electricity or running water - but that was what made it so special to six-year old Peter. There was only one room with a wood stove used for cooking and heating. Peter considers those days to be the best times of his childhood.

His parents started staggering vacations in the summer, so the children could be there as long as possible. School summer vacation in Czechoslovakia was two months, July and August, and there were a few times when the children spent the whole two months there. They were always outside, swimming in the river, running through the forest, and climbing the cliffs. They often picked blueberries, strawberries, and mushrooms, for their mother to use to prepare their meals. Their skin was tanned from the sun, and they were hardy and healthy.

Every morning they would get up before their mother prepared breakfast and run down to the river to brush their teeth and swim for their morning shower. Every so often, the children were sent to the nearest small village to buy fresh eggs and milk. One or two times per week, they would walk through the forest, fields, and meadows, to the larger village with a small grocery store. The store was the size of most people's kitchen. It had basic food supplies such as vegetables, milk, bread, flour, butter, and jam, but they also sold farming equipment such as milking buckets, pitchforks, and also horse whips. People had to bring their own hand bags to the store to carry their groceries home.

There was another somewhat bigger grocery store in a small town on the other side of the castle. To shop there, they had to take the ferry across the river. After walking through the castle and traveling another mile and a half, the road led to a small town with a more modern grocery store. That store had more grocery supplies but no farming equipment. This trip was always special and pleasant to Peter, as they traveled through the countryside.

Chapter Seventeen

ABANDONED CHAPEL

There were crosses and small praying chapels found in unusual areas, and Peter always wondered why they were there. There was one in particular that seemed to be abandoned and had deteriorated through the years. Eventually, he learned the heartbreaking story from centuries ago, about this small praying chapel which was approximately the size of a closet. It involved a young couple who lived in the four house village nearby.

Josef, a young man twenty years of age, lived in one of the four houses in the tiny village. He was tall, skinny, and lively. Living in one of the other houses was Madla, who had long black hair, dark eyes, a narrow waist, and was always full of life and laughter. She was considered a real beauty. It was during the time of the Thirty Years' War,[19] when the young men were being recruited as soldiers into the army for money. If they could not find enough volunteers, they were taking men against their will. Those were the times when young men left their homes to go to war, only to return many years, even decades later, prematurely aged and bitter.

The small village was secluded and the recruiters did not come there very often. When they did, Josef was warned by the neighbors and would disappear deep into the forest before the

---

[19] "Wikipedia," The Thirty Years' War (1618-1648) was one of the most destructive conflicts in European history. The war was fought primarily (though not exclusively) in Germany, and through the years involved most of the countries of Europe. A major impact of the Thirty Years' War was the extensive destruction of entire regions.

recruiters arrived. Josef and Madla were in love. One day, while she was taking a tax payment to the nobleman's house, his typist saw this beautiful girl and wanted her for himself. She would not hear of it because she had given her heart to Josef. The typist made excuses to visit her house often, but she always managed to disappear. This made him mad, and he became even angrier when he was told she was engaged to Josef.

The typist told the recruiters about the young, strong man that would make a good soldier, and gave them the address of Josef's parent's farm. The recruiters searched for him but as many times before, Josef disappeared before they came to their house. They were told that Madla probably knew about his whereabouts, so the recruiters went to Madla's house, pulled her out, and began asking her questions while being somewhat rough. Josef was watching from his hiding place and ran to help her. The recruiters overpowered him, put him in shackles, and took him away. As they were leaving, he turned and called back to Madla, "Wait for me in our favorite spot. I will be back!"

Their favorite spot was a flat rock on the highest point in the neighborhood, close to their village. The view from there was breathtaking. There were white houses with red roofs, green meadows, and golden fields surrounded by dark forest, in the distance. Every day, in the evening when the chores were done, Madla walked to their spot, and stood on the rock looking over the countryside to see if Josef was coming home. Days slowly changed to weeks and weeks turned to months, but Josef was nowhere in sight.

Madla gave birth to Josef's son and named him Jiří. The months slowly spilled into years. The trees were growing taller, obstructing her view. She would bring her young son with her, lifting him on her shoulders to see over them. She would ask him if he could see his father coming. Madla was getting older, and the trees were growing taller, so she brought rocks to stack on top of each other to be able to see across the countryside. Her age began to show. Her eyes were not as sparkly now and her back started to bend. Wrinkles were visible around her eyes, but she continued to go to that same spot every day, waiting for Josef's return.

The rocks were starting to create a wall, and it became bigger than she was. The nobleman's typist that kept chasing her for years had died. Both of her and Josef's parents had passed away long ago. Her thick black hair was starting to change to silver, and her little boy had become a grown man. Her son, Jiří, had married and took over the farm. The war finally ended and Madla felt that Josef was not coming back, but day after day, she went to their place to wait for him.

The rocks were falling apart, so she asked her son to cement them together. She was getting too weak to climb the walls, so they built steps for her and placed lumber on top. She continued going to their spot even though her eyesight was weak, and she could barely walk.

When she was too old to climb on the wood, she continued to go and just sat down on the ground leaning against the wall. She hung a picture of the Virgin Mary on the wall, praying everyday and reminiscing back to the happy times. Soon there was a picture of Jesus and a small religious statue hanging next to the Virgin Mary. Year after year, she would come to this place...remembering...waiting.

She would bring fresh flowers until the time she could no longer get out of bed. Then she asked her son, his wife, or her grandchildren to take flowers to their place and watch for Josef. When she was on her death bed, she told her son, who was an old man himself now, "Don't forget about our little chapel my boy. Your father may still come back." But, he never returned.

The spirit left her body. After her death, they took the rocks apart and built a small brick structure designated for praying. The walls were finished with white stucco and the roof was covered with red clay tiles. It was furnished with a little wooden table and a prayer bench in front of it. A white tablecloth and a vase filled with fresh flowers were always present. Small trees were planted on each side of the chapel. Josef and Madla's descendants continued to bring fresh flowers during the summer and artificial ones in the winter.

The abandoned chapel - picture was taken in 2009. The tree on the right was planted after the original one died many years ago.

A cross erected in the woods away from civilization.

A different chapel along the road by the village of Jickovice.

Zvíkov in the present day. Photograph was taken in 2009.

The individuals involved in this story have died, and their remains disappeared a long time ago. The countryside has changed, but the small white chapel is still standing on the same highest spot, overlooking the countryside. It is clearly visible from all directions, as if still waiting for Josef to return home, hundreds of years later...

*

When Peter and his family started going to this place in the early 1950s, no one was taking care of the tiny chapel. The trees beside it grew so big it would take two people to wrap their arms around the base. As they grew wider, the trunks began pushing on the structure and cracked it. The roof also had a few holes and was leaking, and the building was deteriorating. The view from this place was phenomenal and somehow became spiritual and dear to Peter's family, even before they learned the story behind it.

Many years later after the Communists lost power, the chapel fell under jurisdiction of the nearby village, and Peter's family members started asking why no one was taking care of it. They were informed that the descendents of the family were no longer around, and the village had no money for repairs. Peter's family donated 3,000 Korunas (five weeks wages) to repair it. They also brought new pictures of the Virgin Mary and Jesus Christ. They gave the money to the local mayor, who had previously been a hard-core Communist party member. The next year Peter's family expected the chapel to be repaired, but it was not, nor was it years later.

After the mayor passed away, Peter's brother mentioned the donation to his friend, who was a member of the village board. They looked through the books and discovered that the money had never been registered as being donated. The good old party member pocketed the money and never mentioned anything to anyone. Eventually, the village decided to fix the chapel, and now it is being taken care of as a local landmark.

The cabin with these surroundings was like a sanctuary to them - almost sacred - just being away from the outside world and Communism was priceless. They were totally alone and nobody was watching them. Sometimes Peter's parents would invite visitors, but Stanislav always told them not to bring newspapers or battery powered radios. He did not want to read or hear any Communist lies and propaganda while on vacation. Peter's dad felt that the cabin was the only place they could get away and forget about that dreadful oppressive system.

*

Peter's dad was very creative with his hands. The walls of the cabin were decorated with his paintings and wood carvings, all of which pertained to the American West. The evenings were reserved for playing games, listening to stories, or just sitting around the campfire with the guitar and singing songs. The air was clean since the cabin was far away from any towns. The stars sparkled in the sky with the moon lighting up the forest, creating silver cascades shimmering across the river.

They only used the cabin for sleeping when it was cold or raining outside. Sometimes they slept in tents, but most of the time they slept outside under the open skies. Since he was the youngest, Peter had to go to bed first. He watched the starry summer night skies above, while listening to his dad's songs in the distance, as he drifted off to sleep.

The first thing Peter always did after arriving at the cabin was to take off his shoes. There was one year he stayed barefoot for the entire two months. The bottom of his feet became so callused and tough, that he could run on pinecones or rocks without feeling it. He was eventually able to walk barefooted over hail after a storm. At the end of summer when it was time to go back to school, he had to put his shoes on, and his feet burned like they were on fire for the entire first week.

Those days in the cabin taught and prepared Peter for his future life and his dad had taught him how to preserve nature without damaging it.

"If you need firewood, chop down a dead tree."

He told him to never stick an axe, pound nails, or put wire around a live tree. Don't throw human waste around because it makes the place look ugly and disgusting. Always clean and dispose of everything properly. When you go camping or work in the forest, always leave it the same way as it was before you got there.

Don't make unnecessary noises. If you are too loud, you will not see nature, the animals will disappear before you get close enough to see them. Everybody can hear you and will know where you are. If you are too noisy you can't hear what is going on around you. If you leave a mess or cause damage, everybody will know where you were and what you were doing.

At night, if you are in the light, you cannot see anyone in the dark, but they can clearly see you. It is also the same if you are walking with a flashlight. A person can only see what he is shining the light on, but nothing else. Everybody else can see exactly where you are."

Peter learned quickly how to orient himself in the dark and was not afraid. He realized the forest looked exactly the same as it does at daylight, only at night you could not see it. He also knew that if you can't see others, they cannot see you either. If it is too dark, your eyes start to play tricks on you. Suddenly, you start seeing things that are not there and movements that are not happening. By trying too hard to see, the brain is not concentrating on other senses that are more helpful in the dark.

Peter also learned the sky is always lighter than objects, so if he could not see where he was going, he would look up at the sky. This allowed him to see the outline of the trees, so he knew where they stood. If it was too dark to see anything, it helped to close his eyes and open his mouth, which improved his hearing. In the dark, hearing and touch are two senses that are more important than eyesight.

He learned how to follow a path or trail by just the feel of his feet. Even narrow trails or paths were smoother and harder than the rest of the forest floor. Thanks to many summers spent in the forest, Peter could walk at almost regular speed in total darkness with his eyes closed, and know where the path was and what it looked like. He learned patience while waiting for wild animals and birds, or by sneaking up on them to have a closer view. He learned to depend on himself and how to survive in nature with minimal supplies.

Chapter Eighteen

AWAKENING

Peter was not exactly sure when he first became aware of Communism. It might have been in fourth grade, when they were required to start learning and speaking Russian. Teachers told their students that Russian was the language spoken by most of the people in the world. He also had to join a Youth Communist Organization called 'Pionýr', where children had to attend meetings and specified events. The uniform they wore consisted of blue pants, a white shirt, and red scarf. It was said to be a volunteer organization, but parents did not dare to keep their children from joining. They did not want to 'rock the boat' and attract the attention of party members. Peter hated this. It made him feel like a sheep, by being forced to do the same thing everyone else was doing, but he had no choice. *

Maybe it was during the times when he came home from school talking about history class, and his father would sit him down and tell him the true history. His dad explained how things really happened, but would tell Peter not to repeat it, because it could get him in a lot of trouble and he could end up in prison. The Communists were always changing, twisting, and obscuring history, starting with children in grade schools. For example, the schools did not teach about the American Army liberating parts of Western Bohemia, including the big town of Plzeň (Pilsen) during World War II. The inhabitants of

---

* To read the Pionýr promise and laws, see appendix E in the back of the book.

Plzeň remembered that Americans liberated them, lived in their homes and helped them with food and money. They used to give men cigarettes and children bubble gum and chocolates, which they had never seen before. At some point later, schools in Western Bohemia started teaching the students that those soldiers were actually Russians dressed in American uniforms. The Cold War was raging, anti-American propaganda was seen everywhere, and Czechs being liberated by the American Army did not fit in the Communist scheme. The Russians were supposed to be their saviors, while Americans and Western European countries were considered to be dangerous enemies.

Adults would not openly discuss this situation for fear of persecutions. There were monuments erected in honor of the American soldiers, who died liberating Czechoslovakia during the war. Their names were engraved in stone. The communists started tearing those monuments down throughout the years, until they were all gone. However, the population of Plzeň was grateful to the Americans and continued to place flowers where the monuments once stood. The few that dared to do so, went in the middle of the night to avoid being seen.

The one other thing that made Peter aware of the fact that they were living under Communist dictatorship was their May celebration. The First Day of May celebration was the biggest Communist holiday and every city and town held parades on that day. People had to assemble at a specific place and walk in columns through towns, waving Czechoslovakian and Russian flags. They carried pictures of prominent leaders and founders like Lenin, Stalin, and other Communists. People working in factories and local businesses marched together, while school children who were wearing the party uniform paraded with their classmates. Speaker platforms were erected on the main square, where local high ranking Communists would speak. There was usually a band playing the Communist marching songs.

Citizens were expected to display the Czechoslovakian and Russian flags outside the windows of their living quarters. The apartment buildings and houses built under Communism were automatically equipped with the flag holders on each side of the window. People were expected to tape flags to the windows if they did not have flag holders. Some people hung the flag because they believed in Communism and some did it to avoid attracting unwanted attention. It was a sign of rebellion not to fly the flags - only a few people had the courage to revolt.

Most of the people attended the parade because they did not dare being the only person missing from work. Every place and business had one or two dedicated party members, who were more than willing to snitch on the other people. Peter's parents were always upset about the parade, but went anyway, like everybody else.

Peter hated those celebrations from his early childhood. During his grade school years, he did not have a choice and went to the parade. When he was fifteen-years old, he graduated from grade school and went to plumbing trade school for three years. The trade school was in Prague and he had to get up at 5:00 in the morning to catch the bus. Then he got on the city tram and traveled through Prague to school. This created an opportunity for him to skip the parades. The authorities in his home town assumed he was attending the parade with his trade school classroom. He told the teachers in his trade school that he was a member of the junior soccer team in his home town and was going to the parade with them. Therefore after turning fifteen, he never attended a Communist parade again. It made him feel proud and rebellious, which gave him satisfaction. He felt like he had one up on them.

*

Peter grew up in the small town of Mníšek pod Brdy, approximately 15 miles south of Prague. It was a pretty town with its own school, stores, and even a gas station. The town was nestled at the foothills of the forest ridge named Brdy. Iron ore was discovered in the hills before Peter was born. Samples of iron ore were taken to determine its quality and amount. The quality was low and there was not a big supply of it, but under the pressure from the Russian Communist advisors, the Czech government decided to mine the iron ore anyway. Millions of Korunas were spent building a factory for processing the ore, changing it into raw steel. With the need for factory workers and miners, a new section of town was soon built with new apartment buildings. Peter's dad was hired as the designer for the mechanical parts of the factory in 1952. It was a good job opportunity for him and he accepted the offer. The young family moved to their new home south of Prague.

Mníšek pod Brdy was a small town with a long history. It had a bus and train line connecting it with Prague and the town of Dobříš, which was approximately ten miles in the opposite direction. The center of town was the oldest section with a big square in the middle. There were stores, a few restaurants, and a church. Since iron ore was discovered and the factory was created, a new school needed to be built.

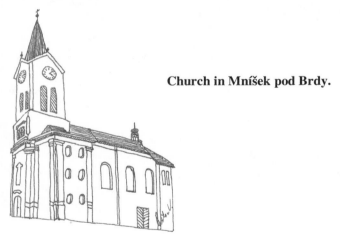

Church in Mníšek pod Brdy.

There was an old Monastery standing in the hills above the town. It was a complex with beautiful old buildings, a prayer alley depicting the Stations of the Cross, and a famous historical chapel. A long time ago, a noble family lived in a small castle-like building. That family was very religious and founded the Monastery on top of the hill. The nobleman was an admirer of Saint Mary Magdalene, who lived in the caves by Marseille, France, for 33 years in penance for her sins. The church was later built above the cave. The nobleman sent a famous architect to France to copy the church, so he could build a miniature replica in the Monastery complex, which overlooked the town of Mníšek pod Brdy. The interior of the chapel was created to resemble the inside of the cave and was finished in 1693.

They also built a road and planted trees on both sides. The road connected the Monastery to the Catholic Church in the middle of town. The trees are large and old, but still present today. The noble family was chased away by Communists and the abandoned, neglected complex slowly collapsed into ruins. Their small castle was also vacant and started to deteriorate. The church in town was the only building still operating, but the Communists did not respect or accept religion and were telling people that God did not exist. Children in schools were being taught to laugh at and make fun of people who attended church and to see them as extremists. Church services on Sunday were attended only by older widowed women, usually less than 20 attendants. This number continued to drop as they passed away.

Catholicism eventually became the only religion left in Czechoslovakia since the Communists had prohibited most religions and tore down their churches. They were afraid of any group that might be organized, fearing that groups of people might be plotting to overthrow the government. It was even illegal to have more than five people standing together on the street at one time. The Communists wanted people to believe in one *religion* only - Communism.

The underground tunnels used to mine iron ore were spreading through the hills. As a result, the earth above shifted and the ground started cracking and settling underneath the historical chapel. Half of the chapel remained on solid ground and the other half began to sink. The walls cracked almost exactly down the middle. One half of the building ended up settling down about one foot below the other. This caused holes and cracks in the roof, which eventually began to leak. The beautiful, unique, religious, historical building was falling apart.

The factory was open for years but never made a profit - it was losing money year after year. It was spewing pollution and smog into the air. During the winter, the snow would turn black as the smog and ashes covered the ground. The creek running beside the factory eventually turned into polluted slime and contaminated the lake it fed into.

The historical chapel above Peter's hometown of Mníšek pod Brdy. The picture from 1974 to the left shows the deteriorating chapel while under Communist reign. The only repairs they ever made was to strap four steel bands around the structure to keep it from collapsing to the ground.

The earth settling caused the building to crack in two different places indicated by the arrows, from the ground to the roof on both sides of the building. The picture on the right shows the fully restored chapel after the fall of Communism in 1991.

None of this prevented the Communists from operating the factory anyway. There were many other businesses spread throughout the country in the same situation. None of them were ever shut down, no matter how unprofitable or how much pollution they created. That was the way Communists operated, but it was also leading to their end. Money to operate the businesses that were not profitable was running out. The buildings and businesses that Communists had confiscated from private hands were never maintained and were slowly deteriorating.

The building that Peter and his family lived in consisted of eight apartments. All the apartments were exactly the same and had only one bedroom. Some apartments in other buildings in the new development didn't have any bedrooms at all, just a kitchen and a living room. The building had three levels. The ground level was called the basement and housed the laundry room used by all of the families. There were no automatic clothes washers and water had to be heated in a big pot with a coal fire. The hot water was then transferred by buckets to the washing machine. There was also a separate machine used for spinning.

The rest of the basement was sectioned out for each of the occupants to use. Each family had two rooms, one bigger than the other. The bigger room had a window approximately six feet above the ground and was used to store wood and coal to heat the apartment. The only heat in the apartments was the stove with metal plates in the kitchen, used also for cooking. Coal was being rationed for each member of the family. The larger the family, the more coal they were allowed to buy. Once a year, a truck would bring the coal and dump it on the sidewalk in front of the building. The family would shovel the coal into buckets and carry it to the basement. If the father was strong enough, he would carry the buckets of coal and dump them through the window. As a result, everything inside the building was covered with black coal dust.

The smaller basement room was used to store food for the winter. During the fall after harvest, the trucks would deliver potatoes. One 50 kilogram (110 lbs) bag of potatoes could be purchased for each member of the family per year. The potatoes had to be spread on wooden grates, so they did not rot. If one started to rot, it had to be removed quickly before it ruined the entire crop. Mothers were canning different kinds of fruit in the fall to last throughout the winter. Above this basement were two more levels with four apartments each.

Peter in Kindergarten with the precious wooden dump truck he received as a Christmas present. Five-year old Lída in her folk dance dress.

Peter's hometown of Mníšek pod Brdy. Peter and Lída both attended grade school here. Arrow indicates the house Peter grew up in.

Apartment in Mníšek pod Brdy, Peter's home from birth to age twenty-four. Their apartment was the balcony on the lower left side and the window to the right of it. The arrow indicates one of the small windows used for throwing coal into the basement.

Initiation into the Youth Communist Organization, Pionýr, in the fourth grade. Peter is the third one from the right.

Peter's school year 1965-1966.

Lida with her third grade class, first one on the left in the middle row.

Kitchen duty at the Boy Scout camp. Peter is standing in the doorway. The stove was made by the scouts from clay they collected in the nearby creek.

Peter and Lída during early school years.

Chapter Nineteen

CHILDHOOD

Peter was really good friends with three boys living in the same apartment building. He was the youngest and smallest one of them. His best friend Patrick was almost one year older, but they were still in the same class. Dan was two years older, and Jarek, Patrick's brother, was three years older. Every morning they would meet in front of the apartment building and walk approximately one mile to school. They would walk back home at different times. The children could not leave the classrooms until the teachers dismissed them. It was not uncommon for the teachers to continue talking after the bell rang, or to keep kids after school as punishment for bad behavior.

The school hours on Monday, Wednesday, and Friday were from 8:00 to 2:30. There was a half hour allowed for lunch and five minutes between each class which was used for bathroom breaks and to move from one classroom to the next. Students were not allowed to use the bathroom during class time. On Tuesdays and Thursdays, classes were from 8:00 to 12:00, with a one hour break, and then continued from 1:00 to 4:00. Each classroom averaged 20 to 30 students.

The school basement was sectioned into small rooms, one for each classroom. They were constructed of heavy duty steel wire with a gate and lock on them. That is where the children stored their coats and changed into their slippers. Each student had to have a fabric bag with his or her name sewn on it, used to store a pair of slippers. Those slippers were worn during school hours.

Peter did not like school. It was hard for him to sit and do nothing for hours at a time. He was not putting any extra effort into learning, doing just enough to get by. He hated the Russian language class most of all, as did most of the other children.

The students were required to address their male instructors as 'Soudruh Učitel' (Comrade Teacher), and female instructors as 'Soudružka Učitelka' (Comrade 'Teacheress'). Peter hated this Communist requirement and could not force himself to do it. Even though corrected numerous times, he addressed the instructors by Mr. Teacher or Mrs. 'Teacheress'. Eventually, they gave up and stopped correcting him. He was the only one in the class that dared to do this.

While in school, children had to sit with their hands behind their back, unless they needed them for writing. If a student was acting improperly, the teacher would smack them or make them hold their hands straight out, hitting them over the fingers with a wooden pointer, which was very painful and caused swelling! For more severe punishment, the child would have to stand in the corner with his hands stretched out. The teacher would place the wooden pointer on his hands. After awhile, the child's arms would get tired and would slowly drop down. If the wooden pointer rolled off, the teacher would add more punishment time. Each student was given a personal notebook, which had to be with them at all times. If the student misbehaved in school, the teacher would document it in that book then the student was required to have a parent sign it. The father would usually discipline the child again at home.

The grading system was from one to five. Number one was considered the best and five was failing. This system was used throughout the ten month school year. It was used on tests, homework, and all school projects. At the end of the year, the teachers would add all the scores together and divide them by the number of tasks throughout the year. If the child ended up with a number five grade in any subject, they had to repeat the entire school year again. This was always a fear for the children because they would have to leave their classmates and friends. They would be in class with the younger kids whom they used to look down at through the year. If a student failed a class and repeated a school year, he would still attend only nine years. He would graduate from eighth grade instead. Peter remembers one boy who ended up failing three times and graduated from the sixth grade after attending school for the required nine years. Student conferences were conducted twice a year. Their parents had to go to the child's homeroom and sit at their child's desk. The teacher would discuss each student in alphabetical order, in front of all the other parents. It was very embarrassing for the parents whose child was not doing well in class.

Children were also required to do after school tasks, such as collecting different kinds of plants. They assumed the plants were sent to Pharmaceutical companies to be used for making medications from herbs like Red Clover, Nettle, Lime blossom, Chamomile, Wild Rose hip, and many others. Only certain parts of each plant could be used. The blossoms were the only part used from the clover and only the leaves from the Nettle. It was a dreadful job and the children hated it. There was a specified amount required they had to collect based on the type of plant. The children could choose which plant they wanted to harvest. Peter usually chose Clover because it was the easiest for him to find.

First, the herbs or plants had to be found, then collected and taken home and spread on newspaper to dry out. After the plants dried, they shrank in size and weight. A full bag of fresh Clover shrunk down to ¼ of a bag. The dried leaves of Nettle resembled butterfly wings. If the plants were not dried properly or turned moldy, they would be thrown away at school and the student would have to do it again.

During the fall, children were required to pick up acorns, chestnuts, or Wild Rose hips. The Wild Roses were growing in big bushes along the country roads. After the petals fell off, a smooth, hard, dark orange berry developed in the center. After the first frost, the berry softened up and was ready to be picked. A thick orange jam-like substance came out when squeezed, having a sweet and sour taste. Mothers used this berry to make jam or dried them to make tea during winter. The dried berries could also be bought at the pharmacy. This tea was supposed to be good for cold and flu symptoms.

*

Peter and his three friends were together a lot. Every day after school, they would go outside to play games and find new adventures. They were pretending to be characters they had read about in books. They made swords and played musketeers after reading The Three Musketeers book and others. Every day after school, they went outside to play soldiers, cowboys and Indians, trappers, or explorers. During weekdays they had to be home at 6:00 P.M. to eat dinner, do homework, and be in bed by 8:00. Going to bed at 8:00 was standard for most children there. On the weekends, they could stay up later. They were getting plenty of sleep, since they did not have to get up until 7:00 A.M. This created quite a problem for Peter when he graduated from grade school. His plumbing school was in Prague, and he had to get up at 4:30 A.M. and walk about ½ mile to the bus station. The bus ride to the suburb of Prague took almost one hour since the bus made many stops to pick up other commuters. The city tram took another 45 minutes to travel through Prague, where he then continued walking the additional ¾ mile to his plumbing trade school, which started at 7:00. He was used to sleeping until 7:00, and getting up at 4:30 was hard for him the first year.

Peter was pretty small for his age and developed later in life, which was common for all the boys in his family. It was a disadvantage when he was playing with his friends who were older and bigger. They never took it easy on him. They often hiked to the forest to play different games or rode bicycles for long distances. In the winter they would ski across the country. When they hiked, the boys would walk really fast so they could get far in a short period of time. In the beginning, Peter had to jog to keep up with them, until he started taking very long steps. Those long steps affected the way he would walk for years to come. When he was a young man, people would make fun of the way he walked due to his long strides. People said his head bobbed up and down with every step, so he taught himself to walk a different way.

During the summer break they would ride bicycles to his best friend's grandparent's house, who lived in a beautiful small town called Karlštejn, on the opposite side of the ridge Brdy, running behind their hometown. There was a large old castle with the same name standing on the hills, overlooking the surrounding area. Peter did not know that many years later he would be married in that castle. His older friends were big enough to ride bicycles with six speed shifters and lighter frames. Peter's bicycle was smaller with a steel frame and only one speed. At eleven, he was not yet big enough for the adult bicycle. He always had to work hard to keep up with them on bicycle trips. Those trips often lasted a whole day. On the way back home, they had to ride five miles of uphill, switch-back roads. The road climbed to the top of the ridge Brdy, before descending into their hometown.

They never brought water for the trip. They were told by their parents that if they started drinking water, they would have to keep drinking and their stomach would become so heavy they would not be able to ride. A few times Peter felt like he was going to die of thirst. There was a creek running down the hill along the road, fed by a spring from the iron mine. The water was red and slimy from all the different pollutants. It took all the strength Peter had not to drink that water. However, that did not stop him from making the trip again a few weeks later.

He was always behind his older friends struggling to keep up. He felt that since he could not compete with them in speed and strength, he had to do more dangerous and crazy things to earn their respect. When they climbed trees, Peter always went the highest, or if they were jumping into the river, he always jumped from the highest point where the rest of them would not. When they were swimming or diving for objects in a lake, he retrieved the deepest one. The summers he spent at the cabin, in the forest, and on the river gave him some advantage over his friends. His experiences and activities build up his confidence and endurance enabling him to be more daring. The other boys did not have a place like that and had to spend their summer vacations at home.

This all was coming to an end when Jarek graduated from grade school, then Dan graduated and moved on. At the end, it was just Peter and Patrick.

Chapter Twenty

HONOR

Late 1967 and early 1968 brought many new changes into Czechoslovakia. People seemed to be more excited and happy. Newspapers also changed and there was less anti-American propaganda. Certain books and magazine articles that had been once prohibited were now allowed to be published. A wave of happiness, excitement, and euphoria, was sweeping the nation. Organizations and clubs started springing up: Boy and Girl Scouts, Sokol, Harley Davidson, Willys Jeep club and others. There was more freedom of speech and suddenly there was more information being released about Communist and Russian atrocities. New faces and names appeared in the government. It was still a Communist government, but they were talking about freedom and independence from the Soviet Union. 'Socialism with a human face' was the new government slogan. There were discussions about opening borders to the west, and to establish exporting and importing trade with Western European countries and America.

Peter was twelve-years old and did not understand much of what the adults were talking about, but he could clearly feel the changes. Everybody was smiling more and talking openly about issues they would not dare to have discussed before. He joined Boy Scouts and went to camp for four weeks in the summer of 1968. The boys were being taught to be truthful and respectful to their parents, and how to assist elderly people and others. They were taught respect for their country and how to be real patriots. The entire summer camp was constructed from scratch by the scouts, including tents and a big fire ring in the middle. There was a kitchen, mess hall, and a flag pole, where the boys raised the Czechoslovakian flag every day. The older boys took turns as night guards to watch over the camp for two hours at a time. The group was broken into teams and each team had to cook one week for the entire camp.

The boys were being taught endurance, patience, and self control. Earning 'Beaver Pelt Awards' was one of their favorite activities. The boys were told the trappers in old west America, hunted different animals for their fur. The beaver pelt was hard to get and was highly prized. Beavers were timid animals that scared easily, which made trapping them quite difficult. It took patience, hard work, and skills to capture them. There were 13 Beaver Pelt awards, some were easier to earn than others. It was each individual boy's choice to earn them since they were not mandatory.

The first yellow 'Beaver Pelt of Health' required the Scout to run 50, 60, and 100 meters in a given time and to jump a required height and distance depending on his age group.

The second light green 'Beaver Pelt of Accuracy' required the Scout to hit the chosen target 80 times from 100 throws with a stone.

The third black one was the 'Beaver Pelt of First Aid' and required the Scout to learn basic first aid skills.

The fourth red 'Beaver Pelt of Swimming' required the Scout to swim 60 meters without assistance.

The fifth dark blue 'Beaver Pelt of Gentlemen' required the Scout to learn respect of others by being well mannered, with no screaming or swearing. This took seven days to earn.

The sixth was the dark brown 'Beaver Pelt of Courage'. The area chosen to earn this patch was usually the scariest place around the camp, like a swamp in the woods, or a remote area with a cross or cemetery. The leader and a boy trying to earn the patch would walk to that place during the day and place some type of symbolic item there. The boy would then go back after dark alone, with or without a flashlight, which depended on the distance, terrain, and his age, and try to bring back the item. If there were more boys trying on the same night, the youngest ones went first.

The seventh dark green one was the 'Beaver Pelt of Nature'. The boys had to be able to recognize and name 50 different plants or trees.

The eighth orange 'Beaver Pelt of Silence' was one of the hardest to earn. It took a lot of self control. The boy could not talk or make noises, including laughing or sneezing loudly, for 24 hours. The boys could choose the time they wanted to start their 24 hour period. Peter did not know anyone who earned this patch on their first try. Sometimes it took two, three, and even more times to succeed. Some of the boys tried many times and never earned this patch. To make the task even more difficult, the leaders would sometimes wake the boy up in the middle of the night and ask him a question. It took a lot of self control and awareness to remember not to answer. The boys were also being taught that lying or not doing a task the correct way would be dishonorable. There was one case when one boy had only one hour left in his 24 hour silent period and started singing in the forest when he was alone outside of the camp. His conscience would not allow him to earn this patch, and the Scout admitted the truth to the leaders.

The ninth pink 'Beaver Pelt of Solitude' required the boy to be alone and invisible to other humans for 24 hours. At night fall, the leaders would take the boy away from the camp and help him prepare for the night. It was not very far away, but out of sight from the other scouts. The following morning, the boy would walk away from his sleeping bag and the leaders would collect it. The scout had a back pack with supplies and food for one day. It made for a long, lonely day, being away from the rest of the scouts for 24 hours.

The tenth purple 'Beaver Pelt of Skill' required the boy to make 13 wooden buttons, bore holes into them, and color them, one for each 'Beaver Pelt' symbol. After earning each award, he had to sew it on his shirt by himself, with no assistance.

The eleventh light blue 'Beaver Pelt of Strength' mandated the boy to accomplish a specified amount of pull ups, sit ups, and pushups. It required being in good physical shape.

The twelfth grey one was the 'Beaver Pelt of Hunger'. The

boy was not allowed to eat anything for 24 hours, not even chew bubble gum or suck on candy, he could only drink water. It took Peter two tries to earn this patch. The first time, he was outside of camp in the woods when he ate five berries from a Blueberry field before remembering the goal. Peter would not be able to enjoy this patch because it would always be on his mind that he cheated and so he returned to camp and told his leaders. Most of the boys felt the same way. The boys had to wait two days before they could try again, because the leaders did not want them to go too long without eating.

The thirteenth white 'Beaver Pelt of Nobility' required the Scout to perform a good deed daily, without being asked for 30 days. This was usually accomplished by helping with extra chores, carrying coal from the basement, chopping wood, or bringing water from the well for elderly, sick, or others in need. Their regular duties such as washing dishes or helping their parents with everyday chores did not count. It was the Scouts responsibility to record his good deeds.

Chapter Twenty-One

OVERCOMING THE FEAR

The Boy Scout leaders in camp decided to find destinations for earning the Beaver Pelt of Courage. One day, each boy was handed a small, solid, wooden block cut from a tree branch, measuring approximately 3 inches in length and 1¼ inches in diameter.

"This will be your object to bring back from your hunt," they were told. "You can paint it, carve it, or leave it the way it is. Just make sure you leave a clean smooth spot to write the date and the name of this camp, after you earn the patch."

One afternoon, the leaders gathered the boys together and went for a hike. "Pay attention" they said, "if you want to earn the Beaver Pelt of Courage, you will have to walk through here alone after dark."

Everybody started following the path behind the camp. The fresh green meadow was warm from the summer sun and had a pleasant smell. There was a narrow wild game path at the point of the meadow, which entered into the pines. After approximately 15 yards, the path crossed an old narrow trail made by horse drawn wagons in the old days. They followed the trail uphill. The boys could hear a creek softly running in a ravine on the right side, obstructed from view by thick bushes along the road.

The forest started getting darker and the temperature was colder, as the tall trees were preventing the sun from reaching the ground. The trail continued up hill and without the sunlight, the forest did not look as friendly as before. After walking for approximately 15 minutes, the forest was getting lighter as the road exited the trees and entered a beautiful meadow basking in the afternoon sun, covered by hundreds of Ox-Eye Daisies. The meadow was bordered on three sides by pine trees, with an island of lime trees in the mouth of it, approximately ¼ mile ahead. The old unused two track dirt road made by wagons and buggies continued past the lime trees, and started descending through the wide open countryside with rolling hills, leading to a simple, quiet village, whose red roofs could be seen in the distance. The group walked up to the lime trees and stopped. An old black steel cross cemented in a big flat boulder was peacefully nesting in a lap of trees.

"Why is this cross here?" some of the boys asked.

The leaders told a sad story about a young couple in love many years ago. They were engaged to be married, but the girl's parents strongly objected to the relationship, as he was from a peasant family and not good enough for their daughter - how they prohibited her from seeing him - how the two secretly became engaged, promising to love each other forever and declaring they would rather die than be separated - how one day the young man, his father, and brother were logging trees in the forest that the Scouts had just walked through - how there was a terrible accident and the young man was crushed to death by a tree trunk rolling off the wagon - and how he was calling the girl's name, until the blood running from his mouth prevented him from being heard. The young girl screamed in agony when she learned about the accident, and ran all the way from the village to be with him, meeting the wagon carrying his dead body at this very spot - by these trees - where she fainted from the sight of his lifeless corpse. When she finally awoke, she was deranged and out of her mind. For more than three years, she wandered around the area barefoot, clothes in rags, dirty and unkept. Her hair had grown down past her knees and was a tangled mess. Most of the time she would sit in these trees and call his name, while crying and sometimes howling like a wild animal. On quiet nights, her inhumane screams could often be heard all the way down into the village. When somebody approached her or traveled by, she would growl like a rabid animal, but most of the time, she would just simply disappear into the forest at the sight of people.

The villagers were often bringing food and clothing for her, leaving it on this flat boulder. One day - they discovered her lifeless body hanging from a thick branch, where she had hung herself, right above this rock. The villagers chiseled a hole into it, and erected this cross in memory of her broken heart. They often brought fresh flowers and prayed to God to forgive her, for taking her own life. Some say that on quiet nights, her cries could still be heard and her spirit could be seen wandering around...

There was dead silence when the leaders finished telling the story. Some of the boys took a deep breath as they had forgotten to breathe while listening.

"Place your blocks on the rock at the bottom of the cross," the leaders told the boys. "This is where you will have to come to earn the Beaver Pelt of Courage. You will bring your block back to camp as proof you made it all the way here, than write the date on it as a reminder of your accomplishment."

*

The walk back to camp was quieter as the Scouts were still submerged in the story, and no one felt like talking. The sun was getting closer to the horizon, and it was almost dark deep in the forest. The mood changed as they emerged from the woods on the meadow behind the camp, which was still basking in the evening sun. The boys started joking once again, talking bravely about how they would go to the cross. One boy was saying how he would jump up to swing on the branch above the cross, but their courage was slowly disappearing as the sun was setting down. The camp was unusually quiet that evening.

Peter's heart was racing in his chest. He knew he should volunteer to go back there that night, but did not want to. He knew the moment when the leaders would ask for volunteers was getting closer. Peter was telling himself that he did not have to go - nobody was making him - it was completely up to him, and that made him relax some. But the more he thought about it, the more he knew he had to do it that same night. If he did not, it would be on his mind all the time, making him nervous until he made the trip. He was one of the four oldest boys in camp. The younger boys were separated into four teams, with Peter and the three older Scouts assigned as a leader for each. Teams earned points through different races, competitions, games, creativity, and how clean and orderly they kept their tents. Peter's group had earned the most points so far, and his boys were looking up to him. He was teaching them how to be strong and brave. He *had* to volunteer first, or he would feel like he was letting his team down, and when the question was asked, he immediately raised his hand. Three more boys also volunteered that day. Peter was the oldest, so he would go last.

Shortly after dark, around 10:00 P.M., the first one of the boys was given a flashlight and whistle. The whistle was only to be used in an emergency, in case the boy became lost or in trouble. The camp was quiet since the boys had to be in bed by 10:00. The only people still up were the four Scouts and their leaders. When the first boy left, the rest of them were anxiously waiting for his return. After what seemed like an eternity, they saw the flashlight in the trees, moving quickly down the hill. The boy ran into the camp sweating and shaking, but with a big triumphant smile, proudly holding his precious wooden log. The second boy changed his mind and did not go. The third boy was gone for quite a while, but returned empty handed... He had made it all the way to the meadow on top, but could not force himself to go close to the patch of trees and eventually gave up.

It was almost midnight when it was Peter's turn. The older boys did not get to use a flashlight, which made it even with the younger ones. They could only light a match while finding their own piece of wood at the cross. The moon shining overhead was illuminating the meadow. His heart was beating heavily in his chest. He followed the meadow to its point, easily finding the deer path. The forest was dark and his focus switched from sight to his feet, feeling the ground. Peter turned onto the old trail and followed it uphill.

The surroundings were getting darker and darker - the creek sounded so much louder than before. Now it was almost deafening in the quiet of the night. He wished he had the power to turn it off, because he could not hear anything else. Peter was straining his eyes trying desperately to see. The bushes on the right looked black, and he started to see movements there. He was forcing himself to stay composed. 'Your eyes are playing tricks on you,' he was telling himself. Calm down! You know how the forest is at night! He had enough experience in the woods at the cabin. The thoughts about the young man from the story that had been crushed somewhere in this area entered his head. He tried to force the thoughts out of his mind. As he was walking up the hill, the sound of the creek slowly began fading away until it was completely silent.

Now he could depend on his hearing again and suddenly - he heard a soft sound behind him. 'What was that!?' he thought, straining to hear better. Someone was following him! He heard a soft, gentle, swishing sound as if somebody was sneaking up behind. Peter thought he recognized the sound of pants, rubbing between a person's legs. Peter's heart was in his throat, he held his breath and stopped - so did the sound! He must be hearing things. Peter started walking again, and the sounds behind him resumed. He decided to pick up the pace some, but whatever was following him also sped up. When he saw the moonlight in the meadow through the trees, he began to run, but the *thing* behind him was keeping up. Peter bolted into the open meadow looking over his shoulder, fully expecting to see someone or something behind him...but there was nothing - only the sound.

Then it dawned on him - he remembered the small box of wooden matches in his back pocket. The box softly rattled with his movements and made noise. When he stopped moving, the noise stopped, and when he ran - the matches bounced around more.

Peter looked around and relaxed a little. The white flowers in the field made everything lighter and visibility was better. There was no one around, but the patch of trees was very dark. His heart started beating faster when he realized - that was where he had to go. Now he understood why the boy before him, could not force himself to reach his destination. 'Let's get this over with,' he thought, 'and the sooner the better.' Peter was about 15 yards from the trees, when something made him stop dead in his tracks...! His heart started racing in his chest. He saw something that looked like a light-colored, torn up dress, swaying back and forth in the trees.

The memory of the girl hanging from the branch in the story, shot through his head. He felt as if ice-cold fingers were squeezing his heart and stomach! Dropping to one knee, he hunched over making himself less visible. He forgot to breath and was straining his eyes to see through the darkness. And there it was - he could clearly see a silhouette of a female body hanging by her neck. In a flash, his whole body was covered in a cold sweat, and then - from the corner of his eye - he saw movement to the right of the trees and a second later, one to the left... He sighed with relief when he realized, it was the mist rising and lingering in the dim moonlight.

He walked the remaining distance in a hurry, easily locating the cross. His heart jumped as he lit the match, casting black shadows moving all around him. He did not dare to look at the branch above! Peter quickly located his carved block, then turned and ran across the meadow until he entered the forest. He jogged down the hill holding his precious prize in one hand, and the box of matches in the other, to prevent them from making noise. He switched to walking just before he exited the woods. Peter gathered himself together and casually walked back to camp, where he was greeted and congratulated by the waiting leaders. He was covered with sweat, but felt very, very, happy and relieved.

*

Peter woke up to the sound of a trumpet. His first instinct was to jump up, but soon he realized he did not need to do it today. He could not see the camp, but knew exactly what was happening there. The boys were scrambling from their sleeping bags to line up in four teams by their height, to raise the flag, and do their morning exercises. That routine was repeated every morning at 6:00 A.M. The boys had 2 minutes to line up before points would be subtracted from the teams total score.

Peter's sleeping bag lying on the pine needle forest floor was warm and very comfortable. The air was crisp and had a pleasant fresh smell. He knew it would be cold while getting dressed, and did not want to get up. He would have the whole day to spend alone. It was the morning of his quest to earn the Beaver Pelt of Solitude. The summer camp would come to an end in a week, then it would be his thirteenth birthday, and the beginning of a new school year would soon follow. He did not like school and was not looking forward to it. He yawned and stretched his body and limbs like a lazy cat.

The boys out of sight were laughing and splashing in the water. The morning line up was over, and they were brushing their teeth and washing in the nearby creek. He knew he needed to get up and disappear before somebody came by, spoiling his chance to earn his award. He dressed quickly, picked up the backpack with supplies for the day, and walked away leaving his bedding behind for the leaders to retrieve.

Peter was walking through the trees for some time, finally crossing the open meadow away from the sight of the camp, to brush his teeth and wash his face in the creek. The cold water washed away the last remains of sleepiness. He loved how strong and healthy it always made him feel.

The last night he decided to follow the creek upstream, to see where it would lead. That way he would not get lost and had a plan for the day. Now he had a new idea, he would first go to the place of the Beaver Pelt of Courage destination, where he walked to a few days earlier. Peter easily found the trail through the woods leading to the meadow with the steel

cross. Now everything was peaceful, quiet, and beautiful in the morning sun. It did not seem at all like the same scary place from the intense night that he had remembered. Looking around, he reminded himself once again, it looks exactly

like this in the dark - we just cannot see it. Some wooden blocks at the bottom of the cross were gone as more boys overcame their fears and accomplished their goal, but there were still many of them left. He told himself to remember to run here on the last day of camp, to dispose of those which would not get picked up. There was no need to litter this special place.

Peter started walking to the woods on the left, slowly circling back to the creek. As he stepped out of the woods onto the grassy meadow, he caught movement out of the corner of his eye. He looked quickly to the right and saw a man with a scythe, cutting hay. Luckily, the man had his back to him. Peter quietly retreated back to the trees, out of the man's sight. Had the man seen him, Peter would have had to start all over again.

He did not have a watch and was trying to judge time by how high the sun was in the sky. When he thought it was about noon, Peter set up a small camp with a fire ring made of stones, and began cooking pea soup for lunch from his supplies. When the soup started to boil, something caught Peter's attention. He took a spoon and retrieved a red object periodically coming to the surface. It was a large hairy spider, which turned red in the boiling water. It was gross, disgusting, and he wanted to pour the soup out, but had nothing else to eat. He had to force his mind to think about other things while eating the soup, as the picture of the boiling spider made his stomach turn.

After noon Peter began making his way back to camp, but he could not return until after supper. Staying out of sight, he climbed a tall tree to see what activity was taking place in the camp. He realized it would be a long time before the evening meal. He must have been sitting in that tree watching for two hours, before fulfilling the requirements for the Beaver Pelt of Solitude.

Chapter Twenty-Two

RUSSIAN INVASION

Peter returned from Boy Scout camp on August 18, 1968. His mother, a Girl Scout leader, was attending training camp. His brother was a tank commander in the military. Every man eighteen-years old, was drafted into the service for two years. During the second year, soldiers were allowed to take seven days vacation, which they had to apply for. This vacation could be denied but the soldiers whose commanding officers felt deserved a vacation, were allowed to leave.

In the morning hours of August 21, 1968, four days before his thirteenth birthday, Peter was abruptly awakened by the loud speakers mounted on wooden poles throughout his hometown. These speakers were used by city officials to get information from city hall to the people. At first he did not understand what was happening, but as he listened, he realized Czechoslovakia was under military attack. Peter was home alone and scared. What he understood was that his country was at war, and he did not know what to do. Around 10:00 A.M. his father came home from work. This was the first time Peter ever remembered either one of his parents coming home early. His dad told him that everybody left work because the country was under Russian attack. The Russian government could not handle seeing the political situation change in Czechoslovakia. They were afraid if Czechoslovakia separated from Russian control, the rest of the Eastern European countries would follow and losing that much power was something they would not tolerate.

The Soviet Union was organizing huge military training operations for Warsaw Pact[20] countries, the Eastern European equivalent to NATO (North Atlantic Treaty Organization). The war games were organized approximately every five years and involved the Russians and all Eastern European armed forces. This time, the Czechs were not invited. These war games took place in countries surrounding Czechoslovakia. In the middle of the night, united military forces entered Czechoslovakia from neighboring East Germany, Poland, Russia, and Hungary, while special trained attack forces of paratroopers were being dropped on Czech airports, to seize control.

Early in the morning hours, thousands of tanks and trucks with Warsaw Pact soldiers occupied all the big cities, including Prague. The enemy forces surrounded all Czechoslovakian military bases, court houses, and railroad stations, arresting some certain members of the Czechoslovakian leadership. The Russians hurried to seize all of the radio stations that were transmitting information and directions to citizens through the public radios. This was very important as the whole nation was listening for updates. The Russians were aware of this and were trying to silence them and cut off all communications.

Peter was sitting in the kitchen with his dad listening to the broadcast. The radio stations were being taken off the air one after the other, until there was only one left. The remaining station was informing citizens about the military movements and government members who had not been arrested or were in hiding. Those government officials were periodically calling in, keeping citizens abreast of the situation. The last radio station was calling for help from the citizens, asking them to surround the building they were transmitting from, since they were the last form of communication, and the Russians were closing in.

Station employees barricaded the front door of the building and the studio door to delay the takeover, stating they

---

[20] Wikipedia-The Warsaw Pact (1955-1991) is the informal name for the mutual defense called *Treaty of Friendship, Cooperation and Mutual Assistance* subscribed by eight Communist states in Eastern Europe that was established at the USSR's initiative and realized on May 14, 1955 in Warsaw, Poland. The states were Albania, Bulgaria, Czechoslovakia, East Germany, Hungary, Romania, Poland, and the USSR.

had only minutes of airtime left. Peter remembers the voice of the brave female reporter declaring the Russian soldiers had broken the front door down and were now in the building. He could hear muffled gunshots in the background as the soldiers approached the barricaded studio door. He remembers her incredibly calm voice sounding the same way as if she was reporting everyday news with a smile, while the soldiers were breaking down the studio door. Then violent Russian voices screaming demands, and furniture breaking could be heard in the background, ending abruptly with her voice being replaced by dead silence. Peter's heart was pounding and he was on the verge of panic.

"Did they kill her dad?" Peter asked almost crying, while desperately searching his father's pale face for reassurance.

"No! They just unplugged the studio microphone to end her broadcast," his dad replied.

As tears filled Peter's eyes, he felt some relief knowing she had not been killed. Later, after Peter became a parent himself, he realized that his father didn't know what fate the broadcaster had endured. He was simply responding, as any parent would, to calm the fears of a child in the middle of a crisis situation.

*

Some groups of people resisted. They set up barricades in the streets of Prague, but had no firearms since the Communists would not allow civilians to have rifles or hand guns. People were making Molotov cocktails* to throw at the tanks. This resistance did not last long since it was weak and unorganized. The Russian occupiers shot some civilians, while crushing others with their vehicles. They were driving through the streets shooting at buildings and into the windows. Historical buildings such as museums, theaters, and other structures in the center of Prague bore bullet holes for years.

The Russians instated Martial Law: anyone on the streets

---

* A makeshift bomb made of a breakable container filled with flammable liquid and a rag wick that is lit just before thrown.

from 10:00 P.M. to 6:00 A.M. could be shot without warning.

Peter was worried about his mom who was with a group of women in the Girl Scout training camp. They were camping in secluded Northern Bohemia and did not know about the attack. A local resident from a nearby town informed them. Finally direction from leadership came, the camp was to be closed, and everybody was sent home. The ladies decided to remove their uniforms, and put on civilian clothes, then went to the nearby train station which was under control of the Russian army, and traveled to Prague. They later arrived at one of Prague's railroad stations shortly after 4:30 in the morning. People spilled out of the train, but could not leave the station due to Martial Law. They had to wait until 6 A.M. to enter the streets so they would not be shot. The ladies wished each other the best of luck and said goodbye. Russian tanks and soldiers were everywhere. The city's electric tram system was crippled. People were crossing intersections, walking directly under the tank cannons. Peter's mother walked about five miles to the southern edge of Prague to catch the bus home, only to find out the buses were not running either. Fortunately, the first car driving by offered her a ride home. She arrived the following day after the occupation.

The Czechoslovakian government was being completely silenced, since all communications had been severed. This left citizens confused because they did not know if government members were alive, dead, kidnapped, or if they had been moved to Moscow. The country was being crippled without government and its leadership.

Most of the Russian soldiers were 'primitives' with little education or none at all. Most of them thought they were in West Germany to fight an imperialistic country. The soldiers were prohibited from speaking to the locals under the threat of immediate execution. Some Czech teachers who spoke Russian were trying to communicate with them in calm voices, asking why they were there and explaining to them that Czech people were not a threat to anyone. But there was no response from the stone cold faces of the soldiers. The Russians sat silently on their tanks, holding weapons in their arms. Czechoslovakian dreams and hopes of new times, freedom, and politics with a human face, disappeared in one single night. The only hope left was that the American government would save Czechoslovakia from Russian occupation, and liberate its people from Russian and Communist oppression. Czech people were hoping the U.S. military would push the Russians back and help them become free and live better lives, but that never happened. People were hoping for some time - hope is always the last thing to die!

Citizens were tearing the red stars (symbol of Russians and Communism) from the roof tops of businesses and factories. They began painting slogans like 'Russians go home', 'Moscow 2000 kilometers due east', 'Go home Ivan, Natasha is waiting for you', and 'we don't like you here' on bridges and roads.

One year later, Jan Palach, a student from Prague, went to Wenceslas Square in the middle of the day, poured gasoline over his body, and set himself on fire in protest against the Russian occupation. He became the symbol of resistance and a hero for the Czechoslovakian people, who were naively hoping that this single act would make the Russians leave.

Ludvik Svoboda, a highly decorated General who led the Czechoslovakian battalions during World War II alongside the Russian Army, was President of Czechoslovakia since March of 1968. He was a Communist collaborator in 1948 when he helped establish Communism in Czechoslovakia. The members of the Czechoslovakian government eventually returned. The Prime Minister of Russia, Leonid Brežňev, let them return home, but they were all mentally broken. Under pressure, they had signed several agreements and apologized for their actions.

The Communists were soon in full control once again. However, it took almost two years of slow changes being implemented in small increments, to take the full effect. The Czechoslovakian borders stayed open until late 1969. Many citizens left before that time and immigrated to Australia, Canada, or America (those were legal immigrations). Czechs and Slovaks applying for an immigration visa were granted them by foreign governments, due to the Russian invasion.

Individuals wanting to leave were allowed to do so by Czech authorities, until the borders were sealed again. Freedom of speech lingered on for some time as well. People were still hoping something would happen and they would eventually end up being free. Such hope was like candlelight - slowly fading away.

*

Eventually all of the East European militaries, except the Russians pulled out of Czechoslovakia. Demoralization in the Russian army was rising and suicides among the soldiers were more common. The Russian leadership felt they could be losing control of their own people and had to deal with bad morale. Executions and punishment of soldiers was on the rise. Russian soldiers started to like it in Czechoslovakia, they did not want to return back home because life in Czech was different, better. The Russian Communists started to worry about uprisings among their own soldiers so they began evacuating them at a fast pace. Some of the soldiers were sent back home, but many of them were relocated to the Russia-Chinese border, where a military conflict was brewing.

It became obvious to everybody that America was not coming to the assistance of Czechoslovakia. Russian advisors were everywhere. Members of the Czech military, police, and STB that expressed unhappiness with the Russian occupation were removed and replaced. Hardcore party members were put in all leadership positions. The cleansing of bodies of control was almost completed. Media censorship was under total Communist control once again. The Communists could not deny that the Russian occupation happened, and so they had to come up with an explanation why the Russian military was there.

"The Russian Army came here to protect and save citizens of Czechoslovakia from imperialistic forces, which infiltrated the leadership and population, and tried to enforce Capitalism on our country," they explained.

New Communist committees were set up in all places of

business. Every employee was questioned about his position regarding the Russian invasion. People were 'strong-armed' into stating that they were thankful to the Russians, for coming to save Czechoslovakia from the danger of 'western forces' - forces that wanted to take their freedom away.

Peter's father was the head designer in a development and invention company at that time. That company was one of the few businesses that had contracts with Western European companies. Stanislav was the chief designer for years and had 40 experts under his leadership. Their work was bringing a lot of hard currency, like German marks and American dollars, to the Communist government of Czechoslovakia. When he was called in front of the cleansing committee, he told them that he disagreed with the Russian occupation, and accused the members of the committee of using scare tactics on Czech people. He reminded some of them about a time not long ago, when they were themselves painting anti-Russian slogans on the road in front of their business. Now - they were the ones punishing, firing, and arresting others - who dared to disagree with the occupation. He also accused them of betraying their own country. Since he was very valuable to the government and was making them a lot of money with his expertise, he was *only* demoted to regular designer.

Chapter Twenty-Three

SOLDIER

Peter's brother was named after his dad, Stanislav (Standa) Vodenka. He was in the Czechoslovakian military serving his obligatory two-year term. Prior to his military service, Standa had attended four years of higher education in heavy industry, which gave him the credentials to be a tank commander. Any person with a rank higher than his was a profession soldier. All professional soldiers were required to be party members.

In the early morning hours of August 21, 1968, Standa was rudely awakened by the sound of an alarm, resonating through the military base camp. One of the officers couldn't sleep and learned about the invasion from the radio. The military officers were running through the barracks screaming commands that everybody was to get up and mobilize, "Czechoslovakia is under military attack. Dress in your full battle uniforms and prepare to pull out."

The commanding officers called Standa and other tank commanders in for a briefing. They were informed that foreign military forces had entered Czechoslovakia from four different directions. There was no communication between command and their leadership. The commanders made the decision to become fully mobilized and wait for two hours. If they did not received orders within that time period, they would pull out of base and attack the invading forces on their own. The tank commanders were sent back to their barracks, to prepare their subordinates and wait for further orders. Most of the soldiers sat down and began writing what some of them believed could be their last letter home.

The tank battalion was located in western Bohemia near the town of Strašice, located in a shallow valley with a tall ridge directly in front. There was a road between the camp and the ridge, running along the bottom of the hill. Daylight revealed a chain of Russian tanks positioned along the top of the ridge, overlooking the camp. The Russian tanks were positioned in such a manner that only their spinning turrets and cannons were visible, preventing them from becoming a target for the camp below.

Each Czech team had a regular tank they were using for everyday training. They also had battle-ready tanks in reserve, parked side by side in long buildings, ready to move out on short notice. Those tanks were not being used in everyday tasks. The soldiers knew if they started the tanks, opened the doors and drove out, the Russian tanks would start 'picking them off'. They decided during the final briefing that on a command, the soldiers would start the tanks inside the buildings with the door closed, and then back up through the back walls, causing the buildings to collapse behind them. This should create a lot of dust, noise, and commotion, which would confuse the Russians and buy the Czechs a little time. Then every tank on its own, would have to make it as fast as possible to the road underneath the ridge, where the Russians would not be able to lower their cannons enough to cover the road. The Czech tanks would drive away at high speed, to reassemble at a designated location. They knew some of them would be hit by Russians, but most of them should make it out.

Before the two hours were over, orders finally came from leadership prohibiting all Czechoslovakian military from any resistance against the Russian invading forces. Most of the soldiers were upset about this decision as they were ready to fight to protect their homeland and country. However, the Czech military was told to lay down their arms once again.

For many months to follow, Russian military convoys traveled on the roads to show their strength and discourage Czechs from any resistance. The situation in Czechoslovakia was slowly settling down.

One year later, during the first anniversary of the Russian occupation, the Communists were expecting an uprising in big cities, especially the city of Prague. They made the decision that Czechoslovakian military and police forces, fully under control of the Communists again, would suppress the uprising. The military, police, and even members of the STB, were mobilized and equipped with helmets, handcuffs, batons, and weapons, then sent to Prague in armored vehicles. The Communists knew that if anything would take place, it would start in Wenceslas Square. The tanks were sent to all streets leading to this square in the center of the capital. A group of eight to ten soldiers was ordered to park their tanks across the street, to block possible movement of a crowd. These soldiers, like Peter's brother, were in the military because it was an obligation and it was only a temporary situation for them. They hated Russians as much as the civilians did.

In the early morning hours of August 21, 1969, Czech civilians assembled in the streets of Prague and started moving towards Wenceslas Square. The people were angry - it was their own Czechoslovakian military standing guard opposite them. It looked as if the soldiers were on the Russian side now. When people saw the barricades created by the tanks and trucks, they started chanting "Nazis, Nazis, Nazis", and ran against them.

The commanding officer behind the soldiers started yelling, "Shoot! Shoot!" but Peter's brother and the other soldiers could not bring themselves to shoot at their own unarmed citizens. They backed away from behind the tanks and into the entrances of the buildings on each side of the street. As people were pouring over and around the vehicles, Standa heard his friend next to him telling people in a muffled voice, "We will be discharged in one month. If you would have waited, we would be there with you." That soldier could be court-martialed if he would have been overheard by his commanding officer. People protesting on the street without weapons had no chance against the well-equipped professionals of the Communist controlled forces. The uprising did not last very long - it was broken down in a matter of a few hours.

After everything settled down, Standa needed to go to the bathroom. He was told to go to a nearby police station. Police in armored vehicles were hauling in people who had been arrested. All of them were bleeding and hurt because the police had 'fun' with them before throwing them into their vehicles. Inside the building, they had created a police corridor on each side of the steps and in the hallway leading to the station on second floor. Citizens were being attacked with night sticks as they walked through.

Standa hated the police as much as everybody else, but because of his military uniform, the policemen looked at him as their ally, talking to him in a friendly manner, as if he was one of them. While exiting the building, a teenage girl was pushed in through the front door. She had a bloody gaping wound on her forehead caused by a club. She was clutching a torn suitcase with her clothes spilling out, clearly indicating she was not even part of the uprising. She must have been caught while traveling through the city of Prague to some other destination. The girl looked helpless, frightened, and began to cry when she saw the chain of policemen waiting for her. Standa took her suitcase and walked her through the column of policemen, thus preventing her from being beaten along the way.

Peter's brother returned from the military in September, 1969. He purchased a U.S. military Willys jeep left behind after World War II. A small number of these jeeps were still used as regular family cars for transportation by civilians.

*

By 1971, the Communists had gained total control of the entire country and were feeling safe again. Most civilians never liked the Russians. They hated them with a passion and saw them as occupational forces forever. The Russian government took over some Czech military airports and bases and used them as their own. In towns where the Russian military was posted, they confiscated apartment buildings. They moved the Czech inhabitants out and used the apartments for Russian families and soldiers. One of these Russian military bases was located in a small town of Milovice, northeast of Prague. It was about a 1½ hour drive and was where Lída's grandparents lived. There was a grocery store and a department store that was now being used by Russians. Czech citizens were allowed to shop in Russian stores, which were stocked with better goods, including food, fruit, and vegetables, than what was available in the Czech stores. However, even though the supplies were better, the Russians were still using primitive means, such as a wooden abacus instead of cash registers.

Some of these Russians arrived to Czechoslovakia after living in shacks with dirt floors in backwoods villages. Many were not used to electricity or running water. The apartment buildings occupied by these Russians, were being destroyed and slowly falling apart. Some employees working for the plumbing company where Peter was later employed would be sent to fix plumbing problems for the Russians on their military base or in their living quarters. The problems these plumbers encountered were sometimes unbelievable. At one time, the main waste pipe connecting six apartments became clogged underneath the basement floor in one of the buildings. The Russians took a hammer and broke the pipe just above the floor. This allowed them to continue taking baths, washing the dishes, and flushing the toilets, with the waste running into the basement of the apartment building, slowly filling it. When the plumbers arrived to fix the problem, the human waste was two-feet deep.

Sometimes tour buses from Russia came over to Prague. Russian tourists were being placed in the biggest and best hotels. Hotel employees used to describe how the Russians stole all of the linens, vases, and ashtrays from the hotel rooms. Everything that could be carried away was taken. The rooms were being trashed and bathtubs were full of human waste. All this was creating a barrier, hate, and resentment, among the Czechoslovakian population toward the Russians.

Chapter Twenty-Four

TRADE SCHOOL

In 1970, Peter turned fifteen-years old. Reaching that age in Czechoslovakia meant receiving 'Občanský Průkaz' (citizen documents). It was a small book about the size of a passport that contained the citizen's picture, all personal information, occupation, employers with dates of employment, changes of employment, and all legal changes such as marriages, spouses, children's names, and birth dates. Children could not wait to reach the age of fifteen and receive this document. It made them feel important, like being an adult. From that moment on, they looked at the younger children as being inferior. They did not understand that their personal information was now at the fingertips of all government authorities. This identity document had to be carried at all times. If they were stopped by the police, the citizen would be asked to present this identification, which would reveal everything about that individual.

Everyone had to be employed somewhere. If a change of occupation or job was desired, the worker had to apply for a transfer with the employer, even though all the companies were government owned. After written notice was given, the worker would be called in front of a board to explain why he wanted to change jobs. If the board decided the citizen had a good reason to quit the job, it would rule on 'six-plus-one', 'six-plus-two', or 'six-plus-three' terms. This meant that this person had to work for another seven months if 'six-plus-one' ruling was made. 'Six-plus-two' would total eight months, and 'six-plus-three' totaled nine months of work before they were allowed to leave the old job. After that time, the person had only three days to start a new one, and get their identity document stamped, showing new employment. If somebody was found without this stamp of employment, they would be sent to prison for being a *parasite of society* and living off someone else.

After students graduated from grade school, they had a few choices. They could go into the work force at the age of fifteen, attend trade school for two or three more years, or enlist in intermediate school for four years to get a higher education. Only children whose parents were party members could receive college or university education. Non-Communist children could go to trade school or intermediate school, but nothing above that.

Peter decided to go to plumbing trade school. This took 3 years, each school year consisting of 11 months with one month summer break. During the first 5½ months, he spent one week in the classroom and one week in the shop learning how to work with steel. He had to make flowers, decorations, and different objects from steel to learn how to use the tools. Everything was made by hand. He learned how to weld, solder, and blacksmith. The second half of the first year and the entire second year, students spent one week in the classroom and one week in the field installing plumbing systems, while under the instructor's supervision.

The boys were retrofitting pipes in old buildings in Prague. These buildings usually occupied one entire block, were seven stories high, and had no elevators. An open courtyard in the center of the buildings was used as a playground for the children. These apartment buildings were over 100 years old and needed to have all the plumbing replaced. The plumbers were being trained to install plumbing systems, including hot water, cold water, waste pipes, gas lines, pressurized air pipes, steam pipes, and hot water heat with pressure tanks and radiators. All the buildings were made of bricks or stone, and the pipes were cemented inside the walls and floors. Old pipes had to be removed by chisel and hammer, since there were no power tools. Seventy percent of the plumber's time was spent chiseling and hammering, while the rest of the time was spent actually installing pipes.

The third year of plumbing school consisted of one day in the classroom and four days working in the field. All the steel pipes were heavy schedule 40 pipe wall thickness and had to be cut by hack saw and were threaded by hand ratchet threaders. Each thread had to be cut three times. Adjustable dies on the threading tool were set up to make the first thread shallow, then deeper, and the third time the thread was cut deep enough to screw the fitting on. Peter quickly learned to cut the pipes straight, since it was difficult to start the threader on the pipe if it was not cut correctly. The pipes that were bigger than four inches were sawed off and threaded by a power machine. Each plumbing shop had one power machine, which was used only on the biggest jobs.

Graduating from plumbing school was not easy. The final exam consisted of three parts. The first part was the written test which took hours to complete. This test included questions on plumbing, heating, math, Czech language, and other subjects. The second part of the examination was an oral test. A large classroom was set up with tables along the walls, with one or two examiners sitting behind each one. The students would stand in front of each table answering questions about gas piping, steam piping, water piping, steel processing, chemistry, physics, and math. Students would spend approximately 15 minutes with each examiner, and then everyone would move to the next table. The last part of the test consisted of working on a job, with a group of examiners following each student. They watched the student work, made notes, and discussed him among each other. If the student passed, he graduated and received a journeyman license and was allowed to join the work force.

Everything in Czechoslovakia was government owned, including the mechanical shops, so there was no competition. Cities were broken up into sections with one plumbing shop for each. If people needed plumbing or other trade services, there was only one place to call. The order would be written up and placed in a basket. There were several plumbing crews working on retrofitting old plumbing systems and a few one-man crews doing service work. They would pick and choose the orders. If the job was far away or looked difficult, the order would sit there for months and sometimes even a year. People could not choose the plumbing company they wanted to do their repairs. If someone was not satisfied with one company and requested a different one, they would be told, "We cannot work there. You will have to call a company that services your area." Every company in the country was providing the same bad service for the exact same high price. People had no choice but to pay whatever price the government decided.

*

When Peter was seventeen, he bought an old World War II Harley Davidson motorcycle. During World War II, when the American military liberated Europe, they brought a lot of equipment and most of it was left behind. The Americans gave the surplus equipment to the United Nations with instructions to distribute it to countries that needed it. After World War II, the Czechoslovakian government received a great deal of surpluses and set up stores called UNRRA (United Nations Relief and Rehabilitation Administration), which sold the left over surplus. These stores also sold food, blankets, clothing, boots, military jeeps, trucks, and motorcycles. When the Communists took over, it was prohibited to buy anything from Western Europe or America. However, there were quite a few American military vehicles, motorcycles, and jeeps left over from the war, already in the hands of the Czechoslovakian people.

Peter always wanted a Harley as he felt it was part of American culture. America was his dreamland. He eventually bought a Harley from a man in Prague who was the second owner, and Peter became the third owner of this beautiful U.S. motorcycle. It was a 750 cc, 1943 Harley Davidson, with only 42,000 miles. It had a foot clutch and a speed stick. Peter loved that machine. It was American and it looked so different from the other motorcycles in Czechoslovakia. It was much stronger, bigger, and better looking.

*

At the age of eighteen, Peter had finished plumbing school. That made him very happy as he hated it and told himself he would never go back to school again. If he could only see into the future, he would have known how wrong he was. He was now an adult - eighteen was the age that all children waited for. Now he could get a driver's license, drink alcohol, get married, and "vote". However, adulthood also brought new challenges. It exposed new horizons and opened new windows in the thing called life. Many experiences became more confusing since he was no longer protected and shielded by his parents.

Many questions started popping up in Peter's mind. If the Russians were our 'big brother', protector, and savior, why did they come over with tanks and machine guns and kill people? If life under Communism was so great and life under Capitalism was so horrible, why would people defect from East European countries, even for the price of losing their lives? Why aren't people defecting from America or Western Block countries to Czechoslovakia, Russia, Bulgaria, or other eastern countries? People should be coming in hoards, he thought.

Why was the Czech version of Boy Scouts and Girl Scouts outlawed, when they were teaching young children to be true patriots to their country, to help others less fortunate, and to be people of honor and respect? Why were individuals like his grandfather, who fought for the freedom of his country against a foreign enemy, stripped of his recognition and medals? Why were men who defected from their country to England in order to raise arms against the Czechoslovakian enemy, arrested and thrown into prison for years by their own government, instead of being recognized and honored upon their return home?

Why were people with no education, no knowledge, and no experience, but with party membership running businesses and government, while the people who were fully qualified and educated to do so, like doctors, professors, and priests, digging ditches, working in the Uranium mines, or rotting in the prison cells? Why did regular people end up in prison for months, for telling a joke or singing a song that could be vaguely translated as anti-Communist, while high ranking party members could commit crimes without punishment?

Why was it illegal to say the American army liberated parts of Czechoslovakia, or how nice and helpful American soldiers were to the local population at the end of World War II? Why was it illegal to mention that Russian soldiers, who also liberated parts of Czechoslovakia, were ransacking homes of citizens, taking their scarce food supply, and stealing their possessions? It was illegal to point out that Russian soldiers were raping women, mothers, wives, and daughters as young as twelve, over and over in front of their families!

Why were monuments erected in memory of the fallen American soldiers who liberated some parts of Czechoslovakia, destroyed and torn down after Communists came to power? Why did citizens fear punishment from their own government, for placing flowers on these places?

There was never ending anti-American propaganda. The newspapers, radio, and TV, were reporting horrible events from America daily, stating that Americans were dying from lack of money for heat or food, and cancer and other diseases were rampant in the U.S.A. The Communists always claimed that unemployment was high, inflation was bad, and named the U.S. stock market 'The Murderer's from Wall Street'.

The TV reports showed people in America dressed in rags, waiting in soup lines, and sleeping on park benches wrapped in newspaper. If someone was sick or collapsed on the street of American cities, reports stated that people would simply step over them - nobody would help. The reports explained how Americans hated the whole world and wanted to conquer the nations to take everyone into slavery. The American soldiers in Vietnam and other conflicts were killing innocent and helpless people, eliminating the entire villages, including women and children.

On the other hand, there was constant pro-Communist and pro-Russian propaganda, boasting Eastern European countries would be living under the slavery of America, if it was not for the generous and helpful protection of Russia. Bad events were never reported from Communist countries by the government-controlled media - no murders, no rapes, no suicides, no diseases, no poverty, no inflation, no crimes, and no natural disasters were ever reported. Only happy people and children were shown from Russia and other Communist countries, people in parades celebrating Communism and freedom, dancing in the streets while welcoming and hugging visiting politicians and leaders of other Communistic, Socialistic countries.

If life in Communist countries was so fantastic and Western Capitalistic countries were so horrible, why were people not allowed to travel there?

*

When Peter was nineteen, he bought a World War II Willys jeep. Owning this vehicle was not easy. It was an American military vehicle which made the owner look like a dangerous and rebellious individual in the eyes of the government. The police did not like the vehicle or the people who were driving them. The Communists thought people should buy Czechoslovakian, Russian, or other East European cars. If somebody spent money buying an old American military vehicle, it was presumed he did not like Communism. Peter and his brother were often pulled over by the police and had their documents checked.

Citizens had to have the small vehicle document book on them while driving. It included the serial number for the engine and frame. It was illegal to have a vehicle with a different serial number than when it came from the factory. This document also listed the color of the vehicle and the owner's information. Vehicles also had another booklet, which was the official title. This book was *not* pocket size and was kept in a safe place at home. It was a book with many pages describing the entire vehicle history, including the make and model, accidents, and each person who ever owned it. New information would be added as each transaction took place.

Sometime in the middle of the 1970's the Communists decided they did not want too many vehicles older than 20 years on the road. The problem was there were many vehicles older than that. Once a year, any vehicle in that category, had to go for the big 'technical check-up'. Special stations were created for that reason. The vehicle would be placed on rollers to lift it off the ground. When the brakes were applied, they had to put the same pressure on all four rollers while they were spinning. The emergency brake was checked the same way. There could be no oil leaks or even oil drops anywhere on the bottom of the vehicle. There could be no delay between the steering wheel movement and reaction time for the front wheels. The vehicle was checked with a fine-tooth comb. If any of these or other defects were found, police would mark the title book as 'unfit' and confiscate the small title book. Without that book, the vehicle was not allowed to be on the road. The vehicle was only good for spare parts if found 'unfit'. Many people did not have the means to buy another vehicle if one was taken away. Interestingly, many of the brand new vehicles manufactured by Communists coming directly from the factory could not pass this test.

After the test, the policeman who was overseeing it, would document everything in the vehicle title book and record the evaluation number. All new cars purchased from a store were automatically given the number one in their title book. Number two was good, and number three was still okay, but number four was bad. It meant the car was useless.

When Peter took his jeep in for the annual inspection, the mechanic conducting the test was making nothing but positive comments about it. Peter had just spent two years restoring the vehicle and it was in 'like-new' condition. The mechanic even mentioned he had seen brand new vehicles in worse shape than that. The Communists hated these vehicles with a passion and were trying to get them off the road. The reason - it was an American military vehicle. The policeman, who was watching the inspection and filling out the paperwork, assigned Peter's jeep a number four - that was not good! Once again, as so many times before in his life under Communism, Peter was filled with anger and helpless feelings. There was no chance to protest or challenge this one man's decision.

Patty in Peter's jeep after the restoration.

Peter and his Harley.

Playing game of Cowboys and Indians with the kids is not very convincing with blonde hair and a feather from a domestic goose.

Peter and his brother Standa in their early cowboy times. Peter and Nelly Gray below.

Chapter Twenty-Five

IRON GRIP

After the taste of freedom from 1968-1969, people were still a little too daring for the Communists, who felt they needed to 'tighten the screws' some more. For example, auto part stores started selling sticky checkered stripes in rolls about one inch wide. Some people were buying and taping them to the sides of their vehicles or painting them with white stripes. It was a refreshing sight as Communist countries were pretty much colorless. Peter's brother, while restoring his American military jeep to its original state, painted a white star in a white circle on the hood. He also added some other markings in white on the jeep, just like in the pictures they had seen from World War II.

One day the police decided to set up check points on all major roads around the country and began pulling all vehicles over. Vehicles with one color, just like when they came from the factory, were allowed to proceed. Vehicles with two colors, white stripes, or checkered stripes, were put through a vigorous inspection on the spot. Those vehicles had their small title book confiscated, since the color was different than originally stated. By having the small title book confiscated, the driver was only allowed to drive to their home address on that particular day. The owner had to repaint the vehicle to its original specified color, and then go to the inspection station. It had to pass the detailed check and be in the same condition as the big title book stated, in order to receive the small title book back.

One day, Peter and his brother were on their way to the

cabin in Standa's jeep, when they were pulled over at one of those check points. There were five policemen yelling at people with vehicles displaying more than one color. After taking one look at the brothers, the highest ranking policeman started running towards them while screaming at other policemen to follow! "Vystoupit a na zem (Get out and get on the ground!)," he yelled. Threats of physical violence and swear words were raining upon them. This situation was serious and worrisome! The beatings could start at anytime, easily followed by arrest. Fortunately, that did not happen - possibly due to the fact that cars with families were all around them.

The policemen went through the jeep with a fine-tooth comb. They could not find anything wrong, but fined them for having a two-toned vehicle. The police made Standa and Peter use screwdrivers to scrape the white paint markings off the jeep and after enough damage was done, they took pictures of them.

Front cover of small title book that had to be carried in the vehicle at all times.

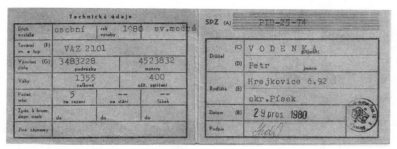

Small title book opened.

"The pictures will be sent to your place of employment, representatives from your home town, and newspapers, where you will be listed as dangerous individuals and bad examples," the highest ranking policeman announced. All this took place in loud screaming voices with no dialogue or conversation. The brothers were not asked any questions, so they did not say anything. All the communication was a one sided chain of threats. The policemen were so busy screaming at them, that they forgot to take the small title book away before they let them go.

Standa repainted his jeep in one solid, olive drab color. The Communists wouldn't allow people to do anything out of the ordinary, even a small change like having an inch wide racing stripe on the side of their car was now prohibited. In general, people were afraid of the police, even the sight of a man in a police uniform or police car would increase the heart rate and create tightness in the chest. On the other hand, if an individual had a relative or friend who was a high ranking party member and told them how

Front cover of the Czech driver's license, unfolded below.

poorly the police treated him, the policeman would be punished without mercy. The policeman would end up apologizing and explaining there was no way he could know everyone, and begged the person to be kind and not mention his name.

The Communist political system was like a big fish eating little fish, and the people in power were mercilessly controlling those below them - people in their own country - the same nationality - and the same citizenship! This was happening by their own so-called 'people's democratic government.' The government they were paying taxes to and providing with a better living than they could ever have themselves.

*

Peter was an adult now, living and working in an adult world, making a living as a plumber. He usually worked on two-man crews and was paid in cash twice a month, as checks did not exist. The money would be sent to their place of employment. The company accountant would sit at a table in the break room and employees would stand in line waiting for their money. The accountant would take paper bills and change, counting out the amount of money for each employee, based on the pay stub which arrived with the cash. The pay stub showed only the gross and net income; the taxes and deductions were not itemized, so they did not know the tax percentage and what the deductions were for. The money and paystub were put into an envelope and handed to the employee. The wages were based on the amount of work completed. The first payroll of the month was calculated based on the employee's productivity for the previous month and was called a down payment. The second pay was the remainder of how much the employee produced, minus the amount of the first payroll.

Every foreman was issued a booklet with tables describing the installation of plumbing parts and repairs. He had to list how many meters of pipe in each size were installed. He also kept track of how many fittings, gaskets, meters of grooves, and trenches they chiseled in concrete floors or brick walls, how many threads they made, and how many fittings they screwed on the pipes. Every task had a value amount written next to it, which was added together at the end of the month.

Some crews with a foreman that was a more 'creative' writer had bigger paychecks.

The workday was supposed to be eight hours, but nobody actually worked that long. Employees in work places with punch cards would ask friends to punch their card for them, in case they were going to be late or wanted to leave early. People working in construction did not have punch cards.

The plumbing company where Peter worked was selling lunch vouchers to the employees. Each voucher was worth five Korunas, but could be bought by employees for only three. Employees could buy one for each working day of the month. These vouchers could be used in any restaurant in the city of Prague. All the restaurants served beer. If two or three men working in the same neighborhood happened to meet in a restaurant for lunch, they would usually start drinking beer and seldom went back to work. That was not uncommon since people generally felt they were working for Communists and did not really care. Concepts like productivity and profit were virtually unknown. There were no safety requirements and training, because it was too expensive and labor was cheap.

There were many different stories and situations related to plumbing work. One day Peter and Marek went to a seven story apartment building, where apartments above each other shared a common supply and waste piping. They had to notify the occupants that on Monday morning at 8:00, the toilets would be out of order for approximately one week, as plumbers would be removing them to replace the plumbing pipes. They would have to use their neighbor's bathroom across the hallway, and then switch while the neighbor's plumbing was being replaced later.

The work started in the basement and the plumbers were moving to upper floors. Peter took the toilet bowl out on the first floor, chiseled the pipe from the wall, and started breaking the cast iron waste pipe with a hammer. The pipe cracked and crumbled to the floor, but another pipe created by decades of human waste was standing in its place. Peter had to smash this artificial pipe made of feces to break it. The rubbish consisting of cast iron pipe, bricks, concrete, and petrified human waste, had to be carried in buckets to the dumpster on the street. After the toilet room was cleared, Peter kneeled in the corner and started chiseling out the pipe leading through the floor to the basement level. The 4 inch waste pipe from the upper floors terminated at the ceiling above him. Then he heard someone on the upper level flushing the toilet. Peter jumped up and ran out of the room, slamming the door shut. After everything inside settled down, Peter and the apartment resident carefully opened the door. The room was full of toilet water, used toilet paper and human waste, splashed high up on the walls and the back of the door. Peter was grateful for his quick reaction to get out on time.

Another time the plumbers were scheduled to start work, but the new toilet bowls had not been delivered to the plumbing shop. Their boss, Comrade Nový, told them to begin the work anyway.

"New toilets will be here any day," he said.

Peter was mad and told Marek this was nonsense, Comrade Nový and everybody else knows very well, that nothing ever happens on time in Communist Czechoslovakia, and those poor people will be without toilets for weeks!

They completed the demolition, but the new toilets did not show up for three weeks. People were angry at them, especially a big burly man living on seventh floor. The plumbers explained the situation, *blaming* everything on Comrade Nový, who was a party member and disliked by every employee.

One day Comrade Nový showed up on the jobsite. The man from seventh floor confronted him and Comrade Nový told him to 'go straight to hell!' The burly man threw a punch, hitting him hard and knocking him out. Comrade Nový was very mad and was going to make sure the man went to jail, only to find out that the man was also a party member, only in a much higher position than him. The Comrade ended up apologizing and new toilets were installed in a hurry. Peter received a lot of pats on the back by his co-workers for what happened to good old Comrade Nový, which was a good reason for celebration by meeting in the restaurant for lunch, drinking beer, and not returning to work for the rest of the day.

A different time, one of the apartments the plumbers were working in was occupied by a middle-aged English couple, probably British Embassy employees. The bathroom they were working in was full of exotic looking toiletries they brought with them from their country. The toothbrushes, toothpaste, bottles of shampoo, soap, and shaving products were so much nicer and smelled better than they had ever seen. At one point, Peter needed to go to the bathroom and he took a small piece of the toilet paper they had in their restroom. He was taken by how soft and soothing it felt, unlike their rough, narrow rolls, with a texture that resembled tracing paper. That experience made enough impact on Peter that when he returned home from work he had to describe it to his mom and brother.

One day, Peter and Marek, were working in the apartment of an elderly gentleman, who told them he was a sailor on an ocean liner in his younger years. (The boys didn't know that Czechoslovakia had an ocean liner and assumed the man was probably a member of the STB working in foreign countries as a spy.) He showed them pictures of many exotic places he had seen: such as Cuba, Brazil, Chile, Venezuela, Egypt, and others. Peter was envious of this man who had traveled the world. He felt disheartened and worried that he would never be able to go anywhere. He felt helpless and discouraged as he was picturing himself aging slowly, living an insignificant meaningless life, and never accomplishing anything - like most of the adults he seen around him - and then being quickly forgotten after his death. He could not stand the thought of it. He knew he had to do something. There must be a purpose for his life, but what? What could he do? He knew he had to get away from this place to escape the feeling of living life in shackles, but how? That was when the idea of defection began brewing in his head.

All these experiences were like links connecting together in his mind, creating the chain of events leading to defection.

Chapter Twenty-Six

LUMBERJACK YEARS

Peter did not like plumbing work, so he started looking for a different job when he turned twenty-one. Tom, one of his friends from his hometown, was a lumberjack logging trees in the surrounding forest. This job sounded really intriguing to Peter. It would eliminate traveling to Prague for 1½ hours every morning and afternoon, and allow him to work in nature, which was close to his heart. He submitted his notice to the plumbing shop, but had to persuade the required committee with a good enough reason to quit the job. If he told them he did not like the work or did not want to travel to Prague, they may not allow him to quit, because those were not considered good enough reasons. Peter made up a story that he needed to work closer to home because of his mother's poor health, and he was the only one who could take care of her since his brother had a family of his own. He was given permission to leave and was granted 'six-plus-one', which meant he had to work for another seven months before he could quit.

He started working for the forest company and was one of five men from his hometown working with chainsaws. There were also three female employees who were planting new trees. One person would drive the company four-wheel drive Russian military style vehicle - GAZ (*Gorkovsky Avtomobilny Zavod)*, with a tarp roof, two seats in front, and two benches along the sides facing each other in the back.

Peter received an old beat up Husqvarna chainsaw, and one of the forest rangers who was his immediate supervisor, showed him how to operate it. Peter was not assigned a helmet, ear and eye protection, with the explanation that he was new and inexperienced.

"You will get those things when you improve at your job and deserve them," he was told.

There was no safety training whatsoever. He would be paid by the amount of cubic meters of wood he processed. Every tree had to be measured and marked. There was a minimum quota each lumberjack had to meet, but the more work they did, the more money they made. Some men were more productive than others and were consistently making better wages.

Trees were being logged for different reasons. Sometimes the trees were needed for electric or telephone poles. These trees had to be a required height and size, with all the branches smoothly cut off and the bark removed. Other times they were logging trees to be used for shoring in underground mines. Some lesser quality trees were being cut down for paper mills, while others were used for lumber or railroad ties. It was very hard and physically demanding work, but Peter loved it. It was his favorite job. All year round, they started working at sunrise. The driver would pick everyone up and drop them off where the logging needed to be done, then go to work himself. During the winter they would start as late as 7:30 A.M., but in the summer they started as early as 4:00 A.M.

Peter was lucky to be working on the same crew with the most productive man of all 68 lumberjacks working for the same company. Peter worked very hard and when his first day was over, he had done less than 50 percent of what the number one logger had accomplished. The second and third day he tried to work even harder, but ended up with the same results. Peter could not understand that since he was so much younger and stronger than that man. How could it be? The next day instead of cutting trees, he followed and watched the best worker for two hours. He learned more in those two hours than he would learn in 6 months on his own. Later, he received his helmet, eye and ear protection. With further experience, the work became easier and more fun, and eventually, Peter became one of the top lumberjacks in the company.

Due to a lack of proper warm clothing, working during the winter was more challenging. They wore rubber boots without insulation, so they did not get wet, but were always cold. The heater in the truck was not adequate for the tarp roof, so when they arrived at work they were already cold. Their fingers were frozen before they even started. The first hour of work was treacherous as it felt like a hammer was hitting their fingers from the vibrations of the chainsaw. The first thing they did was to build a large fire when they reached the worksite. This would be their workstation where they ate lunch, refilled oil and gas in the chainsaws, and sharpened the chains. Sometimes they would bring spare clothes to change into, as they would always get wet from snow falling on their backs from the trees. One set of clothes would be drying by the fire, while they were working in the other.

Peter loved the variety of different settings they worked in. Some work was on top of the hills overlooking the countryside. Other times they worked on the cliffs high above the river, deep in the forest, or next to the villages. He loved seeing the sun rise daily, as each season brought different changes.

However - his conscience started to get the best of him. The workers would enter a beautiful section of woods with a forest floor covered by an undergrowth of blueberries, raspberries, strawberries, and mushrooms. Pleasant smelling pines created a protective green canopy above. And when they were done, there were no more trees and the forest floor was ripped up by heavy machinery, and covered with dying branches and tree tops. It looked as if a bomb had exploded!

One day the crew was sent to log a section in the hills above his hometown. This section of the woods was majestic. Peter and his three friends used to play there in childhood. It would take all four of the boys to encircle each tree by joining their hands around the base. The tree tops connected with each other, creating a natural Cathedral-like ceiling above. It was a magical, fairytale-like place to Peter, and now he was one of the men destroying it. He was sad knowing that his children would never experience anything like this. Peter understood the trees would be cut down even if he was not involved, but he had a hard time dealing with being one of the tools controlled by Communists to destroy this monumental beauty, which should be preserved for future generations.

Representatives from Germany and Austria were buying the trees for lumber while they were still standing, thus preserving their own forests. The government was selling them for hard currency while knowing trees like that would never grow in Czechoslovakia again. Peter could not bear to be a part of the destruction and eventually quit his favorite job.

*

It was during his lumberjack years when Peter met his future wife. He met her through one of his co-workers, a logger named Josef, a strange man who was married to Lída's older sister. In Peter's early lumberjack days, he worked together with a strange man named Josef. After they were dropped off at their assigned section of forest, Peter was anxious to start working and fired up his chainsaw. Josef started yelling at him to be quiet, because it was too early and he wanted to snooze. He found a nice, soft dip in the ground, filled with pine needles, curled up in it, and drifted off to sleep. Peter sat around bored out of his mind, nervously waiting for Josef to wake up, knowing he was not making any money.

While everyone was bringing lunch to work, Josef would only bring beer. He usually brought four to six .5 liter bottles with him. He opened one immediately in the truck and drank it on the way to work in the early morning hours. He drank more beer throughout the day, while filling his chainsaw with oil and gas or sharpening the chain. While everyone was eating lunch, Joe was drinking beer. On the way home, he usually asked to be dropped off at the local bar, instead of his house.

He was dangerous to work with, as he did not pay attention where other workers were or what was happening around him. He was very careless, and most of the time his tree landed in a different place than he intended. Many times Josef endangered other worker's lives, and it was a miracle that no one was ever seriously hurt.

One day while logging trees side by side, one of Peter's co-workers had cut down a tree and was working along the trunk removing the branches. Josef cut his tree which once again did not fall where he had planned. It was falling in the direction of the co-worker, who was working on his tree lying on the ground. All the men started screaming, yelling, and whistling to get the co-worker's attention. Of course, because of the ear protection and noisy chainsaw in his hands, he could not hear anything. The tree landed with a thundering crash right where the man stood. They all expected him to be dead - but when the dust settled, the man was shaken but standing there unhurt. His head was sticking out of the mass of tree branches and needles. The tree trunk barely missed his body, while two other large branches the size of an adult man's leg, landed one in front and one behind, framing him on three sides.

A different time, the men were logging trees in parts of the forest with thick, waist-deep undergrowth. Peter dropped his tree and was working his way along the trunk, cutting off the branches. When he was at the end, he jumped on the tree trunk to walk back, avoiding the undergrowth. Then he remembered he was working with Josef and looked up to see what he was doing. He saw Joe step back from the tree, which begin falling directly in his direction. Peter dropped the chainsaw and started running, making giant leaps to avoid the thick brush. The tree landed close behind him, shook the ground, and created a strong gust of wind that knocked Peter's helmet off. Everyone was mad and yelled at Joe, but he just laughed.

"I have never seen you move quite that fast before," he told Peter. "You were jumping through those bushes just like a deer."

After that, everyone swore to keep a safe distance from him. There was also another problem involved with Joe. He was not a big fan of soap and water - and it could be quite torturous to be in the same vehicle with him.

Chapter Twenty-Seven

MEETING FOR THE FIRST TIME

Peter was the youngest lumberjack and the only single one.

"My wife's youngest sister, Lída, is stunning," Josef would tell Peter. "You need to meet her." One day on the way from work, they were passing through the village where Joe's in-laws lived and stopped by to visit. It was the first time that Peter met Lída - however - he was not very impressed.

"Is this what you call a stunning sister-in-law you idiot?" he told Joe when they were back in the car! "You don't get out much, do you?"

One Saturday about a month later, Peter and a group of his friends went back to that same village for a dance party with live music. Peter ran into one of his co-workers from the forest company who was there with his girlfriend, and they started to talk. Suddenly, Peter noticed a beautiful girl walking toward them. She was wearing a light pink and green checkered dress that stopped just above her knees. Her hair was dark brown, and she had a slim waist with round hips and bust. She was tall with long muscular legs and nice calves. The outline of her strong thighs was visible through her dress as she was making strides. She was the most attractive woman in the entire building. It was Lída. Unknown to Peter, she was friends with his co-worker's girlfriend, and joined in on their conversation. They talked and laughed for a long time, and while Peter never enjoyed dancing and was not very good at it, they spent the rest of the evening dancing together. That was when they fell in love - even though she was constantly leading - making him trip and stumble a lot. Lída was eighteen and Peter was twenty-one years old. Eight months later they were married.

*

Peter always dreamed about being married in Zvíkov castle near their cabin. Unfortunately, the castle was only open for two summer months and their wedding was scheduled for March 23, 1978. Peter was disappointed. They decided to get married in the castle of Karlštejn instead, which was located only ten miles from his hometown.

After work on the day before his wedding, Peter and his three friends started drinking. It was a tradition for a young man getting married to go on a drinking spree with his good friends, to say 'goodbye' to their single life, also known as 'Rozloučení se svobodou' (departure from freedom). These celebrations always took place the night before the wedding. They moved around a few local bars in his hometown, ending up late at night at one friend's house in a small village located about three miles from Peter's home. They kept drinking until the early morning hours.

Peter woke up later than he planned and walked three miles to his home. He arrived around 8:00 A.M. and was greeted by his mother, who was very angry. He was half drunk, hung over, and not looking very good. She did not know where he had been all night long. She was afraid something had happened to him or that he was too drunk and would miss his own wedding. She heated water for him to take a bath, but taking a bath at this point was beyond Peter's abilities. Over his protests, which were not doing him any good anyway, she started giving him a bath and while washing his hair, smacked him periodically on the head, while telling him how stupid he was. He was twenty-two years old. Later his brother came and they drove to the florist to pick up the flowers to take to Lída's house. At 10:00 everybody left for the wedding ceremony, which would take place at 11:00 in the castle of Karlštejn.

Castle of Karlštejn where Peter and Lída were married on March 23, 1978.

Wedding day!

The wedding ceremony seemed to last forever as Peter's stomach was still upset from drinking and he was trying not to throw up. Instead of listening to the Judge, he was constantly swallowing, trying to prevent running down the aisle with his cheeks filled with vomit. After what seemed to him like the longest ceremony ever - it was finally over. The wedding party exited the castle and pictures were taken on the draw-bridge.

The wedding reception followed in a nearby restaurant, located in an old building still in the castle complex. After the reception, the entire wedding party returned back to Lída's parent's home. The living room furniture had been removed and tables and chairs were set up for the dinner and wedding party.

The next day was Friday and Peter and Lída traveled to their cabin. Monday was the Easter holiday so they spent a long weekend there. That was their honeymoon.

Chapter Twenty-Eight

LIVES OF OTHER PEOPLE

Lída's parents were somewhat different than Peter's family. Her mother, Vlasta, was a very devoted member of the Communist party since she was eighteen-years old. She fully believed in the Communist ideology and was a member because of her beliefs, not for the benefits like many others. Vlasta was married once before. Her first husband was a Russian soldier, who ended up in Czechoslovakia at the end of World War II. He was shot through the lungs and met Vlasta in the hospital, where she was a nurse. They had two daughters, Vlasta and Alexandra (Saša). He never completely recovered from his wounds and eventually died from his injuries. Vlasta met her second husband, Karel, while he was working in the uranium mines near the town of Příbram.

Karel was a tough, strong person, and a miner by trade. He finished mining school when he was eighteen, was rebellious, rough, and always fighting. He found a job in a coal mine located in the northwestern part of Czechoslovakia. In 1949, as the Communists were tightening their iron grip on the country, Karel decided to defect to the west.

The border separating Czechoslovakia and West Germany was not as secure yet, as it would become later. He did not know how to cross the border, so he needed a guide to lead him. Karel learned about a man who guided people to Germany for money. The contact was made, and he was supposed to meet the guide at a specific table in one of the restaurants in a border town. Unknown to him, the secret police had learned about this person and was trying to trap him. They received information that the guide was supposed to meet someone in a restaurant on a certain date and time. That someone happened to be Karel.

The police set up a 'sting operation'. Every person in the restaurant, including the bartender and waiter, were undercover policemen. At the scheduled time, Karel walked into the bar and sat down at the designated table. The guide learned about the sting operation and never showed up. When Karel entered the bar, the police thought he was the man they were looking for. One of the secret policemen sat down across the table from him, thinking Karel was the guide. Karel, on the other hand, thought the secret policeman was the guide he was supposed to be meeting. Karel was packing a gun.

The two men began talking, but after awhile, it became obvious to Karel that this was a trap. He did not know that he was completely surrounded by undercover police. The situation deteriorated quickly - Karel pulled out his gun and shot the policeman across the table in the head. The bullet just grazed the man, knocking him unconscious. In a flash, every man in the bar was on top of Karel. He lost his gun in the scuffle, but tried to fight his way out. He ripped out a small cast iron wood stove standing in the middle of the room, connected to the wall by a chimney pipe, and used it to defend himself. Karel was fighting against big odds and eventually was overpowered and arrested.

There were four allegations brought against him. He was carrying a weapon, planning to defect, resisting arrest, and the most serious one, attempting to kill an undercover policeman.

Karel was facing 30 years or possible life in prison. As luck would have it, his parents who were highly respected in the community, were invited to a friend's wedding. Among the wedding guests was a man with bandages on his head, seated at the same table. Eventually, he was asked what had happened to him. He told a story about being shot by a young man during an arrest. Karel's mother began to suspect this could be the man her son had shot. Later in the evening, she approached the policeman and asked him about the circumstances, realizing that it was him. She pleaded with the policeman, telling him that Karel was a good boy, but a little hot-headed. After building a rapport, the policeman promised to talk to the judge about Karel's case. As a result, Karel was sentenced to a hard labor prison in one of the Jáchymov[*] mines for only four years.

When Karel arrived at one of the Jáchymov camps, he was assigned prison clothes that were made from a hard, scratchy, burlap-type fabric. The prisoners were driven from the camp to the mine on the back of military trucks with canvas tops, to work eight hour shifts. The men were sweating while doing the backbreaking work, and their clothes and boots were always wet from the water constantly dripping off the tunnel ceilings.

Most of the time, their transportation back to the camp was not there when they emerged from the mine. During the winter months, their wet, muddy clothes would freeze on their bodies. The men had to run around, jump up and down, or huddle together to stay warm. Sometimes they waited for many hours for transportation to arrive. The trip on the trucks back to camp was torturous, with the freezing wind blowing through the tarp tops, open in the back.

During certain times when the camps were overpopulated, three prisoners each were assigned to one bunk in the wooden barracks. One prisoner was working his eight hour shift, while another one was sleeping, and the third one had time off. They slept with their filthy clothes on to prevent them from being stolen by other prisoners. In the cold winter days with the frigid wind blowing through the barracks, the only way to dry their clothes was by their own body heat under the blankets.

There was no training or safety equipment furnished. The men were handling uranium ore with their bare hands. While underground, they occasionally washed with and even drank the radioactive water. The blasts at the front of the tunnel caused a fine dust to linger through the air for hours. The dust covered their hair and clothes, entering their lungs and slowly

---

[*] To the Czechoslovakian population, the name of Jáchymov became synonymous to imprisonment in hard-labor camps by the Communist government, just like Siberia in Russia.

destroyed their health and immune system.

The camps and mines were surrounded by high fences with guards in watch towers, ready to shoot for any reason. One day, while the prisoners were waiting for the truck to pick them up, one of the guards threw a cigarette butt on the ground and some of the prisoners started to fight over it. The guards announced they were looking for two volunteers to race down the hill made from mine tailings. The winner would get an entire cigarette and the loser would get a beating. Karel volunteered. At the bottom of the hill was a wire marking a section of land, off limits to prisoners. Beyond that was the outside perimeter prison fence.

Karel was making big jumps moving down the 45 degree hill, but something did not feel right. At the last minute he fell on his back, stopping short of the wire. His competitor passed him, jumping over the wire at the bottom. At that moment, a salvo of machine guns tore his body apart. When Karel crawled back up the hill to join the other prisoners, he was beaten by the guards for losing the race.

Prison food consisted of a small piece of bread given to the inmates every three days, which had to last them for breakfast and dinner. They were given a cup of watery coffee to go with it. For lunch they usually received some potatoes, dumplings with gravy, or something similar, with a small piece of meat.

Those who were too weak or too sick to meet their daily work quota, were placed in solitary confinement and their food rations were cut in half as further punishment. They slept on the bare ground without a blanket and sometimes even their clothes were taken away. Beatings were not uncommon. Such treatment made them even weaker and sicker and it usually continued until they were taken away, never to return.

Eventually, there were 16 such Gulag type concentration camps in the vicinity of Jáchymov. Nobody will ever know the exact number of prisoners (Mukls)[*] that did time in those camps between the years of 1948 and 1989. It is estimated that

---

[*] Mukl: Muž určený k likvidacy - man bound for elimination.

over 200,000 prisoners, or modern day slaves[21], were sentenced by judges to serve their time in one of these camps, of which approximately 200 were executed by the rogue decision of the guards. In addition, an estimated 8,000 were tortured to death, beaten to death, or died in prison. The Communist's motto was, 'The dead ones don't talk!'[22]

The prisoners that managed to survive these camps were living skeletons, often weighing less than 100 pounds when they were released. Some of them were coughing blood or had bleeding sinuses. Many of the men that survived the camps succumbed to cancer at a young age.

At one time while being transferred to another place with other prisoners, Karel saw his chance and managed to escape. Guards with dogs chased him, but he succeeded to lose them. He was on the run for five days but had no place to go, so he decided to go to his parent's house. The police were expecting him to do that, and had people hiding throughout his hometown, secretly watching the family home. When he showed up hungry and tired, they arrested him and sent him back to prison. An additional 1½ years were added onto his sentence. After 5½ years, he was released from prison and later married Vlasta. He was mean, angry, aggressive, and often stated, "I hated the whole world."

Karel moved in with Vlasta's family. Her village Nová Ves pod Pleší was under control of three local brothers, who ruled and somewhat harassed the villagers. Karel was an outsider - the newcomer. He was not one of the locals, and the three brothers were looking for the chance to show him who was the boss. Karel became friends with a local man he worked with in the mines. The brothers felt they had to teach that man a lesson for associating with an outsider.

One day the friend came over to Karel's house where they played cards and drank beer late into the evening. Around

---

[21] There were times when Russian advisors felt the uranium ore production was not high enough, so they ordered the Czech government authorities to deliver more workers. The authorities complied by arresting and sentencing citizens on phony charges to increase the work force in the uranium mines.

[22] Čestmir Čejka, Pražské Slovo, June 1990, Uran z Pohledu PolitickéhoVězně

midnight, the friend went home and Karel and Vlasta went to bed. Suddenly, the friend was back pounding on the door.

"The three Mach brothers are waiting for me on the road in the middle of the village. Can you walk me home?" he begged.

Immediately - Karel became enraged and was *ready to go.* When they reached the point where the brothers were waiting, words were exchanged. His friend got scared, jumped over the fence, and disappeared into the darkness, leaving Karel alone to face the three brutes. Karel ripped a piece of wood from a picket fence and started beating the brothers until they were on the ground bleeding. He continued to hit and kick them, until his friend watching from a distance came back and stopped him - which probably saved the Mach brother's lives! By this time, they were like bloody rag dolls, unable to move. The 5½ years of frustration, rage, and hate were finally erupting from his soul. That was the end of the Mach brothers reign. From that moment on they became regular citizens. As a result of this incident, Karel became somewhat of a celebrity and was also more at peace with himself.

Lída, his only daughter, was born in 1958. She was born with asthmatic type symptoms, cried constantly, and had a lot of difficulty breathing. She was unable to eat and was only skin and bones. She was sick for months and they were concerned that she may soon die. Eventually, the doctor recommended rubbing her chest four times a day with dog lard. But where would one get this? They talked to a dog catcher who had five daughters. His family was very poor and survived by eating dogs. He admitted he had an abundance of lard. Once the dog was roasted, the drippings were allowed to cool, and the white fat in the roasting pan was collected in a jar. From then on, whenever they needed it, the dog catcher sold them a jar of lard to be used to rub on Lída's chest. This treatment eventually cured her breathing problem forever!

As if her body was catching up, she became a chubby child, but by the time Lída started school, she was slim and taller than the rest of her class. She was considered a tomboy. Whenever the boys were picking on girls, Lída 'taught them a lesson'. She got in trouble a lot in school because of this behavior. Her father did not have any interactive skills and the only way he knew how to deal with the problem was to beat her. He continued this type of punishment until Lída married Peter. It was difficult to understand why Karel would be so aggressive towards his own blood, but never physically punished his stepdaughters.

*

It did not take very long for Peter to discover the dynamics in Lída's family. Her mom and one sister were party members, believing in all the Communist propaganda. Her father hated the Communist system, because of his experience in the Jáchymov mines. Her oldest sister was not a fan of the Communists either. Many times, heated arguments broke out about the Cold War and the political situation between Russia and America. Peter often got very upset and said more than he should have about Communist dictatorship, 'Russian Red Danger', and freedom in America. Afterwards, he would be mad at himself for losing control and saying too much. Eventually, Peter had learned to control himself and did not respond or become involved in these useless arguments and dangerous conversations.

In April 1978, Lída became pregnant and a decision had to be made about a name for the unborn child. Since there were no ultrasounds, parents did not know the gender of a baby until it was born. Before the mother went to the hospital to give birth, paperwork had to be filled out, stating a male and female name for the baby. The name for a boy was usually easy, as it was custom in Czechoslovakia for the first born son to receive his father's name. It was not uncommon for the first born daughter to bear her mother's name also, but Lída did not want her daughter to have the same name. Peter wanted an American name for a girl, but that was not an easy task.

Czechoslovakian calendars had individual names written on each day of the year, except for holidays. The government only allowed children to be given a name that was written on the calendar. One day, Peter and Lída went to see an American movie, called 'Stuntmen', in a tiny local theatre. One of the main female characters was named Patty. That was it - the name they were looking for. They wanted to name a girl Patty, but since that name was not in the calendar, it would not be allowed. The name on the calendar closest to Patty was Patricie, so they decided to name her Patricie and call her Patty.

The government required their baby to be born at the hospital in a county town named Příbram. This hospital had a really bad reputation for high infant mortality rates. Peter was afraid of this facility, but did not have any other choice - unless he could pull some strings and get her admitted into a different hospital.

*

One day on the way from work, the loggers stopped in a small bar in the middle of nowhere to have a few beers. Peter was the designated driver and stayed until the evening hours while his partners got drunk. This small bar was in a recreation area surrounded by cabins, where people from Prague came on weekends. When the loggers were ready to head home, a distinguished older gentleman drinking at the bar asked if they would drop him off at his cabin. Peter agreed and the man got into their vehicle. As they were driving closer to his place, this strange man said, "I really appreciate you guys driving me home. If anyone of you has a pregnant wife, let me know and I will deliver the child." As luck would have it, he was a doctor specializing in childbirth and was working in one of Prague's prominent hospitals.

Peter saw his chance and went back the next day to talk to him. Eventually, this doctor personally delivered both of Peter and Lída's children in the hospital in Prague, but because it was in a different county than they were required to go, the doctor told the officials that Lída was his niece. That proved to be good luck for Peter's family, because of their daughter's difficult birth. There were complications, and without the extra help and care, she probably would not have survived at the hospital in Příbram.

At that time they were living with Peter's mom in a one bedroom apartment. It was crowded with three adults and a baby, plus they were also planning to have one more child. The combinations of a small apartment along with Peter's desire to have a horse and work with cows were reasons to find work that would combine all of these. Eventually, he would learn about the shortage of workers on government corporate farms and the possibility of being assigned an apartment. They decided to look for a job in Southern Bohemia, an area with picturesque colorful villages and beautiful countryside.

Karel and Vlasta's wedding picture.

Patty and Peter at the cabin.

In the woods above the Vltava River, where Peter was logging trees.

Different view of the woods. The arrow in top left corner indicates the clearing after the trees were logged out.

Chapter Twenty-Nine

GETTING CLOSER

He found a job in a small village called Litochovice. Lída was at home with their infant daughter, while Peter started working with cows on a corporate farm and was assigned to the steer barn. After calves were weaned off the bottle, the baby bulls went to the bull barn where they were raised until ready to be butchered, and the cows were moved to the steer barn where they were chained to the troughs. There were four rows of steers chained side by side. His job was to feed and wash them, remove manure, bring fresh straw for bedding, and watch for them to go into heat so the inseminator could be called. The cows had to be tended to twice a day, seven days a week. Work started at 4:00 in the morning. The farm had been privately owned before it was confiscated and used by the Communist government. It was designed for a specific number of animals, but as usual, the Communists crowded in twice as many.

The steers stayed in this barn until shortly before giving birth. At that time they were moved to the milk barns where they were again chained to a trough. After the calf was born, the cow was milked for the first time. Cattle spent their entire life chained up. All they could do was stand up or lay down. Because of this treatment, the cattle did not know how to walk, so as they were moved, they walked clumsily and sometimes even fell down.

This type of work was new to Peter. His superiors told him to stuff straw into the vent openings to keep the cattle warm during the winter, but that prevented proper ventilation. The heat from the cows and their excretions created a fog, making it look like a sauna, except with a lack of oxygen and foul smell. Lack of proper ventilation and animal overcrowding made Peter and the cows cough constantly. He did not believe this was the right thing to do, but he did it since management told him to do so. One day Peter remembered reading about American farmers playing music to their cattle in milk barns, which helped the cows produce more milk. He brought in a radio and played music to his steers. Local people laughed and made fun of him, saying he was a little eccentric. Years later, a well known movie director from a nearby village, made a successful movie based on one young man working on a government farm playing music to the cattle. Peter's family in Czechoslovakia continues to tease him to this day, saying he was "the star of the show!"

As there was no hourly wage, people were making money by the product. In the milk barns, workers were paid by the liters of milk the cows produced. Peter was paid by the weight the steers were gaining as they were maturing. Once a month, a large scale designed for livestock was brought in and every cow was weighed and recorded, one at a time. Peter's predecessor was a lazy man who did not do his job well. Peter was told there were times when the man did not show up for an entire weekend, and the cows were mooing from hunger. When Peter took over the job, the ribs on the cows were visible. He wanted to feed the cattle as much as he could, but was limited by the amount of food that was delivered on a daily basis.

One time Peter did one of the tractor drivers a favor and in return, the driver was bringing more food than was rationed for the cattle Peter was tending to. The steers started filling out quickly, catching up from the days of being hungry. The first month they gained a lot of weight and as a result, Peter's paycheck was very nice. It was the biggest paycheck he had ever received. After that, the steer's growth leveled out, but he was still making more money than he made as a lumberjack. He also volunteered for extra work between feedings.

Chemicals and different hormones were being added to

the cattle's diet and many of them were becoming sick and unable to stand. The veterinarian would then be called to treat them. Sometimes the treatment worked, and the cow would improve, but most of the time it did not. The workers continued to milk the cows even while they were lying on the floor dying. When it appeared the cow was about to die, she was dragged from the barn and placed on a wagon. She was then rushed to the slaughterhouse, to be butchered while still alive. If the animal died before getting to the butcher, the meat could not be used for consumption.

The slaughterhouse was in a nearby town and served about ten farms. The butcher's living quarters were located in the same complex. The butcher was a tall, burly, dark-haired man with a German name, who had a reputation as being an angry, mean person. He was a real nightmare for tractor drivers when a dying animal had to be delivered in a hurry to the slaughterhouse, especially after working hours or on weekends. As soon as the tractor driver pulled into the complex, the doors to the living quarters flew open and the big butcher appeared. He was always wearing an apron splattered with blood, waving an 18" butcher knife, swearing, screaming, and threatening to cut the driver's throat as soon as he stepped off the tractor. The butcher would hit and kick the tractor while waving his knife. The scared driver would be sitting inside, frantically holding the door shut. This usually continued for a few minutes until the butcher calmed down, then if the driver dared, he would exit the tractor and unload the dying animal, while still being the object of swear words and threats. Some of the drivers were frightened enough to drive away, causing the animal to die before being butchered, and losing any chance for the farm to make money.

Peter went there a few times while helping other drivers. When the time came for him to deliver an animal on his own, he was very nervous and scared. He remembered the butcher's red angry face, bulging eyes, puffed up veins, and spit flying from his mouth from screaming, while waving the butcher knife and wearing the bloody apron. As he was getting closer, his heart began beating faster - than he had an idea. He drove into the building complex as fast as possible, threw the vehicle in park while jumping from the tractor at the same moment the butcher appeared in the door. Peter slammed the tractor door shut as hard as he could, and started kicking the wheels while swearing and raving about the idiots who sent him here on his time off - on the weekend - when he had plans with his family. But no, THEY had to screw it all up for him. He had to deliver THEIR stupid sick cow while THEY were sitting on THEIR butts and enjoying the weekend with their family. Peter was pacing back and forth next to the tractor, using every swear word he could remember, and kept yelling about THOSE who caused him to change his plans. The butcher stopped dead in his tracks, his jaw dropped while watching Peter yell, swear, and carry on. When Peter finished, the only thing the butcher said in a calm, relaxed voice was, "Come on let's unload that stupid cow so you can be on your way home."

From then on, Peter always volunteered when it was time to take a sick animal to the slaughterhouse. He was paid extra money for doing so, and no other tractor driver ever challenged him. They just could not understand why he would want to do that. The key was to start yelling sooner and louder than the butcher and use more swear words. However, Peter never revealed his secret to anyone!

Peter became friends with an older man who took care of a team of horses on the same farm. This man had a couple of old saddles at home, so Peter asked him if he could ride one of the horses. The black work horse was large and very strong. However, there were two problems - Peter didn't know much about horses - and the horse did not know anything about being ridden. The horse had been pulling farm equipment while working in the field his entire life. He always walked and never trotted.

The man helped Peter saddle the horse. Peter mounted him and entered the back road leading into the open fields, but the horse was used to being part of a team and never walked alone. He would walk only to the end of the yard, then turn around and walk back to the stable. He would let Peter turn him around again, but at the same spot, the horse turned and walked back to the building. It continued like this for three days. Peter was very frustrated and did not know what to do. He asked the man for advice, but he did not understand it either. The only thing he thought might help was to break off a small stick and use it as a whip, hitting the horse between the ears when he turned around. While Peter felt bad about this method, but it managed to get the horse's attention. Once past that turn around point, the horse continued to walk into the fields.

Peter only rode the horse a few times a week but the experience was getting better. Eventually, he felt comfortable enough to trot, but that was very uncomfortable so he decided to pick up the pace. While trotting, Peter continued to push the horse until he changed into a gallop. But the problem was the horse had never galloped before and did not know how to do it. He was clumsy and uncoordinated, but was quickly improving.

Their times together became more pleasurable for both of them. Peter soon told his brother about his experience and when Standa came to visit, Peter asked if they could borrow the other horse. Then, for the first time ever, the brothers went for a ride together. That was one of the most exciting times in their lives - to ride horses like cowboys side by side, through the fields and woods. It was a dream came true for both of them.

Lída was pregnant with their second child, and in October 1980, she moved in with her parents who were living closer to Prague, where she would be giving birth again. In November, four days before Lída's birthday, their baby boy, Peter, was born. This was a surprise to Peter, as he felt Lída was carrying another girl.

The distance from Litochovice to their families was very far, so they decided to move closer. Six weeks after the baby's birth, they moved to the town of Hrejkovice, where Peter began to work on a different government farm. This small village was still in Southern Bohemia, but was closer to their hometowns. Hrejkovice became their favorite place to live. It was a nice, clean, small village, close to Peter's cabin in the part of the country he loved. They lived there for 2½ years prior to their defection from Czechoslovakia.

Chapter Thirty

FINAL STAGE

The wages people earned working on farms were above average, and to make the jobs more attractive, the government did not withhold any taxes. However, tending to animals was considered substandard work since there was no education needed and it was unskilled labor. The young people working with animals were considered simple-minded individuals, who were too dumb to get an education or could not do anything else. Peter and Lída's family thought he was degrading himself, by lowering his standards to work with the cattle. To Peter's surprise, he was making more money than his father, who had a high education and a key position in a prominent company.

It wasn't easy to support a family in Czechoslovakia, since everything was very expensive there. The cost of food was outrageous and stores were poorly supplied. The village of Hrejkovice had one small grocery store, consisting of one room approximately 20 feet long and 15 feet wide, and had a wooden countertop which ran the length of the room, separating it in the middle. Covering the wall behind the counter was a large wooden case extending from the floor to ceiling, with a number of smaller open compartments filled with bread, pastries, butter, flour, sugar, and other products. People would stand in line and point at the groceries they wanted, while the clerk would place them on the counter. Once all the items were selected, the clerk would write down the prices on a small piece of paper and add them up by hand, while the customers would place the groceries into their handbags they brought with them. Once the supplies in the store were gone, people could not purchase more until the next delivery.

Meat was delivered to the store twice a week on Tuesdays and Thursdays. Customers had to come to the store on those days and order the amount of meat they wanted, which would be delivered a week later. One Kilogram of meat (2.2 pounds) cost about 60 Korunas. The average pay was anywhere from 11 to 13 Korunas per hour. Fresh fruit was only available during the summer. A kilo of strawberries or peaches cost about 80 Korunas while watermelon and other fruits would cost 50 to 60 Korunas each. Stores in the big cities were separated into meat, produce, and grocery stores, which carried the largest selection.

When Peter was a little boy, most stores were better supplied with food than when he became an adult. Butcher shops used to have quarters of animals hanging from hooks behind the counter. The next person in line could choose how much meat they wanted and it would be cut from the bottom of the quarter. If the next part was the ribs, that was what the person would receive. The butcher would chop, cut, and saw the meat off, including the bones which were considered part of the animal, and as the meat was weighed, so were the bones. The customers ended up paying the same amount for the bones as for the meat.

Even basic needs like toilet paper or sanitary pads were sometimes unavailable or were being rationed per person. There were times when people were using newspaper instead which was crumpled and rubbed together to make it softer and women had to use cotton or cut up rags for sanitary pads. So when the news spread that toilet paper had been delivered to the store, different members of the family would separately rush there to buy a roll each, before it would be sold out.

Peter worried that his children were not receiving enough vitamins. His family could not always afford to buy fruit and vegetables, which were only available during the summer months anyway. That was another reason why he wanted to defect to a western country.

Right after their marriage, Peter began pointing out and explaining to Lída what was happening around them in the

Communist environment. He was also talking to her about Communist propaganda, the Cold War, the differences between Eastern and Western European countries, and the difference in the lifestyles. Her eyes were slowly opening and soon she also began to worry about their children's future. The subject of defection came up more often. It would not be easy to leave their families, friends, homeland, and all their possessions, but Peter knew in his heart - it had to be done.

Peter always worked hard and was able to provide for his family better than most people his age. They lived in a nicely furnished apartment, owned a television, new car, and a horse. Even some middle-aged people didn't have these things. The government would only let citizens have limited prosperity, unless they were party members of course. He hated the thought of his children growing up under this system. Peter and his wife were young as well, and he felt they should also have a better future than what their homeland could offer.

He knew if they defected - it would be permanent. They would become political criminals, which meant they would never be able to go back to their homeland again. They debated what their defection would do to each member of their family - grandparents, parents, and siblings. How were they going to react to it? How were they going to feel about it? What would happen to them during their interrogation?

There was another danger they had to discuss. Some people who had emigrated from their homeland in the past would eventually become homesick, remembering only the pleasant things from their previous life. Some returned and ended up in a lot of trouble. They would then regret their return, but it was too late. They would have to live with the consequences for the rest of their lives, and some even committed suicide. Peter heard that some homesickness could eat people alive, affecting their judgment enough to make them think irrationally, and causing illogical decisions. That was a situation they needed to prepare for and be able to deal with, in case it occurred.

Peter eventually came up with an idea how to deal with homesickness. They would force themselves to recall bad memories from life under Communist dictatorship, and since a person cannot feel sadness and anger at the same time, the feelings should level out and prevent them from making absurd decisions.

Neither Peter nor Lída spoke English or German. The only foreign language they knew was Russian, which they hated and were trying to erase from their memories.

"How will we communicate?" she asked.

"We will learn English in America."

"But I am not good at learning foreign languages. Russian was very hard for me."

"Yes, but it was a different situation. We did not want to learn Russian, we hated it. When we get to America it will be easier to learn English, because we will be exposed to it all the time."

"What will we do for a living?"

"We will find something. I don't even care what it is. I will do the worst, most disgusting work, even a job that nobody else wants to do, as long as it is legal."

"But America is so big, where are we going to go?"

"I don't know that answer," he said "but we will make it work."

"How are we going to find a place to live?"

"I don't know that either. It might be in God's hands, but anything is better than staying here. Look at our lives now. We cannot travel, we cannot see the world, and we can only do what the government allows us to do. We don't know if the children are getting enough vitamins, and most of the year, we cannot even provide them with fruits and vegetables. What future will they have here when they grow up? They will not be able to get a higher education since we are not party members. They have no future here, and by staying, we are sentencing them to the same life that we have. Since we are still young, the two of us will also have a brighter future there than we have over here."

"Okay," she said, "let's do it!"

Part III

Chapter Thirty-One

CROSSING THE BORDER

He walked swiftly back to his car and told his wife, "This is it! We have to do it now! Let's wake up the kids and put their shoes on!" Both children woke up but were dizzy, confused, and sleepy, as it was almost 2:00 in the morning.

"Remember, we told you that we would have to wake you up in the middle of the night and go somewhere?" he said. "It is time to go and you cannot cry!"

He searched for his wife's hand and held it in his silently for a few seconds. He started the car and drove back onto the road. This time he knew what was around the corner. He knew the guard facing them would be looking into the headlights and would not be able to distinguish the model of the car or its license plate. The guard would most likely assume it was a Western European car coming to cross the border, he thought.

At the last moment, Peter turned onto the dirt road in front of the guardhouse which led into the fields. It was very muddy with many potholes filled with water. The car was slipping and sliding, but they were continuing to move forward. He did not want to drive too far and become lost in the darkness! He knew they would need to stop and walk to the left. In his headlights, he could see a waist high crop growing on the left side of the road. It would be difficult to walk through there he thought, so he continued on. Suddenly - the field changed to a different crop that was just sprouting out of the ground. There was a narrow grassy path between the two fields. He stopped the car and quickly shut off the lights and engine, leaving his keys in the ignition.

He jumped out of the car and quickly opened the back door, grabbed the bag throwing it over his shoulder, then scooped up his son with his right hand, while closing the door with his knee. At the same time, his wife opened the door on the other side, and snatched her bags while pulling her daughter out. Then she closed the door and walked around the back of the car. Everything was happening in a big hurry now!

Earlier, he had been trying to think through every detail, but one thing he forgot about was the dome light. When they opened the car door - the light went on. The watching guards saw them taking the children and bags from the back seat and assumed they were making a run for the border. It took the family about ten steps, than it felt like all hell broke loose! The situation by the guardhouse exploded! Voices started yelling commands! Someone with a powerful military flashlight was running from the guard house in an attempt to cut them off. Dogs started to bark. Peter heard a car engine roar as it turned on the dirt road. All this took place in a matter of seconds. He turned his head back and called into the darkness behind him, "Run as fast as you can!"

Peter started running with all he had, but immediately realized he needed to slow down as Lída and their four-year old daughter could not keep up with him. At that moment it felt as if his brain switched into a different gear, everything became foggy. He did not concentrate on anything in particular, but knew exactly what was happening around them, as if his mind had split. There were five points of focus which his brain was processing all at the same time. The invisible border in the darkness in front of them - the soldier to the left running along the border in an attempt to interfere with their path - the car with the revved up engine closing in - his wife and child in the darkness following in his footsteps - and the firm surface of the ground beneath his feet.

Suddenly - it felt as if his spirit left his body. He saw the situation from a different angle. He felt as if he was watching everything from above. Even though it was completely dark, somehow he could clearly see himself with his wife and daughter running behind. He knew how far the border was, and he knew they would be there earlier than the soldier trying to cut them off. The car racing on the dirt road was slipping and sliding in the mud, which was slowing it down. As soon as it arrived at Peter's abandoned car, there would be more soldiers chasing them. He knew he must stay on the solid grassy strip to avoid the muddy fields on each side. His brain was processing all this information at the exact same time.

The situation was changing now. The car came to a stop behind Peter and Lída's vehicle and two men with flashlights jumped out to chase them, but the lights could not penetrate the sheets of water coming down. Somehow he knew the man on the left was of no danger, so his mind blocked him out. The biggest threat to them at that moment was the two men behind, moving a lot faster than his family was. He felt he was pulling away from his wife and slowed down some - but he also knew - the men behind her were closing in.

He was told there would be a hill leading to the woods which were supposed to be in Austria. Peter was expecting the ground to start rising up towards the woods at anytime now. He closed his eyes as his sense of sight was of no use to him in the dark. His entire focus was on his feet. If he stepped on the soft muddy field, he would have to correct himself immediately to avoid falling flat on his face. Finally - there it was - a few steps uphill as the ground began rising. We are close he thought. We will make it! But his next step found no ground under his foot. In a flash, his running changed into a free fall that lasted only seconds, but felt as if he was falling forever.

He tried to rotate his body to the right to land on his left shoulder and prevent himself from falling directly on his face, while also keeping his son on top of him. Immediately, there was a splash and the fall loosened the grip he had on his son, but he scooped him up quickly and stood up. The water was only knee deep. He felt for the bag that was on his shoulder seconds ago and picked it up, but the strap had broken off. A couple more steps and they were on the other side. He could hear his wife and daughter close behind, but could not tell how far back the guards were.

"There is water here, but it is not very deep," he said into the darkness behind in a hoarse, whispering voice. He intensely listened for splashing as he started to climb the steep hill on the other side, but there were no sounds in the dark behind him. She must be afraid to get in the water, he thought with a jolt of panic.

"Get in the water, get in the water, it is not deep," he said with utmost urgency, "they are coming!" He crawled to the top of the short hill and there stood the woods - their goal - and their safety. He heard Lída and Patty behind him now.

"We have to keep running," he told the girls, "to disappear from their sight." He didn't want to slam into tree trunks and knew from summers spent at the cabin, that trees were always darker than the sky. Peter looked up to see the outline of the trees, but there were none. The night was completely black with heavy rain pouring down. He felt the dense undergrowth and was pushing through it with his chest. His little boy in his right arm began to cry.

"Shh," he told him, "you cannot cry right now, remember we talked about this yesterday..." As if with the flip of a switch, the child quit crying.

On the move, Peter looked over his shoulder to see where the pursuing lights were. To his great dismay, they were in the woods. He was expecting the guards to stop, not to cross the borderline. Their lights continued sweeping from side to side, illuminating the dense undergrowth between them and his family. The lights never stopped on Peter and Lída as they were searching back and forth. The rain and vast forest made the family invisible to the guard's eyes.

"They did not stop and are still chasing us," he called back to his wife. "Drop everything - so we can move faster!" He dropped the bag in his left hand and kept pressing on. His son started crying again, but he stopped after Peter's reminder, just as he had done before. After a while, Peter realized the guards were not chasing them anymore, it was just an optical illusion. They *had* stopped at the border and *did not* enter the forest!

The border guards were not allowed to fire their weapons

in the direction of foreign countries. But there were some cases when Communist guards shot people in secluded areas and dragged them back to their side, documenting that those people were actually shot before crossing the border. Would that have happened if the search lights had found his family?

Once realizing that they were not being chased anymore, the family stopped to huddle together, making sure everybody was okay and unhurt. It was still dark, but the rain had stopped as if its *protective cover* was no longer necessary. They started walking again veering left, back towards the road they left earlier in a different country, creeping to the edge of the woods overlooking a narrow meadow with a road behind it. Peter did not want to leave the protection of the woods yet - not until he had gathered his thoughts and figured out what to do next. To the left they could see the lights from the guardhouse. It was not the same guardhouse Peter had seen earlier. This must be an Austrian one, illuminated by the street lights Peter had seen earlier in the distance, beyond the Yugoslavian gate. There was a flag flying, but Peter and Lída realized they did not know what the Austrian flag looked like. They hoped they were in Austria, but were still not one hundred percent sure. It was early in the morning, June 21, 1983.

The whole family was soaking wet. Peter and Lída were wet from the rain and the sweat pouring off their bodies while they were running. The children were very tired and shivering from the cold.

"Where is the bag?" Lída asked Peter. "We need to change the children's clothes."

"I don't have it," he said. "I dropped it when I told you to throw everything, so we could run faster."

"But I didn't throw my stuff away," she said. "I still have both of my bags, and Patty has her backpack. We need to do something. The children are going to catch pneumonia." They removed the sleeping bag from its cover and placed it on the wet ground. After stripping off the children's wet clothes, they put them inside the sleeping bag, where they immediately fell asleep. Peter and Lída were trying to decide what to do next. Peter was mad at himself for not knowing what the Austrian flag looked like. They decided they must be in Austria - if they were still in Yugoslavia, the guards would have kept chasing them. Dawn was approaching and the sky was getting lighter. They were still worried and nervous about being captured.

"Let's get away from here before daylight, because if the Austrian guards see us, we could be arrested and handed over to the Yugoslavian authorities. We need to get as far away from the border as we can," he said in a hushed voice.

"What are we going to do with the children?" she asked. "We cannot put the wet clothes on them and we don't have any dry ones."

"I will carry them inside the sleeping bag."

He took the sleeping bag and threw it over his shoulder with both children in it, but soon realized that was an almost impossible task. There was no other choice, they would have to wake the children and dress them in their wet clothes.

It was shortly after five in the morning, and with daylight approaching, they noticed a bloody cut on little Peter's face. The cut went from his nose, across his cheek, and all the way through his left ear. There were dried bloody streaks clear down his neck. What happened - was he shot? Then Lída noticed a similar smaller wound across the right side of her husband's face, which he had not been aware of. There must have been a branch or something between the two of them, causing the cut while pressing through the undergrowth. That must have been why he had started to cry, they assumed.

It was hard to imagine what could have been going through a child's mind - running in the soaking rain - in a totally dark forest - pushing through wet bushes - and getting snapped in the face by an invisible force! They could not believe a two-year old child with such a large painful wound would stop crying, just because his father reminded him he had to be quiet!

Chapter Thirty-Two

MOTHER'S FEAR

With her heart beating strongly in her chest, Lída watched Peter disappear into the dark. She was scared and worried. Her two little children were sleeping on the back seat and her husband walked away in the direction of danger. She felt alone and helpless! What is going to happen to us if he doesn't come back, she thought? What if the children and I get arrested and hauled away before he returns? What am I going to do if somebody knocks on the car window and begins to ask me questions in a foreign language? Many such questions were racing through her head. Why isn't he coming back? Why has he been gone so long? With her heart beating heavily in her chest, she was hoping for the best, but expecting the worst. She was expecting to hear gun shots. She was expecting the guards to bring Peter back in shackles, beaten up and bloody. Her heart skipped a beat when she saw a person appear in the dark next to the car door! She sighed with relief when realizing it was her husband, and opened the door so he could get in. He was gone only 15 minutes, but it felt like an eternity.

"We are going to do it now!" he said. "Let's get the kids ready." She gently woke up the children and put their boots on while they were sitting on the back seat. Her husband started the car, switched the lights on, and turned towards the direction of the border. As the car came around the bend, she recognized the familiar site. Seeing the guardhouse, the streetlights, and the guard with the weapon on his shoulder standing next to the gate, sent a surge of panic through her entire body. As they were getting closer, she gasped for air, realizing she had forgotten to breathe for a while. She was expecting to see the guard swing his weapon off his shoulder - then Peter turned right just before the building. The muddy road with potholes was reflecting in the cars headlights. There was dead silence in their vehicle as they were slipping and sliding, while making their way forward. Abruptly, Peter stopped the car.

"Let's go, hurry!" he said. She opened the door and exited the car as fast as possible, swinging the back door open and grabbing her daughter by the hand, pulling her out of the car. Lída snatched the sleeping bag and the bag sitting next to it as they had practiced earlier, while pushing the door closed with her knee and walked around the back of the car in a hurry.

After a few steps, she looked towards the guardhouse in the distance as it suddenly erupted with activity. She saw car lights as it drove on the dirt road behind them, and also noticed a light carried by an invisible person moving quickly in their direction. Then she heard her husband's voice in the dark in front of her, "Run as fast as you can," and she immediately started to run.

It wasn't easy to run on the wet uneven surface, while holding a four-year old child by the hand and carrying the bags in the other. She was praying to God to give them wings. She wasn't aware of her surroundings, all her being was focused on one thing - not to lose Peter who was invisible in the dark in front of her. Suddenly, she heard water splashing and stopped, her husband's voice was echoing from somewhere below. When she realized there was a steep bank in front of her, she sat down and pulled her daughter next to her. They slid down the wet grass on their butts, and when her feet hit the water she stood up. While turning around, she grabbed Patty's hand and swung her over the water to the other side. She retrieved the bags and proceeded to climb the steep bank, pulling her daughter behind.

"Get in the water, get in the water, it is not very deep!" she heard her husband's voice. Why would he be saying that, she thought? I am already across! Following her husband, she ran in the woods. It was easier to follow him now since she could hear the breaking of branches. At one time she held her breath as she thought she heard her son cry, and tried to concentrate on it, but there were no sounds. I must be hearing things, she told herself.

Lída came to an abrupt stop as she felt something tangle around her ankle. She quickly reached down trying desperately to untangle her foot. Patty was tugging forcefully on her hand, "We have to hurry mom, or they are going to catch up to us!"

"Wait a minute, I have to let go of your hand for a second."

Whatever was restraining her had pulled off her shoe. She scrambled to place it back on her foot, and grabbed Patty's hand while starting to run again. From the wet darkness in front of her, she heard the muffled sound of her husband's voice. She listened intensely to hear what he was saying, but could only make out the words, "...throw everything away so we can move faster!" She could not understand why he was saying that.

"I don't want to throw my backpack away mom," her daughter said.

"That is okay honey, you don't have to," she told her in a reassuring voice. After sometime they caught up with Peter.

"We can slow down now," he said out of breath, "they are not following us anymore." They came close to the edge of the woods and stopped.

"We have to change the children's clothes," she said, "they are all wet. Where is the bag?"

"I don't have it, I threw it away," he replied. Well, that is not good, she thought! We don't know what is going to happen next and we don't have any spare clothes for them. They walked to the road and started traveling north.

*

Lída kept reminding Peter about the bag.

"We need to have clothes for the kids. We don't have spare underwear or socks for them. We don't know what is going to happen to us or where we will end up. They are both soaking wet and could get pneumonia! You have to go back there and find the bag," she told him numerous times.

Eventually - Peter agreed. He figured out it would be better to go back now, since the sun was not completely up, and they were still close to the border.

"Okay - I will go back there, but you must wait for me by the road. If the police drive by, they will probably try to arrest you and take you away, but you cannot let them! Somehow you have to explain that I am also here and you cannot leave without me. If we do get separated now - I don't know how we would find each other again. No matter what it takes, you cannot let them take you!"

She sat warily in the ditch with the children on her lap. Peter started walking back towards the Yugoslavian border. He felt as if he was walking back into the 'lion's den'. His heart was beating faster with every step. How can I find a bag that I dropped in the darkness of the night somewhere in the woods? He was thinking about it hard and then had an idea. If he could line himself up at the edge of the forest with the small path between the two fields, he should be in the right area.

He was quietly sneaking through the trees, trying to avoid the Yugoslavian guards. It was almost light now and the first sunrays were shooting through the trees like golden arrows. He was looking around and could not believe his eyes. The forest was clean and well kept with mature majestic trees. The forest floor was wide open - except a 150 foot wide strip covered with dense undergrowth - through which they had been running for their lives a few hours earlier. A little farther right or left of this section and they would have been wide open - clearly visible to the guard's flashlight! God guided our steps, he thought.

He continued carefully to the edge of the woods. In the distance to his right, he could see the Yugoslavian guardhouse. A beaten path used by the guards was running along the edge of the woods. He cautiously looked both ways making sure there were no guards in sight. Now - in the daylight - he could see what the border really looked like. Approximately 20 feet from the edge of the woods parallel to the trees, was a man-made berm. The top of the berm was about 2 feet high and was lined with white stone pillars which were approximately 50 feet apart, marking the border. The ground behind it dropped down into a man-made water channel then rose back up to an identical berm on the other side. The problem was, since the ground went up, down, and back up again, he could not see over it to locate the path between the two fields. He would have to leave the safety of the trees, slide down to cross the water channel, then climb up the other side in order to see the land beyond. He decided not to take that tremendous risk. We made it, he told himself. We are in Austria and I will not risk being arrested or shot by the people in the guardhouse. We will have to do without the extra clothes - we will find a way, he thought!

He turned around and walked away from the border for the second time. And there - right in front of his feet - was the bag. On top of the bag was a small colorful snail followed by a narrow, slimy trail sparkling in the sunrays. That scene soothed Peter's unsettled nerves, spilling a complete sense of peace throughout his body! He bowed his head and thanked God for protecting and guiding them through that horrible night!

Chapter Thirty-Three

FREE COUNTRY

Fortunately, his family was waiting in the same place he left them. They quickly changed the children into dry clothes. Peter and Lída also had an extra pair of socks in the bag, and putting them on made their feet feel a lot better. By this time, the clothes on their bodies were almost dry.

Things were really looking up now! It was a perfect early summer morning, with blue skies and no clouds in sight. The sun was raising higher, heating up the soggy ground from the previous day's rain. Mist caused by evaporation was lingering over the fresh green grass. Everything was peaceful and calm. They walked by colorful, traditional, German-style farmhouses with carved wooden decorations, vibrant flowers outside the windows, and well kept gardens. A door opened and an elderly man walked out carrying a wooden milking bucket, while a cow inside the barn began mooing as the farmer stepped in through the door.

The young family was feeling euphoric and happy, as they finally realized they had made it out of a Communist country alive and unhurt! This is where their new lives would begin! A brighter future was awaiting them - starting with this beautiful, peaceful day. They felt as if one life had ended and a new one was beginning. A few short hours ago they left a Communist country where everything was gray, colorless, and gloomy, and now they had entered a country filled with blue skies, green grass, and the sun shining over the countryside, with well kept houses and freedom - freedom! They could feel it! They could taste it! They could smell it! Their spirits were flying high! It felt as if a big load had been lifted from their shoulders. The difference was unbelievable. Just one border line - a few miles apart - only a couple hours away - and everything was so - so much different.

*

It was only 7:00 in the morning when they walked into a small town called Bad Radkersburg. When they entered the suburb, beautiful single family homes appeared on each side of the street. Flowers were everywhere - growing in gardens, in the trays outside the windows, roses climbing the fences in front of the houses. By now the children were very tired. They could hardly walk and were tripping over their own feet, falling asleep standing up. They were not able to go any further. Peter and Lída decided to rest and sat down on the grass. He felt this town was big enough to have a bank. He told Lída to stay there with the children, while he continued walking towards the center of town to see if he could find one. He reminded her once again not to let anyone take them away. In the main square he found a bank, but it was too early for it to be open yet.

As he walked back, he could see his family was not where he left them - they were nowhere in sight! He stared in disbelief at the spot on the ground where he had left them an hour earlier. Immediately, tremendous exhaustion from the previous night's pressures overwhelmed his body and he had to concentrate to avoid collapsing to his knees. He felt tightness in his chest as fear and a sense of helplessness overcame him. He felt weak and empty as if all his energy and strength had been drained. Then - a wave of relief and happiness filled his heart as he heard Lída's voice calling his name from the house across the street.

An old wonderful lady who lived there had come out to water her flowers and saw Lída sitting on the ground with two small children sleeping in her lap. She called to them, inviting them in. She spoke only German and they could not understand her, but somehow they were able to communicate. She gestured that it was breaking her heart to see the children sleeping by the road. She began asking Peter what they were doing there, while feeding them warm milk and big pieces of bread with butter. He tried to explain to her they had defected through Yugoslavia just last night. It seemed as if she could not comprehend what he was talking about. Peter asked for a map of Austria and she pointed at the location of the town they were in. He saw the road they had traveled on while crossing the border, which gave him a better understanding of where they were now.

At 9:00 in the morning, Peter left his family with the lady and nervously towards the bank. He would try to exchange their money for Austrian Schillings, but could not speak German and did not have proper documents. Since they were still close to the Yugoslavian border, he thought the best choice would be to exchange the Yugoslavian Dinaras. The teller took the money and placed it in the money exchange machine, without asking questions. The exchanger counted the currency and ejected the Austrian Schillings. It was a lot easier than Peter had expected. For the first time since he was fifteen-years old, he was not required to show his identification. He then decided to try to exchange the Czechoslovakian Korunas, handing them to the teller. The same thing happened once again. Peter produced the small amount of Hungarian Forints from his pocket, and once again, it was exchanged without questions. This entire time he was expecting the clerk to call the police. Peter walked away with *hard currency* in his pocket. Life is getting easier already, he thought. There was absolutely no chance that would ever happen in a Communist country!

From the bank, Peter walked straight to the post office on the opposite side of the square. He knew that most European post offices had a phone booth inside, where the postal clerk would dial the desired phone number on the switch board behind the counter. The customer would talk on the phone inside the booth, and then return to the counter to ask what the charge was and pay the employee based on the length and destination of the call.

Peter called the family back in Czechoslovakia to tell

them to go to their apartment in Hrejkovice. He was not aware that a few days after they left on vacation, the authorities had sealed their apartment, thanks to their nosy neighbor.

If the defection would not have been successful, their plan was to return home as if nothing happened. They would destroy the letter and go on with their lives. Unknown to them, if they returned home, they would have been arrested immediately and the children would be taken away.

In the meantime, back in Czechoslovakia, their family members did not even know that Peter's family had gone to Yugoslavia. When they arrived at the apartment, they found the door sealed with police tape. They knocked on the neighbor's door and asked what was going on. The neighbors told them the whole village was talking about Peter and Lída's defection. The police had already been there, classifying the apartment as a 'crime scene'. The neighbors also told them that sometimes during the night, trucks had come and people hauled furniture and other stuff away. Those people were probably policemen and local Communist authorities that had learned about the defection. They were robbing the apartment, taking everything they could, before the official investigation began. Of course - those were the people who had seals for the doors, so they would re-seal it after each time they went there. This always happened at night, under the cover of darkness, but none of the residents would dare ask who they were or what they were doing, but everybody knew it was the government.

One of the things left behind in the apartment was the clothes washer. Clothes washers, like everything else, were very expensive and people often saved for years to purchase one. Peter and his wife could not afford to buy one, so Lída's parents had given them one as a present. In order to keep the washer after the defection, her parents had to go to the authorities and apply for it. They told the authorities it was theirs and they had loaned it to their daughter's family until they could afford to buy their own. Her parents had the receipt proving they bought it, so the authorities set up a time with a party member, most likely STB, to let them in.

While getting the washer, Lída's father noticed her baby

picture lying on the floor in the doorway to the children's room. Some of the family belongings were spilling out from the drawers and were scattered on the floor, but most of the stuff was already missing. He bent over to pick up the picture. The party member started yelling, "You don't have the rights to do anything like that, you are only allowed to get the clothes washer and you should be thankful we even let you do that!" Lída's father was not allowed to touch anything, not even the picture of his own daughter.

Lída's mother was a co-signer for a government loan to buy their bedroom set. Now, she was responsible for paying the loan since Peter and Lída were not around anymore. She really wanted to keep the furniture, so she talked to the authorities. They told her she had to go to the auction and bid on it. Vlasta ended up buying the furniture from the government auction and still had to keep making payments to them for the furniture loan. The Communist government kept all the money.

The letter Peter and Lída had left behind for their relatives had been confiscated by the STB and they were not allowed to see it.

Scratches Peter endured while on the run across the border. The dried blood on his face and neck has already been cleaned up.

Lída, Patty, and Peter with the helpful Grandma in her rose garden.

*

The following day Peter, Lída, and their two children, ended up in a refugee camp in a town called Traiskirchen. The camp was located in an old military base that was abandoned some years ago. It was in the middle of town surrounded by fences and had guards at the entrance. There was a three story building and a number of smaller ones, used as housing for refugees and the camp administration offices. All of the new refugees were required to go through the registration process. Peter's family was placed on third floor in the main building, which had steel bars and guards blocking the stairways. They could not leave this floor until their paperwork was processed and they had been interrogated. All four members of Peter's family were assigned bedding, military-style aluminum dishes, silverware, a towel, and a bar of soap. Three times a day, the refugees were assembled and led by guards to the mess hall, where food was dumped into their dishes. They could not eat their meals until they were back on third floor behind bars.

The first and second floors were used for housing single

male refugees. Most of the windows were broken and shattered glass from alcohol bottles was littering the ground around the building. Drunken voices and sounds of breaking glass were heard throughout the night. Peter and Lída were embarrassed and ashamed of the behavior of these refugees. They could not understand the way they were treating the Austrians, especially after receiving their help, hospitality, and protection.

On the third floor were two big rooms with 60 beds each and two smaller ones. These were the temporary living quarters for those who had just arrived. People of different nationalities, backgrounds, and colors, were staying in the same room. Some were from Eastern bloc countries, others from the Middle East, others from Africa. Everybody spoke a different language. It was a little eerie for people from different parts of the world to sleep together with all their worldly possessions simply sitting in the bags underneath their beds. Luckily for Peter's family, they were placed in one of the smaller rooms with beds for 8 people. Two hours after Peter's family had checked in, another family from Czechoslovakia arrived, who also had an older girl and younger boy. They were placed in the same room and they all became very good friends.

Since the building was built as a military camp, there was only one big room with a number of showers and toilets to be shared by all - men, women, and children. Anytime Peter's wife or children needed to take a shower or go to the bathroom, he went with them to stand guard.

The first step in the emigration process was to attend an interview with the Austrian authorities, probably a member of the secret police, who was not very friendly. He began asking Peter and Lída many unpleasant questions separately, checking to see if their answers matched. These questions were about their lives in Czechoslovakia, any problems they experienced with the police or government, their defection, their families, and so on. It took three days for Peter's family to be released from the third floor and receive an ID card, allowing them to get in and out of camp. At that time, they were put on a bus with their new friends, Zbyněk and his family, and were taken 100 miles west to the small picturesque town of Ramsau. Here they were housed in a Gasthof owned by an Austrian family, who was subsidized by the government for providing housing and assistance to refugees. It held approximately 50 families and also some single people, all from Czechoslovakia. Every family and person in the Gasthof had a different story of defection. Some had made it without any problems, some had a very hard time, some stories were unusual, and some people had defied death.

The lower level of the Gasthof consisted of a large dining room, kitchen, and a bar. The owners were cooking three meals per day and everyone was called in to eat in the dining room or during the summers in the courtyard. The second and third levels had a number of single rooms, with one shared bathroom on each floor. Each member of the family was assigned some toiletries such as toothpaste and toothbrushes, soaps, shampoo, and towels. The father received shaving supplies and also some money.

Peter was required to write his immediate family history, including the date he and Lída were married, their occupations, and how and why they defected. They also had to fill out an application for entering the country where they wanted to go.* The paperwork was then translated into English and forwarded to the U.S. Consul. Once a week, the U.S. Consul had a day assigned for interviewing refugees applying for residency in the United States. Some applications were denied and those people had to apply numerous times. A few people ended up living in refugee camps or in Gasthofs for over two years.

Peter and Zbyněk, who spoke a little German, found a job clearing the undergrowth from the forests surrounding the town of Ramsau, to make a little extra cash to begin their new life in America. The work only lasted about three weeks, but every little bit helped.

During this time, life was quite simple and easy for Peter and his family. They had a roof over their heads, three meals a day and basic supplies provided. The family went for walks

---

* Most of the refugee applications were for the United States, Canada, and Australia. Some people desired to go to New Zealand, Sweden, Germany, or stay in Austria.

everyday in the beautiful countryside surrounding Ramsau. The town was located at the bottom of a long valley, with a crystal-clear creek running through it. The road and line of houses wound back and forth parallel to the creek. Behind the Gasthof was a small swimming pool, fed by a brook running next to it, where they spent hours basking in the sun. But more than that - they were living in a Western European country, Austria.

Peter had a hard time enjoying this carefree lifestyle. No matter how beautiful - this was just the place in between - the waiting period. They had applied for the United States, but did not know if their application would be approved. He knew their new beginning was going to be in the United States, but they did not know where and when they would end up in America. They wanted to learn English and start building their new life as soon as possible.

While in Austria, Peter kept close watch over his family. Stories were circulating about cases where Communists staged kidnappings, forcing entire families to return, in an attempt to keep them silent. The STB set up elaborate covert operations to kidnap a child and take it back to Czechoslovakia. The petrified parents were notified about the child's whereabouts, which ultimately forced their return. Peter religiously kept a watchful eye on his loved ones. He eventually concluded those men were probably more important to the Communists because of the knowledge they possessed and allowing them into a foreign country where they could talk, would be very undesirable. Peter felt he was not important enough for the Communists to risk exposure on the international level.

Chapter Thirty-Four

THE PROMISED LAND

The two religious organizations, Catholic and Protestant, had offices located in Traiskirchen camp. These organizations were translating refugee applications and letters for the U.S. Consul. The meeting with the U.S. Consul was eventually scheduled in Vienna for Peter's family. They were interviewed by him with the assistance of a translator. They were asked questions such as why they defected from Czechoslovakia, why they were looking for asylum, and why they would choose America instead of another country. This entire process lasted approximately 45 minutes. After the interview, all members of the family were sent for a complete medical examination. A few days later, they received their approved application. That was a big relief and a reason for celebration with their friends!

The next step was to have a sponsor in the United States. This process was also handled by the religious organizations in Traiskirchen. People were not allowed to go to the United States or any country without having a sponsor first, even after they were approved by their Consul. A few days later, Peter received their paperwork stating the Protestant organization had located a sponsor for his family. Their sponsor was the First Lutheran Church located in Beach, North Dakota. The parishioners of the church decided to sponsor a young family with small children from Czechoslovakia. The pastor contacted the Immigration office in Fargo to notify it of their intentions. The Immigration office checked their records and came across Peter's family. The church group decided to sponsor his family after they received their information. Unknown to Peter, his family was sponsored before they were even interviewed by the U.S. Consul.

Peter, Patty, and little Peter in Vienna, after their interviews with the U.S. Consul.

Eventually they received all the required documents and then on Wednesday, September 7, 1983, left Austria and flew to their new home - the United States of America. Their time in Austria lasted only 2½ months, an all time record according to other refugees staying in the Gasthof.

Zbyněk's family went with them to the Vienna airport to say goodbye forever, since they had chosen to begin their new lives in Australia. The day before departure, the transportation to Traiskirchen camp picked them up at the Gasthof. They went through final paperwork clearance and were given airline tickets to the United States. Their last night in Austria was spent in a small Gasthof across the street from Traiskirchen camp. They had to be in a refugee camp early in the morning to board the bus taking them to the airport in Vienna. The bus was full of refugee people of different nationalities, all traveling on the same plane to America, most of whom Peter's family did not know. The whole group, as well as regular passengers, boarded the plane at Schwechat Airport in Vienna. That plane took them to Frankfurt, Germany.

Peter was still very nervous because of a story he had once heard about a Czech refugee family flying the same way from Vienna to Frankfurt. The weather was bad in Germany and the airports in the surrounding areas stopped receiving air traffic. The plane had to be re-routed to Prague until the weather cleared in Frankfurt, which should have been only a matter of a few hours, until the bad weather passed. The passengers were required to exit their plane in Prague and as they entered the airport, Czech authorities verified passports, making sure the same number of people leaving the plane re-entered later. The refugee family was caught due to their Czech names. Because of the bad weather, the plane that was supposed to take them to freedom, delivered them back to their homeland instead, where the government they were trying to escape, persecuted them.

After Peter and his family landed in Frankfurt, the entire group of refugees was met by one person, who led them to the next gate to board the plane to America. There was not adequate layover time, so they were rushed, almost running, through the airport to reach their next flight on time. The America bound plane was a Boeing 747, the 'Jumbo Jet'. Peter was surprised. He remembered when he was a teenager and the Boeing 747 was introduced to the public transportation system, during a big international air show in France. The jumbo jet was the biggest commercial airplane of all times. As usual, the Communists immediately started another anti-American campaign. According to the news broadcasts, the plane was nothing but American propaganda. The Communists claimed the Americans had built this plane as more proof they were superior. They also claimed the plane was built only for show and it was way too big and heavy to actually fly. The Communists said only three of these planes were produced and were not fit for public transportation. At that time Peter believed it, as did most of the people in the country. But now he was sitting in a Boeing 747 and while looking out the window, he saw at least five more identical planes.

"Guess that was one of the many lies we were constantly being fed," he told his wife.

Peter had flown on a commercial plane once before, but he was shocked and could not believe the size and the amount of passengers this plane held. He was fascinated by the separate compartments throughout the length of the plane, and the size of the engines and wings were unbelievable to him. Many thoughts were going through his head. We are leaving Europe - possibly forever! Peter never dreamed of even making it to Austria or Germany and now they were leaving those countries behind. Czechoslovakia, their homeland, was just across the border, not very far away. His brother's family and parents were there - right now - in places he knew, while his family was sitting in this humongous plane ready to depart the continent. Then he started to second guess himself. Okay he thought, I heard about America, I read about America, and I saw the maps. Soon we will be in the air, flying into the unknown. What if there is no America and the continent doesn't even exist? And if it does, what will happen to us? He did not know if anybody would be there waiting for them. What was ahead of them? They did not know where they were going, what to expect, and what it would look like. Would they survive? All these questions were rushing through his head. But then the plane started moving and the excitement changed his thinking process. It is true - we are on our way to America - right now - finally - this is it! His lifelong dream was about to become reality! His family was on their way... they were on their way to the 'promised land'...

From his seat he could see the tip of the left wing. The wing was bowed down and the end was even with the bottom of the window as they started moving across the runway, picking up speed. The plane soon lifted off the ground and its weight transferred from the wheels to the wings. The wing flexed up and was now in line with the top of the window instead of the bottom. And - this giant American made machine was taking his family through another link on their *journey for freedom.* At that moment, he became truly emotional. Tears started flowing from his eyes, rolling down his cheeks. He looked across the aisle at his beautiful family. That was the happiest day of his life!

When the flight attendant came with the refreshments, Peter asked for a Coca-Cola and whiskey. He never liked hard liquor, but this time it would be symbolic. He was flying in an American made plane to the U.S.A., so he ordered what he believed was a typical American drink. He never had Coca-Cola before. Peter had tasted whiskey and did not like it, and it still did not taste good, but he drank it because it was special to him. On the other hand, he liked Coca-Cola a lot.

He could not believe the number of televisions on the airplane. There were still many people in Czechoslovakia who didn't even own one.

After an eight hour flight, the plane began descending into New York City. At one point when the airplane tilted sideways, Peter saw the Statue of Liberty far below. It appeared to be the size of a baby's finger, but the sight of it was overwhelming. Interestingly enough - since that day, he has flown through New York a few other times, but not once, has he seen the Statue of Liberty again!

When they landed, people on the plane started clapping. Peter and Lída were looking at each other with excitement, while hugging and kissing their children. Then they entered the airport - for the first time in his life, he set foot on American soil. Peter couldn't be more excited if he would have stood on the moon! Since this was the first stop in America, they had to retrieve their luggage and go through customs before they could enter the airport.

*

Peter was standing among hundreds of other travelers at the New York City airport. Hanging on the wall was a large clock showing the local time. Everybody began to change the time on their watches. Peter also removed his watch from his wrist, pulled the knob to move the hands to the correct position, and realized it was already set to that time. His mind flashed back to the time when he was eighteen and his brother found out that the New York City time zone was six hours behind Czechoslovakia. They had both turned their watches to that time zone. It made them feel closer to life in America by knowing what people were doing at any particular time of the day. If it was 7:00 on his watch, he knew people in America were getting up for work, or at 5:00 in the evening, they were eating dinner. There were times when Peter, Standa, and their friend Tom brought in the New Year in Czechoslovakia, then stayed up six more hours to celebrate the coming of the American New Year.

The commotion in the airport snapped Peter back to reality. Peter became overwhelmed with emotions when he realized - destiny finally brought him to the time and place he belonged...

After going through customs, they walked into the main level of the airport. There was a man holding a sign with their last name. He led them out of the airport to a shuttle bus. They drove into the streets of New York City, seeing the skyscrapers in the distance, the yellow taxi cabs, and six lanes of freeway surrounding them. Until that moment, they had only seen these things in pictures or at the movies. Now, they were seeing it in real life and it seemed somewhat unrealistic.

After driving for about 30 minutes, they got off the shuttle in front of a hotel. The guide, who spoke broken Czech, walked them into the hotel lobby and helped them with checking in. He explained that they would have to stay there overnight, as their connecting flight to Minnesota would not leave until the next day. He told them to get settled into their room, then go down to the hotel restaurant where dinner would be ready. He would be back tomorrow morning at 7:00, to take them to the airport.

The outside temperature was really hot - hotter than they had ever experienced. The hotel room was also hot. There was an air conditioning unit in the window, and the person that let them into the room turned it on. After he left, Peter wanted to cool the room down so he opened the window. They never slept in a hotel before - never heard of air conditioning - and did not know how it worked.

After awhile, they walked downstairs to the restaurant. All four of them received a half chicken dinner with salad, potatoes, and vegetables. It was an entire half of the chicken in one solid piece, laying on each of their plates. They were not very hungry since it was 1:00 in the morning in Europe, and their bodies had not adjusted to the time change. Little Peter took two bites and was done, and Patty did not eat much more. Back home, it was considered rude to leave food on the plate, so that night Peter ate three half chicken dinners, as he cleaned his children's plates. It was not an easy task and he barely wobbled back to their room after he was done.

They could not sleep much that night because of all the excitement, heat, and the time change. They dozed off for a few hours, but Peter and Lída both woke up at 1:00 in the morning, which was 7:00 A.M. in their homeland. They heard children's voices outside on the street. Peter looked out the window in disbelief, and to his amazement, he saw four small black children playing on the sidewalk. That was something Peter and Lída could not comprehend. Where were their parents? How come they were playing outside at 1:00 in the morning? How come they were not sleeping? Didn't they have to go to school tomorrow? They could not understand what was happening. Something like that was simply unheard of in Czechoslovakia.

Chapter Thirty-Five

NEW HOME

The same person that picked them up from the airport the previous day came to get them in the morning. He rode with them on the shuttle bus to what they thought was a different airport and escorted them to the plane departing for Minnesota. Another person holding a sign with their name was waiting for them when they arrived in Minneapolis. He was a young man and spoke only English and Polish, not Czech. He led them through the airport to a different gate, where they waited for a few hours for the plane bound for Bismarck, North Dakota. Only a handful of people exited the plane in Bismarck, so the family assumed the plane continued to another destination.

The airport in Bismarck was small and did not even have a Jetway for people to walk off the plane. As they stepped down onto the tarmac, the heat in the air startled them. First they thought it was the heat coming from the airplane's engines, but as they walked away, it did not subside. As they approached the building, they could see people through the window waving and jumping up and down with excitement. Peter and Lída looked behind them to see who they were waving at, but everybody else was already inside the building. Then they noticed the sign with black letters pressed against the window, "VÍTÁME VÁS VE VAŠEM NOVÉM DOMOVĚ V BEACH!" (We welcome you to your new home in Beach). It was written in Czech! They looked at each other in disbelief - how is this possible? As soon as they stepped into the terminal, those people came running, hugging and welcoming them. The lady had tears in her eyes, which Peter and Lída could not understand. This is how you welcome your long lost children, not strangers you do not know anything about. We could be bad people! They don't know us, but yet they are so happy to see us. Something like that would not happen in our homeland. People kept their distance and were guarded - especially around strangers. Back home they did not hug - not even their loved ones - they just shook hands! The group consisted of Pastor Sam Johnson from the First Lutheran Church in Beach, North Dakota, with his wife, Robin, and an older gentleman named Vance from Dickinson, who was a Czech descendant fluent in both languages.

After retrieving their luggage, they all walked to a big old typical American car in the parking lot. The trunk seemed to be the size of an entire Czechoslovakian car. All of them fit easily and comfortably inside the vehicle. They crossed the Missouri River and entered the western part of North Dakota with wide open spaces, rolling hills, and unbelievably big blue skies. The feelings Peter felt were hard to express. They were riding in a big comfortable American car on a big wide road visible all the way to the horizon, and open spaces all around them. He was looking out the window where the vast open spaces continued to spill into more and more open spaces. You can only see this far looking across the ocean, he thought. And all this time, the thoughts, this is America - **WE ARE IN AMERICA** - driving on an American road through the American countryside, were going through his mind. The strong feelings in his chest were overwhelming! His heart was full of happiness! His spirit was flying high and his eyes kept welling up!

They dropped Vance off at his house in Dickinson and stopped to eat a quick meal. They ate a big American burger for the first time in their lives. How tasty this food was! A few years later when they became accustomed to American culture, they realized it must have been either McDonalds or Burger King. After the meal, they were each handed an ice cream cone. It was humongous - everything in America seemed to be big, even the food portions. Little Peter's ice cream seemed to be bigger than his leg and was soon dripping on the backseat.

Peter and Lída struggled to keep up with the children's melting ice cream, along with their own. Peter was still full from eating the chicken dinners the night before and could hardly eat his own, let alone his children's.

When they left Dickinson, the sun was already setting over the horizon. Their destination was the town of Beach, 60 miles away. Everybody was very tired as they did not sleep much the night before, and still were not adjusted to the time change. It was after midnight in Europe and they all quickly fell asleep in the car. Suddenly, Peter woke up as Robin was talking to him. She was pointing at the patch of lights glowing in the distance. Somehow, he understood what she was saying, "That is Beach, your new home."

They pulled up to a two-story white house on the right side of Main Street. Next to the house was the First Farmer's Bank parking lot. Robin pointed to the lit up sign next to the bank. The sign was flashing the time, temperature, and then words - the Czech words started to move across: "PETR VODENKA S RODINOU VÍTÁME VÁS VE VAŠEM NOVÉM DOMOVĚ BEACH NORTH DAKOTA." (Peter Vodenka and family, welcome to your new home Beach, North Dakota.)

Peter and Lída were overwhelmed with emotions. They could not understand how it was possible for the writing to be in Czech! That slogan circulated day and night for the next three weeks. Anytime they looked out the window or walked on the street, they could read it. That meant a great deal to them and made them feel more at home. No one else in town could read what it said - only them!

It was late evening, September 8, 1983, and the beginning of their new life. The only possessions they had when they arrived was $600, a small duffel bag with footwear, a small old black scratched up suitcase they found thrown away in Austria and now filled with extra clothes, the handbag with the broken strap they carried across the border, and a sleeping bag. They also had a suitcase made of paper with reinforced corners, filled with books Peter's mom had mailed to him while they were living in the refugee camp in Austria. Peter always loved reading books. He had been reading books his whole life, and had many which he wished to keep for his children's sake, so they wouldn't lose the Czech culture and language.

The Johnsons led them into their new house. It had a small living room, a kitchen, and a bathroom on the main floor. The bathroom was small and its ceiling was sloped down because it was built underneath the steps which led upstairs to the three bedrooms. The house had no basement, just a hole dug in the dirt with the furnace and water heater sitting in the middle of it. The house was completely equipped with furniture, food in the cupboards and refrigerator, towels, linens, and all the other necessary things, even including toothbrushes and toothpaste. The parishioners in the church had donated furniture, clothes, and money to buy provisions. The owner of the house donated three months of free rent. Peter and Lída could not believe their eyes. This was so much more than they expected! They walked into a fully furnished, fully equipped house. There was no end to their happiness.

There was one interesting thing about Americans, even though they knew Peter and Lída did not know English, they were talking to them as if they did. The words and sentences were just raining upon them and when it stopped and the person kept looking and waiting, Peter would finally realized there was a question which they were expected to answer. That was hard to do if you did not understand what was asked. Then instead of choosing simple and easier words, that person would repeat everything exactly the same way, only much louder. Robin was the worst. She would get closer and talk directly into their ear in a very loud voice. Soon she developed the habit to always talk to the family this way. At one time, Pastor Sam told her in his quiet calm voice, "They are not deaf my dear, they just don't understand English." She put her hand over her mouth and burst into laughter, then apologized. However, the next time when they saw each other, she was shouting all over again, like there was no tomorrow.

Peter and the children in the Minneapolis airport, on the way to North Dakota.

Family Photo taken a few weeks after arrival.

Peter and Lída's house in Beach.

VÍTAME VÁS
VE VAŠEM NOVÉM
DOMOVĚ V BEACH

Welcome sign in airport window.

Little Peter's baptism at the First Lutheran Church in Beach, ND. The ceremony is being performed by Pastor Sam.

Chapter Thirty-Six

FIRST AMERICAN JOB

At the end of 1982, Beach was a small thriving town with a population of approximately 1,500. It was mostly a farming community, prospering due to the strong crude oil industry in the plains of North Dakota. There was a grade school, high school, public swimming pool, department store, two grocery stores, four restaurants, lumber yard, two auto dealerships, three banks, post office, a movie theater, and even a hospital. Then the oil industry went into recession. When Peter and his family arrived, the population in the town had already shrunk by ⅓ and people continued to move away.

Two old widowed sisters with Czech descendents lived in Beach and were members of the First Lutheran Church. They both were fluent in Czech and were the reason the church decided to sponsor a family from Czechoslovakia. Aside from the two sisters, communication was difficult as nobody else spoke Czech. Peter and Lída used a Czech-English dictionary they brought with them.

Most of the time, they were in contact with Pastor Sam and his wife, Robin. Eventually they became accustomed to each other and were able to communicate and understand, without speaking the same language.

Peter immediately started asking for work, but was told the Beach economy was bad and unemployment was high and rising. People from the town stopped by often to visit Peter's family, and he continued asking everyone about employment opportunities. Soon he came across somebody that knew a farmer looking for a farmhand. The farmer, Greg Larson, and his wife Donna, had seven boys, and she was pregnant with another child. Peter was hired and started working on their pig farm on September 15, for the minimum wage of $3.35 per hour, with no benefits or overtime paid. He was working nine hour days, six days a week. Greg's family also provided Peter with coffee for the morning coffee break and lunch at noon. He ate lunch with Greg's entire family, a full dinner with soup, potatoes, meat, vegetables, and such. Everything was served in large bowls in the middle of the table. Peter was eating only small portions as he was uneasy eating their food. People in Czech did not eat at another person's home, unless it was their immediate family or they brought food with them.

The night before Peter's first day of work, snow started falling with a cold, blowing wind. Peter was not properly dressed to work outside all day in the freezing temperatures. Greg Larson must have called Pastor Sam, because when Peter returned home from work that night, Pastor was waiting to take him to the department store to buy warm boots, long johns, a warm hat and gloves, and a pair of insulated coveralls. The snow stayed on the ground for two days, and then it warmed up again, lasting through the end of November. December brought very cold freezing temperatures, even though there was no snow on the ground. For a couple of weeks, the temperature did not rise above 40 degrees below zero. The wind-chill factor was recorded at 60, even 80 degrees below zero, and one day, the wind-chill in Bismarck was reported at minus 100 degrees.

Greg and Peter were working outside all day long, other than the 10 minute coffee break and 30 minute lunch. One day while working, Peter was thinking how easy it would be to freeze to death or get frost bite in these conditions. At the same time these thoughts were going through his head, he looked at Greg's red face and saw a pure white dot the size of a pea on the tip of his nose. It was very unnatural and white as snow. At first Peter thought Greg had something stuck on his nose, but then he realized it was the color of his skin. It startled him since he had never seen anything like that before. Right in front of his eyes, the white dot changed to the shape of a drop with its point spreading quickly up the bridge of his nose. To his horror, Peter realized he was witnessing frost bite in progress. He started gesturing to Greg, trying to explain to him what was happening, but he was just waving his hand as if it was no big deal. Peter continued to tell him in Czech he needed to go in or he would lose his nose. It must have been the expression on Peter's face that finally made Greg realize that something was seriously wrong. He went into the house, returning about an hour later with two rags to cover their faces so only their eyes were visible. With the first breath they took, the rags changed into ice, but it kept their faces warm, except their eyelashes were sticking together as they blinked.

One day Peter was working away from the farm and needed to go to the bathroom. He went behind the haystacks to be protected from the wind. It was a difficult task in his insulated coveralls and all the layers of clothing underneath. His gloves were off for only about two minutes, but his fingers became so cold, that he could not hold the zipper to pull it back up. He ended up squeezing the zippers between the palms of his hands to pull them closed. After the New Year, a blizzard came that lasted for three days. The snow covered the main street up to the bottom of the second floor windows and stayed on the ground for two more months.

Peter and his family went to church on their first Sunday in Beach. The church was packed as all of the members wanted to meet them, even the local newspaper editor came to take their picture on the front steps of the church for an article in the newspaper. Two older ladies who spoke Czech, Mrs. Jones and Mrs. Swanson, stopped by to drive them to church. Mrs. Jones, the older sister who had weak eyesight and decreased hearing, owned the car and had a driver's license. The younger sister was healthy and in good shape, but had never driven a car in her entire life. The car was a 1963 Ford Galaxy, a twenty-year old car with beautiful shiny black paint, a lot of chrome, leather seats, and had only 45,000 miles since she was only using it to drive a few blocks to church and the grocery store.

When they arrived to pick Peter and his family up, Mrs. Jones stopped her car at an angle in the middle of the main street, while her sister walked to the house to get them. When they arrived at the church, the parking lot was already full, but Mrs. Jones saw an opening between the cars that were parked on the street. First she tried to pull the vehicle in forward, but half of it was sticking out. After a few attempts, she realized she would have to parallel park. On the fifth try she was in the right position, but pulled in too far and hit the car behind her. She put the car in drive, pulled forward, and hit the car in front of her. After repeating this three times, ⅓ of the vehicle was still in the road, but she was finally satisfied. After getting out of the car, Peter stole a few quick glances at all four bumpers, trying to avoid embarrassing her. To his amazement, none of the vehicles were dented or even had a single scratch. Peter expected to see damage because the hits were not *gentle*. He credited the lack of damage to the excellent American workmanship. This whole process was repeated again the following Sunday.

After the service was over, the sisters told them, "We will pick you up at the same time next week."

"Don't worry about it, we all need the exercise and since church is only four blocks away, we can walk there," Peter said.

Robin told Peter and Lída to start sending Patty to Sunday school, which would help her learn English by exposing her to other children and to meet new friends. They had no clue what Sunday school was. People in Europe went to church only for the Sunday sermon. There was no Sunday school, no after church dinners, and no other activities ever offered. Peter and Lída started taking Patty to Sunday school, but she didn't like it because she could not understand the teacher or the children. She was coming home crying and unhappy, until they stopped taking her there.

One day while Peter was at work, Lída ran out of one ingredient she needed to prepare dinner. She gave Patty, who was almost five, some money and told her to go to the grocery store to get the item she needed. "You just need to give the sales clerk money," she said, "and they will give you some change back. You don't even need to talk to them."

The grocery store was only about four blocks down Main Street, but across the railroad tracks. "Make sure to look both ways before crossing the tracks. If you see a train, wait for it to pass before you cross," she told her.

A member of the church was driving by and saw Patty on her way back from the store. The lady thought Patty was lost or had run away. She stopped and tried to offer her a ride home, but Patty just put her head down and kept walking. The lady came to their house and told Lída in a panicked voice, that Patty was walking on the street alone. Lída was trying to explain that it was okay, that she had sent her to the grocery store. In the meantime, Patty had returned. The lady must have told people in church about the incident, because Robin immediately came over to explain they could not do that. Peter and Lída did not understand why, it was only one single item. There should be no reason why a child could not accomplish this simple task - their parents used to send them to the store when they were little. It was a common thing to do back in Czechoslovakia. But it created a lot of commotion, and they figured out it would be better not to do that or they could be considered bad parents.

Soon, they had to start paying rent which was $200 per month, utilities included. Peter was making between $600 and $650 per month. Money was tight, but they were managing. A few months after they came to Beach, Sam and Robin took Peter's family to the doctor for a routine checkup. A few weeks later, the medical bill for $340 arrived. Peter's entire two week paycheck, including money from their pocket, was used to pay the bill. They didn't have one penny for two weeks until the next paycheck arrived. They were not aware they did not have to pay the bill immediately or did not need to pay the entire amount at once.

Chapter Thirty-Seven

DIFFERENT CUSTOMS

At the beginning, cooking was difficult for Lída since she could not read the labels and did not know what was in the cans. One time she opened a can of food and dumped the contents in the pan to fry. The food was burning while she was mixing it and was not edible. Sometime later they found out it was pumpkin pie filling. Another time she opened a can of beans assuming it was an entire meal. She served it on a plate and they ate it with bread for lunch. There were many different items in cans and containers they had never seen before and did not know how to use. There were different salad dressings with pictures showing the contents being poured on lettuce or fruits, but it tasted horrible when they tried it. One day they opened a large can of tomato juice. The only juice they had ever seen was orange juice, which was sweet and tasted good. This juice was horrible - the taste startled them and made them gag. Peter ended up running to the kitchen sink to spit it out before he hurled. The kitchen cupboards and fridge were full of food that they did not know how to prepare, so they were kind of hungry. They did not know what most of it was and could not read the cans, but with time it all improved.

One thing they could not figure out was the American's fascination with corn. There were many cans of corn in their cupboards. There were also a lot of different kinds of corn in the grocery stores - small cans, large cans, plain corn, cream of corn, frozen corn cobs, fresh unpeeled corn - corn everywhere. Why is there so much corn they wondered? It looked very strange to Peter and Lída. Back in their homeland, people did not eat corn. It was grown in the fields to feed pigs and cows. Why would grocery stores sell pig feed and in such small amounts, they thought? One can or a few husks would not feed a pig.

One day they were invited to dinner at a friend's house and saw people eating corn. Everybody was commenting on how good it was. Peter tried one corn on the cob and it tasted exactly as he expected pig feed would taste. It took a few years before they started eating corn and liking it themselves.

Some locals were trying to teach them English, but none of them spoke Czech. Slowly they all gave up except one lady named Jane Kowalski. She was doing a very good job and kept teaching them for the rest of their time in Beach.

When Peter started working on the farm, he needed to have a car to drive there since it was about 20 miles away. Someone from the church gave them a maroon 1969 Ford Galaxy 500. It was their car for the next six years.

"What about a driver's license?" Peter inquired.

"You can drive for three months with your Czech license before you need to get a new one," he was told.

The driver license examiner came to Beach once every two weeks. Pastor Sam scheduled an appointment for Peter to take the test.

"You need to bring your own car to the exam," Pastor Sam said. That seemed strange to Peter and made him nervous.

"How can I legally drive a car to take the test when I don't have a license? Am I going to get into trouble? What if I don't pass, do I have to leave the car and walk home?"

"No, you won't," Sam responded, laughing.

"But I cannot read or write English," said Peter.

"Don't worry about it; they have a test designed for people like you." Peter shrugged it off as another unusual behavior of American life - more proof of how simple and easy things were in America.

The test consisted of a number of pages with cartoon like drawings. For instance, one picture showed an intersection with two cars coming from different directions, and the next picture showed the cars in an accident. The third picture showed one car going through the intersection, while the other was waiting and the fourth picture showed the opposite scenario. Peter had to point at the correct picture. He could not believe his eyes as this was effortless, like a test for small children. There was no need to study, since it was pretty obvious which picture was correct. It is a miracle that there is not a lot more accidents in America, since anyone can pass this test, he thought. Then it dawned on him, there are not as many accidents in America as there were in his homeland, because the rules are simple and easy to understand. The driving regulations book in Czech was approximately 150 pages long, with many complicated rules difficult to memorize and understand. Students had to attend evening classes spread over an eight week period, before they were allowed to take the examination.

After the written test, Peter drove through the streets of Beach with the examiner. He passed the test and was given his first American drivers license, still not understanding how he could be allowed to drive away if he had flunked.

*

Peter was worried that he was not advancing in life while working for farmer Greg. He wasn't exposed to people, so he was not learning English as much as he would like. The work on the farm was repetitious, and soon he knew the daily chores that needed to be done. He worked alone all day, except the few minutes in the morning when Greg told Peter what he needed him to do. The only other time he came in touch with people was at noon, but talking during lunch was not allowed. Peter also wanted to find work closer to Beach, since gasoline was $2.28 a gallon. His car was only getting six miles per gallon before the carburetor was adjusted, therefore half of Peter's income was spent on gasoline driving to work.

The highlight of Peter's time working for farmer Greg was when Greg received a phone call from his neighbor, stating that his fence was down and his cattle were on the neighbor's land. Greg asked Peter if he could ride a horse. Peter explained to

Greg that he owned a horse in Czechoslovakia and felt he could hold his own. At that time, Peter did not know that Greg owned 60 head of cattle and four horses. He had never seen any other animals beside the pigs around the farm. Greg went behind the farmhouse and started yelling while beating a metal bucket with a wooden stick. Eventually Peter spotted four horses approximately two miles away running towards them. They saddled two of the horses, got in the pickup truck with the windows open, and started driving away while holding one horse on each side of the vehicle, through the window. They drove to the hills on the horizon, where the farmland changed into the Badlands, left the truck, and mounted the horses. They continued riding the horses for an hour until they found the hole in the fence where the cattle had escaped. Soon they spotted the cows with calves and started herding them together. The cattle were wild and running in all directions, trying to disappear into the rough ravines. Once some of the cattle had been rounded up and the herd was getting bigger, Greg stayed with the group to keep them together, and Peter had the opportunity to round up the stray cows. There were times when he had to ride the horse on a full gallop in order to cut the cattle off before entering the ravines. Peter was in his height of glory as he was herding, chasing, and pushing the cattle. He felt like a true cowboy in the American West. And to top it off, all this was taking place in the rough beauty of the Badlands of North Dakota.

Once the cattle were back on Greg's land and the fence was mended, Greg asked Peter to ride along the fence line, check for weak areas and fix them, while he returned to the farm. That made Peter even more euphoric as he realized that he would have to ride the horse all the way back to the farmhouse. Peter spent the next four hours riding along the miles of fences, exactly as he had always desired and dreamed. Peter was so excited about this adventure that when he returned home that evening, he wrote a detailed letter describing the magnificent experience to his brother back in Czechoslovakia.

...Greg's broken fence was like a gift from God to Peter and he felt like he was in Heaven...

*

Peter always kept his eyes open for better employment opportunities. Finally, he learned about a place close by, called Home on the Range for Boys in the small town of Sentinel Butte. They were looking for a farmhand. Peter applied for the job and was hired and gave Greg a two week notice. Peter was hired for $5.00 per hour, and this place was only half the distance of Greg's farm.

While working on the Boy's ranch, Peter became friends with the farm manager, Luke Brown, who moved to Beach from California with his wife and three children. He was hired the day before Peter's first day and was very interested in hearing about Peter's life in Czechoslovakia, their defection, and their occupations. One day he invited Peter and his family to his church to share the story about their defection from Czechoslovakia, and why they wanted to live in America. People in the church were amazed and fascinated.

Peter also told Luke about his favorite job as a lumberjack back in Czechoslovakia. Luke explained he had some relatives in Oregon, a state with a strong logging industry. His relatives offered to help Peter find a job as a lumberjack, if they moved there. Peter and Lída pondered the new opportunity and decided to move to Oregon, so Peter could make more money.

*

Peter and Lída were keeping in touch by mail with Zbyněk and his family, who were still living in the Gasthof in Austria. Peter described his love of America and how the people were all so friendly and helpful. He explained how the church had a house set up with furniture and all the other necessities they would need, even a car was provided. Peter wrote about the owner of the local movie theatre, who refused to take their money and allowed them to see movies for free, in an effort to help them learn English.

In the meantime, Zbyněk's family had applied for and been approved to live in Australia. After receiving upbeat letters from Peter about their new lives in America, Zbyněk and his wife, Irene, decided they would rather try their luck in America and notified the Australian Consul. Eventually, a First Lutheran Church in Taylor, North Dakota, only 80 miles east of Beach, decided to sponsor their family.

When Peter and Lída found out, they could not believe it. From the entire United States of America, their friends were being sponsored by a church so close to them. A pastor from the Church in Taylor asked Peter if he would go with them to pick Zbyněk's family up at the airport in Bismarck. It was a very exciting reunion for all of them.

Their two families spent free time and holidays together, enabling them to carry out some of their Czech traditions.

Chapter Thirty-Eight

ADVANCING IN LIFE

It was late April 1984, when Peter gave his two week notice at the Boy's ranch. They also informed people in church about their decision to move to Oregon. People in the church were worried about this transition and tried to talk them out of it. Pastor Sam thought Peter should go to the State School of Science in Wahpeton, North Dakota, to attend the plumbing course.

"You are a plumber by trade," Sam told Peter. "Why don't you get your license here in America?" Peter would not hear of it, and since he always hated school, he did not want to go back again. But Pastor Sam and his wife continued to worry, and encouraged Peter daily to attend plumbing school in Wahpeton or stay in Beach.

"The logging industry is down causing the unemployment rate in Oregon to sky rocket. If you get your plumbing license, you could have a good job!"

Peter was torn, not knowing what to do, and once again was waiting for the answer to come to him. And then - two days before they were supposed to leave for Oregon - the answer came. Lumberjacking was hard work and he knew he would only be able to do it for approximately ten more years. He decided to attend school to get his plumbing license first, so he had something to fall back on if needed, then he could go to Oregon and become a lumberjack. If he did not get his license now, school would be more difficult later. Now, their only problem was they could not move to Wahpeton until June, when the students from the current year graduated and an apartment for married students became available.

Peter's replacement at the Boy's ranch had already started, and Peter did not have a job anymore. He happened to run into Doug Kramer and his brother, Rick, who were carpenters. Peter had met them a few months earlier when they were roofing farmer Greg's barn. Doug was telling Peter he had heard they were moving to Oregon. Peter explained what had happened and that he needed work for a month until they could move to Wahpeton. Doug stated they would be building a new house in Wibaux, Montana, and could use some help. Peter agreed and started working on Monday morning for $6.50 an hour.

Early in June, the family moved to Wahpeton. They said thanks and goodbye to the people in Beach at their going away dinner. Pastor Sam and Robin borrowed a truck from Ben and Rose Carson, an older retired couple living in Beach, who had become Peter and Lída's friends. They loaded their furniture on the farm truck and drove across North Dakota to Wahpeton. Sam went with Peter to the school office and helped him register for the nine month plumbing course. They moved to an empty apartment in one of the college complex buildings, but school did not start for another three months and Peter needed a job. The next day, after Sam and Robin left, Peter and his family decided to drive around Wahpeton to see the town and look for employment opportunities. Wahpeton was a well-kept town with a population of 10,000 people. The whole family was excited and happy.

Peter was jokingly explaining to the children how to find a job.

"Drive around until you see smoke and then follow it. Smoke is an indication of a factory, and factories always need extra help."

Soon, they really saw smoke rising on the outskirts of town. Peter drove towards it until they came upon a farmer burning a wood pile in the field.

"Well, that is not the right kind of smoke," Peter told the children.

They followed the bypass road when they spotted a lot

more smoke rising on the north side of town. The smoke was coming from a sugar beet plant. Next to it was a factory called Wahpeton Canvas Company.

"That looks like a great place to ask for work," Peter said.

He walked inside and told the receptionist that he was looking for a job.

"Where are you from?" she asked. "You have an accent!"

"I am from Czechoslovakia."

"Please wait here, I will be right back," she exclaimed.

She returned followed by a smiling, friendly middle-aged man. To Peter's surprise, the man started speaking Czech to him, asking if he was alone.

"My wife and children are in the car," Peter replied.

"Let me get them," the man said and walked outside.

Lída was shocked when a Czech speaking person came to her window. His name was Eric Sherman, and he was the owner of the company, who was born on a farm in the Wahpeton vicinity. He had Czech ancestors who spoke only Czech to their children, so Eric did not learn English until he was in first grade. Peter was amazed that he still spoke fluent Czech. Eric told Peter the story about his mother, who always had a damp cleaning rag over her shoulder and if he came home from school and spoke English, she would snap the wet rag across his face. That was his motivation to continue speaking Czech until he left home.

Peter told him they defected from Czechoslovakia a year ago, and he was starting school in September. He was looking for work through the summer months until school started. Eric hired him for a night shift maintenance job. They became good friends for many years to come.

*

Peter and Lída decided to try to invite Peter's mom for a visit. They had heard about an international agreement that even the Communist governments signed, which stated the government was supposed to allow immediate family members to visit, even if some of them had defected. They sent an invitation letter to his mother and she applied for permission to leave Czechoslovakia and to everybody's surprise, she was approved. Peter thought she was allowed to leave because she was retired, and if she did not return, the Communists would not have to pay her retirement.

Peter's mother arrived shortly after his family moved to Wahpeton. They drove to the Minneapolis airport to pick her up. It was an exciting and emotional reunion, since they were not sure they would ever see each other again.

Peter worked the entire summer until school started, and then Lída took over and worked to provide for the family. When they moved to Wahpeton, Peter was the only one in the family who spoke a little English. Lída and the children didn't learn much because she was home with the kids all day, and the children were not exposed to English while they lived in Beach. That all changed when they moved into the college complex. The apartment building was full of young families with small children.

The children picked up English in a very short time. It was as if one day they had walked out of the apartment to play with other children and returned home speaking English. The whole family went through a transition of language changes. At first they all spoke Czech, and then the parents spoke Czech while the children responded in English. That raised quite a few eyebrows when they were out in public. Eventually, the whole family spoke English all the time. Initially, Peter and Lída tried to prevent the children from losing their native tongue. When the children communicated in English, they made them repeat it in Czech, but with time it was getting harder for the children to do, especially after starting school. It became a losing battle and eventually, Peter and Lída gave up.

Peter's mother stayed with them for the entire year, while Peter was going to school. She found a job working nights, so she and Lída could take turns taking care of the children.

The first two weeks in school were the most frustrating times in Peter's entire life. He received a stack of school books that he could not read. The entire week, he sat in class with his mouth gaping open, unable to understand a word the teachers were saying. When the students were told to take notes, Peter had no idea what he was supposed to do. He felt like an idiot, was frustrated, and mad at himself. At the end of the first week, he came home from school, threw the bag with the books in the corner, and swore never to go back there again.

Lucky for him, his mother was there and gave him a *parent pep talk*, "You can do this - it will work out - you will get it - you are a smart boy - you will see, it will get better!" Peter was twenty-nine years old at that time.

He thought about it over the weekend and calmed down, deciding not to let his language barrier beat him. When he was in grade school, Peter used to sit in back of the class to hide from his teachers and do as little as possible. Now he sat in the second row to be closer to the teacher, so he could see and hear better. Peter had a fear that his language barrier was going to put him at the bottom of the class, but refused to let that happen. He carried his Czech-English dictionary with him at all times. Not only did he have to learn the subjects, he also had to learn the English vocabulary.

Peter locked himself in the bedroom each day after school to study. He studied as much as he could - he studied at night - he studied on the weekends. After they went grocery shopping, he hurried home to study, or when they took the kids to the park for a walk, as soon as they returned, he studied.

The subjects included Plumbing, Cooling and Heating, Electric, English, Math, and others. Shop class was the easiest subject for Peter, because they were learning how to run the pipes and install plumbing fixtures, which he already knew from his years of plumbing in Czechoslovakia. However, he had to memorize the English words for plumbing components. Words like pipe, wrench, valve, fitting, sink, drain, vents, water supplies, etc... When he started school, he did not know any of these words. Peter was studying his books so much, he started memorizing the shape of the words.

The teachers were giving tests all the time. Peter soon realized that taking tests in America was simple. The tests had multiple choice or true and false answers. They give you the answers he thought, you just have to pick the correct one. In

Czech no such tests existed, their questions required the student to write out the entire answer. The English words began to look more and more familiar to Peter. Even if he didn't know what the word meant, he recognized what it looked like. Some words were longer than others and some were shorter. Some words had different groupings of letters. Some words were repeated many times in his textbooks. When he saw a familiar word in one of the answers on his test sheet, he marked that answer.

His hardest subject was Introduction to Modern Business. During one class the teacher explained two lessons at once, and in the next class they were given two tests. There were a total of 30 questions on each test. The students had 50 minutes to answer 60 questions. Due to his word translation, Peter could not finish the test on time. His teacher noticed and told him he could take the tests in the library with one-on-one supervision. Peter welcomed the opportunity and started taking all of his business class tests in the library, with no time limit. After the initial struggle, Peter started doing well on all tests and his reading and writing skills improved tremendously. At the end of the first term, he had all A's except one B in Introduction to Modern Business. At the end of the second term, he had all A's and one B in Archery class. Peter had all A's on the final term.

There were three different books just for plumbing class. One of these books had 380 multiple choice and true or false questions, with the answers written in the back. Peter studied this book so much, that he had memorized all the questions and answers without even realizing it. One day Peter's plumbing teacher, Mr. Adams, told the students to open the book. He started randomly reading questions, calling on students for the answers. If the student gave him the right answer, he picked another question. If the student did not know the answer, the teacher asked if anybody else knew. Peter seemed to always know the right answer.

The teacher was impressed and said, "Let's see how much you really know!" He asked the question and before he could read the answers, Peter said "B." The teacher was surprised and asked a different question, and Peter responded "C" before the answer was read. They both began to realize, that Peter had memorized the entire book.

"Just for fun - what is the answer to question number 84?"

"D" Peter replied.

"Question number 212?"

"A" was his response.

Everybody - including Peter himself - was surprised and could not believe it.

One day his classmates told Peter about a school dinner he and his wife needed to attend. He did not understand what it was about and did not want to go, because he and his wife did not feel comfortable around others, due to the language barrier. They were still experiencing many embarrassing times when people talked to them and they did not know what was being said. Since Peter's friends were also invited to this dinner, he felt more comfortable and eventually decided to go.

The dinner was hosted for the students on the Dean's Honor Roll, which Peter did not know anything about. After dinner, the students were called individually to the podium in front of the dining room. The student's name and grade point average was announced as they received their recognition. Peter was one of the last ones to be called and was awarded a plaque for having a 3.85 average. The Dean said a few words about him being from a foreign country and having defected from a Communistic government. The people in the room stood up and were applauding and whistling as the Dean presented Peter his plaque. Both Peter and the Dean became emotional and embraced. That was the first time Peter had touched another male, other than a hand shake. Friends in his class continued to tease him for a long time for being 'fresh with a man!'

Peter's brother, Standa and his family saying goodbye to his mother at the airport in Prague. She is flying to America for the first time in 1984.

Lída preparing the car for their move to Colorado after Peter's graduation from plumbing school in Wahpeton, ND.

Peter with his mom, Jarka, and Patty on graduation day. He is wearing the same suit he had when they ran across the border and also for the interview with the U.S. Consul.

Wahpeton, ND during a visit in 1987.

Chapter Thirty-Nine

SEARCHING FOR PLACE TO SETTLE

Job openings for plumbing apprentices were posted on the bulletin board located in the classroom. Plumbing companies from Minnesota and the Dakotas were looking for workers. The posted beginning wages were usually around $4.00 per hour. There was also an opening for an apprentice with a company from St. Paul, which was installing fire sprinkler systems. The job was offering $7.25 per hour, with excellent benefits. Three of Peter's friends called the number and set up a job interview for the following weekend. When they returned to school on Monday, they talked about the opportunity. The pay schedule and benefits were far superior to anything the plumbing shops were offering. His friends told Peter that the owner was looking for somebody like him, who already had experience installing pipes and could run jobs as a foreman in a short period of time.

The Administrator for foreign students who was helping them write their resumes, told Peter to send a copy of his grades from the first two terms and a letter of intent. Peter mailed it to the owner of the fire protection company.

The first week in May before school ended, Peter and two friends, Ron and Dan, asked for a week off to go job hunting. They were granted leave and drove to Denver, Colorado, where Ron had some relatives. From there they traveled all the way to Phoenix, Arizona, where he had even more relatives. They visited plumbing shops in Denver, Frisco, and Breckenridge, Colorado, and then drove through Flagstaff and Sedona, to Phoenix, Arizona. Every plumbing shop they visited wanted to hire them. Ron liked Sedona and wanted to move there. Peter liked the Rocky Mountain area and decided to move his family over there after graduating. After returning, Peter described the beautiful mountains to his wife. There was also a letter waiting for him from the fire protection company in St. Paul. The letter stated the owner was very interested in hiring him. He was looking for somebody with experience and felt Peter had it. The owner, Fred, asked him to call right away to set up an interview, but Peter and Lída never responded because they decided to move to Colorado.

Peter's mother returned to Czechoslovakia two days after he graduated from plumbing school. They began to prepare for their move to Colorado. They packed their necessary bedding, fragile possessions, and camping supplies in the car.

Eric, Peter's friend and owner of the Wahpeton Canvas Company, told them they could store their furniture in one of his warehouses.

"I have semi-trucks driving all over the United States," he said. "When you find a place to live and settle down, give me a call and I will have one of my drivers drop off your furniture."

The students graduating from plumbing school had to have 8,000 hours of on-the-job training, before they were allowed to take the state test and become journeyman plumbers. Peter's plumbing teacher, Mr. Adams, was good friends with the State Plumbing Inspector in Bismarck, North Dakota, and explained to him that Peter already had six years of plumbing experience and held a journeyman license in Czechoslovakia. The inspector told Mr. Adams that if Peter gave him a copy of his journeyman license with a translation, he would let him take the test as soon as he graduated.

The test consisted of three parts: a written part, designing a complete plumbing system for a multi-level building, and an oral test with the inspector. Peter used seven of the eight hours he was allowed for the test. The test was very hard and he was sure he would not have passed, had he not been fresh out of school. Peter scored 98 percent on the test.

While he was in plumbing school, Peter's friend Luke from the Boy's Ranch, quit his job. He moved his family to New Salem, located west of Bismarck, to manage a dairy farm. After Peter and his family left Wahpeton, they drove to New Salem and stayed with Luke and his family overnight. The next day Peter left his family there, while he took his test in Bismarck. Peter went back to New Salem to pick his family up, then drove to Beach to say goodbye to their friends.

They decided to spend a week moving to Denver, and planned to stop in the Black Hills of South Dakota to visit historical places that Peter had read about, while he still lived in Czechoslovakia. They visited the historical town of Deadwood and went to Number 10 Saloon where Wild Bill Hickok had been shot. They stopped to see Wild Bill's and Calamity Jane's gravesites, which Peter had seen pictures of in his books about the Wild West. They also visited Mount Rushmore to see the carvings of the four United States Presidents in the mountain. He had seen a picture of Mount Rushmore as a youth, but never dreamed he would see it with his own eyes. They drove through Custer State Park, stopped at the historical ghost town of Rockerville, and toured Keystone, Hill City, and Crazy Horse Monument.

Peter liked the Black Hills, the vast open prairies, and the nearby Badlands.

"Let's settle in Rapid City," he told Lída.

But her heart was set on Colorado with the beautiful Rocky Mountains Peter had described to her before, so they continued on through Wyoming to Denver. They drove to the plumbing shop in Breckenridge, Colorado, to work for the man Peter had talked to while looking for a job a few weeks earlier.

But the man was just shaking his head, "I don't know what happened, but I don't have any work!"

Peter visited all the other places he stopped at before, and all the plumbing managers were saying the same thing.

"We have been in business for 20 years and have never experienced this before - all of the construction has stalled - we are laying people off." The Denver area was at the beginning of a slump in the construction industry.

Lída and Peter's mom had saved approximately $1,200 from their paychecks, but the money was quickly running out. The family had been on the road for three weeks now. At first they stayed in motels, then in campgrounds, and eventually slept in the car.

The car appeared to be closer to the ground everyday as the springs were compressed from the excess weight. They found a small log that Patty placed under the bumper every night, while Peter and Lída lifted the back of the car, to ease the weight on the springs.

The family's fully loaded Ford Galaxy 500, somewhere in Wyoming.

Peter was eventually offered a job doing maintenance in an apartment building complex. He was offered $7.20 per hour, and an apartment in the complex for only $400 a month. Peter decided he wanted to think about the opportunity and said he would call the employer back. He discussed it with Lída and made a few other job inquiries, but the situation was not looking very good, so the following day, Peter called the owner of the apartment complex back and told him he could not take the job. The owner offered to increase the pay to $7.50 an hour, while lowering the rent to $350. Peter and Lída seriously considered the offer, but eventually decided to go back to Rapid City to try their luck there.

They arrived in Rapid City and spent their first night at a campground. The next morning they packed up their tent, which was set up on a hill overlooking the town. They drove into town where Peter bought the local newspaper to search the classifieds for a place to rent. They found a duplex for $240 a month in a section of town called Star Village. Peter went to a pay phone and called the number listed in the advertisement. The owner gave him the address and directions, saying he would be there in 30 minutes. They rented the two bedroom duplex on the spot, and lived there using their camping gear until their furniture arrived.

On Monday morning, Peter went to Job Service and was told about a company looking for a journeyman plumber. Job Service called the owner and set up an interview for that same day. Peter started working the next day for $8.50 an hour, and was one of 30 people working for Dave's Plumbing. He was teamed with another journeyman named Jack.

Peter's family enjoyed living in Rapid City. Lída found a few part time jobs which she worked in the evenings, after Peter came home from work and could take care of the children. They spent weekends in the Black Hills, where they met many interesting people and found beautiful places. Peter was able to fulfill one of his lifelong dreams by purchasing his first gun, a six-shooter with a hip holster.

He will never forget the man they once met on the outskirts of Rapid City. He was performing in shootouts during the summer tourist season in Rockerville and looked like a true cowboy from the Wild West. He also resembled the actor Lee VanCleef and it turned out he had been his stunt double in many movies such as "The Good, The Bad, and The Ugly." The man showed Peter how to do tricks with his six-shooter.

*

One day Peter answered the phone and it was their good friend Jana, a movie director from Czechoslovakia, with whom they used to share their common interests of America. Her brother immigrated to Canada sometime in 1969. Jana told Peter she and her daughter were visiting him in Canada and had decided not to return to Czechoslovakia. They had talked to the Canadian Immigration office, filled out the necessary papers, and applied for political asylum. The Canadian authorities told them it could easily take six months before their paperwork would be processed. In the meantime, they were not allowed to stay in Canada, which meant she was not permitted to get a job and her sixteen-year old daughter could not go to school. Jana asked if it would be possible for them to stay with Peter and his family, while their paperwork was being processed.

Peter and Lída agreed, and Jana and her daughter Brenda arrived by Greyhound Bus in early September of 1985. They both spoke English well. Brenda was a very smart child and wanted to be in school, so Peter took them to the local high school and talked to the principal explaining their situation. He asked if it would be possible for Brenda to attend school, until they returned to Canada.

The Principal agreed, "Of course - we cannot let her be without an education!" She started school the next week.

Peter called the Immigration services in Minneapolis and explained Jana and Brenda's circumstances, while asking if they could apply for political asylum in the United States. He was told that she would have to fill out the applications and mail in the paperwork. After the applications were received, Jana was notified of a meeting with an Immigration officer who came to Rapid City once every two weeks. They were both approved and given a Green Card and Social Security number, which made it possible for Jana to apply for work. This entire process took only approximately four weeks.

The duplex Peter's family was living in was small. The living room, kitchen, and two bedrooms were tiny. It was okay for a family of four, but with two additional people it would be too crowded. Peter and Lída decided to give Jana and her daughter their bedroom. It would be easier for them to sleep in the living room, since he had to get up early for work and Lída made him breakfast and lunch at that time.

The work load at Dave's Plumbing started to diminish and the manager was not contracting any new jobs. He was letting his plumbers go one-by-one, until only Jack and Peter were left. A few weeks later Dave informed the guys he was out of work. He told Peter to apply for unemployment and he would call him back as soon. Jack, who was married to Dave's cousin, stayed on working on a day-to-day basis.

Peter did not want to be collecting unemployment and went directly to Job Service again. There was an opening with a different company called Sheescie's Plumbing. Once again, the interview was set up for the same afternoon, and Peter started working the next day. The manager asked Peter how much he was making at Dave's Plumbing. After he told him $8.50, the manager offered him $7.50 per hour. Peter accepted the job but was worried because there were rumors about construction work slowing down.

Peter remembered the name of the fire protection company from Minnesota, which had a sister company in Rapid City, and decided to check it out. He looked up the address, walked into the shop and talked to Matt, the President of the company. Matt told Peter that work was pretty slow at that time, but Fred in St. Paul was very busy and could use somebody skilled like him. Peter remembered their unpleasant experience picking up his mother from the Minneapolis Airport during rush hour. At that time, the family had decided they would never move to a big city, since they preferred the country. Besides, he already had a job and was just checking other options.

Every so often, Peter would call his teacher at the plumbing school to tell him where he was and what he was doing. In the meantime, Fred, the manager of the fire protection company Peter had mailed his resume to, was trying to locate him. He continued to contact the school checking on Peter's whereabouts, but every time he tried to contact him, they were already gone as they were on the move. Now Fred found out that Peter was in Rapid City, and called to offer him a job in St. Paul.

Peter's response was, "No thank you, we really like this area and don't like big cities," but Fred would not take no for an answer. He would call all times of the day trying to persuade him to accept the job. Peter continued insisting they did not want to move.

One day Fred called and said, "If I purchase you an airline ticket, would you come to St. Paul and let me show you what I have to offer?" Peter felt he had nothing to lose, and would enjoy the opportunity to see a little bit more of America. Peter and Lída discussed it and the next time Fred called, Peter agreed.

The ticket was mailed and Peter boarded the plane for Minnesota early on Saturday morning, October 12, 1985. Fred was waiting for him at the airport and they spent the entire day together. Fred showed him the company office, pay schedule, and benefits he had to offer. He also took Peter to one of the construction sites and showed him the drawings of the fire sprinkler system. They had lunch together and in the evening, he took Peter back to the airport. Fred offered a starting wage of $9.25 an hour, with three weeks paid vacation after one year, eight paid holidays, and medical and dental insurance. Once Peter started running his own jobs as a foreman, he would get $2.00 an hour raise. He would still have to go through the apprenticeship program for installing the fire sprinkler systems, but as long as he studied the books and took his tests, he would get an average pay raise of $0.70 every six months. Peter and Lída discussed the opportunity at length and decided to take the job.

They explained the situation to Jana and asked her if she wanted to stay in Rapid City or move to St. Paul. She said they would move with them. Peter called Fred and accepted the offer. Fred offered to find a rental for them, asking how many bedrooms they would need. Peter told him they would need three bedrooms to accommodate their living situation.

He started working for the fire protection company on

October 25, 1985, about two years after arriving in America. All projects were out of town so Peter left for work early on Monday mornings, worked ten hour days, and returned home on Thursday nights.

Lída's parents, Karel and Vlasta, during their first visit to America in 1985.

Peter, Lída, and Patty in front of their first house purchased in 1987 in White Bear Lake, MN. The picture was taken by their son, Peter.

Chapter Forty

VISITORS

Lída's parents were very angry at Peter after his family defected from Czechoslovakia. He had taken their daughter and grandchildren away - not just to the next town - but halfway across the world to America, the country the Communists hated most. Peter could sense the hostility and anger towards him in letters they received from her father. On the other hand, Lída's mother and sister were pleading with them to come back to their homeland, telling them to think about their children who would end up homeless, poor, and begging for food, living on the streets. It was obvious that Communist propaganda was deeply embedded in their heads.

Peter and Lída invited her parents to come to America for a visit. One of the questions on the American visa application asked if the applicant was a member of a terrorist, fascist, or Communist organization. Vlasta marked it yes since she was a proud Communist, but she was granted a visa by the U.S. Consulate anyway. They arrived in Minneapolis a few weeks after Peter's family had moved there from Rapid City. The place they were renting was a three bedroom duplex in St. Paul, and for three months, five adults, one adolescent, and two children would be living there together.

On the way from the airport, Karel was already fascinated by the size and amount of cars, the width of the roads, the large number of gas stations, restaurants, churches, and stores. He was surprised by how colorful everything was. Vlasta didn't say much, but it was obvious how startled she was with the sights around her. Everything was the total opposite of what she had expected.

A few days later, Peter and Lída took them to a local grocery store. They entered the building in the produce section. The store was brightly lit and there were large piles of oranges, bananas, red and green apples, grapefruits, pineapples, peaches, grapes, strawberries, blueberries, watermelons, and vegetables. Every kind of fruit and vegetable they knew, and many they did not even know existed. There were aisles upon aisles filled with food - flour, sugar, salt, bread in many sizes and brands - and not just one of each. The meat department was loaded with packaged meats, poultry, and fish - not behind the counter - just laying there in the open to touch, pick up, and select. Peter couldn't help himself and had to rub it in a little - he picked up a big package of nice meat and stated, "This costs less than one hour of my wages!"

The color disappeared from Vlasta's face and she turned white as a ghost! She walked along silently - didn't say one word. After they came home, she went straight into their bedroom, and stayed there for three days. She came out to eat and use the bathroom, but did not take part in any family conversations or activities. She never talked about it and they did not know what was going through her head at that time. Did she realize that she had spent her whole life as a victim of Communist propaganda and lies? Was she upset with the party? Was she disappointed that America wasn't the way she believed it would be? Was she happy that her loved ones were living in a better place? Was she mad at herself for being wrong? They didn't know and Vlasta never explained.

Three months later, Lída's parents returned back home to Czechoslovakia. Jana and her daughter Brenda received asylum and were approved to stay in America permanently. They moved to Santa Monica, California, where they had some distant relatives. The lives of Peter's family slowly settled into an everyday routine. Their children were in school now, and Lída worked at Burger King while continuing to look for a better job, eventually ending up in the medical field.

Peter was an apprentice for only two weeks before Fred

advanced him to foreman and he began running jobs. The company was growing and needed more employees. Peter told Fred about his friend Jack from Rapid City, and Fred hired him. The company continued to grow and Peter told Fred about his friends from the school in Wahpeton. One year went by and Peter's three friends Mark, Ben, and Doug, graduated from the HVAC course, which they took after completing the plumbing course. Because of Peter's recommendation, Fred hired all three of them. In the meantime, Peter's Czech friend Zbyněk and his family were still living in North Dakota. When another position with the company opened, Peter mentioned what a good worker and family man he was. Fred decided to hire Zbyněk, and assisted his family with their move to Minnesota.

As the company grew, there was a need for a Labor Superintendant to coordinate the entire field, working with different crews of craftsmen. In 1987, Peter was promoted to that position. That same year, Peter and Lída fulfilled their American dream by purchasing their first house in White Bear Lake, Minnesota.

Chapter Forty-One

AN AMERICAN PATRIOT

One day Peter and his family went to a rodeo in St. Paul. When the National Anthem was being sung, they honored the American flag by holding their hand over their hearts, which was always a very emotional experience for them. Unknown to Peter, one of his co-workers was seated on the opposite side of the arena with a friend. They were both upset due to a group of people who were talking, laughing, and showing disrespect during the anthem.

Peter's co-worker saw him and pointed them out to his friend stating, "Look at that family. They are foreign, but are paying respect to the flag, while these red-blooded Americans don't have enough courtesy to show any respect at all."

The following Monday at work, the co-worker asked Peter, "I saw you this weekend at the Rodeo and I would like to ask you a question about something I don't understand, but I don't want to offend you?"

"Go ahead."

"Why would you honor the American flag when you are not from here and you have your own flag and anthem?"

"It is very special and touching for us to finally be free and be able to honor the American flag!" Peter replied. "We left everything and everyone we love behind - we risked everything we had, including our own lives - for the *privilege* to call the American flag *our* flag and the American Anthem *our* anthem."

The End

EPILOGUE

After five years of living in America, the young family was eligible to apply for United States citizenship. The process consisted of an oral test with an Immigration officer, which lasted approximately one hour. It included questions about the U.S. Constitution and its amendments, structure and function of the U.S. government, Civil War, different U.S. presidents, term lengths of senators and congressional representatives, whose faces appear on American currency, and many other similar questions. Peter and Lída passed the exam and they all became United States citizens.

In 1989, after 41 years, the Communists lost power across Eastern Europe. The new times brought many changes, and the country of Czechoslovakia was divided into two, the Czech Republic and Slovakia. The country of Yugoslavia also ceased to exist.

Peter, Lída, and others were pardoned for their defections and cleared of their accused crimes, no longer being considered political criminals. Since that time, they can travel freely back and forth to their Czech homeland.

Peter's dad died as a result of a stroke on September 20, 1988, one year prior to Communists losing power. At that time, Peter could not return - even for his dad's funeral. One thing that Peter is saddened by most is that his dad never lived to see the end of Communism.

Twenty some years after their defection, Peter's father-in-law told him, "I am glad you guys are in America, because of all the mess that is happening around here." This made Peter feel as if he had finally received his blessing.

In 1994, they sold their first home and purchased a second house with six acres of land north of the Twin Cities, allowing them to own horses again, thus bringing their life *full circle*.

In 1999, Peter became Vice President of the fire sprinkler company. In 2002, after 16 years in the business, Peter and two of his friends started their own fire protection company.

Peter and Lída have worked their whole lives. They have never collected unemployment, food stamps, or applied for any government handouts. The family succeeded without any government assistance. The only people they ever depended on - were themselves.

Lída is working in the medical field. Patty graduated from college with a degree in Graphic Design, is married, and the mother of four children. Peter (son) joined the United States Marines after graduating from high school and was in the first wave of soldiers marching into Baghdad in 2003. He is now working as a foreman in the fire protection business.

APPENDIX A

The events of defection as seen through the eyes of a four-year old child. The following story was published in the book "Teens Write Through It" and earned Patty second place in the competition.

Escape

****

Written by Patty Vodenka

My name is Patty and I live in Minnesota. I just realized that some people don't understand. They think that immigrants are bad for our country. Some are, but there are others who come to make life better for their families.

Like my father, who came to America with two suitcases, one sleeping bag, a wife, and two kids. My father hated it in Czechoslovakia (now known as the Czech Republic). He didn't like the Communists telling people what to think and what to do. He didn't want his children growing up in such an overpowering world, such a horrible life. So he told my mom, even before they were married, that one day he would go to America and be free. It was a dream a lot of people shared, but not too many accomplished.

On June 17, 1983, my family accomplished this dream. We went to visit our cabin on the Vltava River. We often went to our cabin, so my grandparents, aunts, and uncles thought it was nothing more than an average trip. We could not tell anybody that we were planning to escape, because someone might try to stop us. If the government found out, they might have put us in jail. Then we never would have been free.

Fog flowed over the river. There was a quiet swish of the water as it lightly waved against the rocks of the cliffs. The moonlight flowed over the trees and into the window of our small, one-room cabin. My dad was out putting the bags in our little blue European car. He packed everything we could take with us. It was quiet in the forest. As I slept, I dreamt that my brother, Peter, and I were swimming in the river. I inhaled the sweet smell of the forest, when a whisper called to me. I slowly left the river and returned to the small room. I hesitantly opened my eyes. My mom leaned over me, whispering "It's time to go, Patty. Get up." I sat up. Next to me, my brother woke up whining. I looked around the small, cozy room. A few oil lamps were lit, hanging from the wall. As my eyes adjusted to the light, I looked around and saw all the drawings and carvings my grandfather had done. I did not know that this would be the last time I would see those wonderful creations.

I looked out the window. It was still dark. I was confused; it was too early to go anywhere. My mom handed us some buttered bread and a glass of water. After we ate, she helped us get dressed. Dad came in. "Hurry," he whispered, then he left again.

We finished our bread, blew out the candles, and rushed to the car. My dad turned around and looked one last time at the dark river and the shadowy cliffs. The run-down old cabin stood lifeless. I didn't think about it then, but now I understand. My father grew up in that cabin. It was the most beautiful place in the world.

Once in the car, Peter and I fell asleep. We slept most of the way. A few hours later, my mom woke us. It was raining. She frantically got us into our raincoats, but since she couldn't reach us from the front seat, she had to come around and open the door. My mom wouldn't let me take my umbrella, or even my doll. I complained, of course, because my umbrella was pretty and it was raining. The trunk closed and my dad ran up behind my mom. "Quick," he said in a panicked voice, "They know we are here and they are coming." My mom pulled my brother out of the car and gave him to my dad. She dragged me out next and didn't bother to close the door. I stopped and waited for my mom to get a bag out of the car. My dad and brother started running.

I saw the doors swing open on and old, gray, run-down cement building. Dogs were barking, men were yelling. My mom grabbed my hand, and we took off after my dad and brother. They were already a good distance in front of us. In the dark, we couldn't see which way they went. My dad called to us to follow the sound of his voice.

We were running for our lives, not knowing what was going to happen. Not even knowing if we were running in the right direction. My heart was pounding, my little chubby legs running as fast as a four-year olds could. I was slipping on the mud, splashing in the puddles. We were running into a black hole. Flashlights from behind us and gunfire in front of us lighted our way. I could hear feet splashing through the puddles. The dogs barked.

Then there was a scream somewhere up ahead. We kept running, not knowing if my dad and brother were hurt or even dead. We kept running into the darkness, not knowing how far we had gone, how far we had to go. Not knowing if they were going to catch or shoot us, like so many they had caught and killed before us.

Something appeared on the ground in front of us. It looked like a body. My dad? Oh, God, no, - it was a bag. My mom was freaked. I guess she wanted to pick it up but didn't have time. Then the ground disappeared and we stumbled down a hill. I heard the water before I saw the creek. My mom picked me up by one arm and made her way slowly, dragging me across the water without being able to see just where she was stepping.

Once we got to the other side, we started up another hill. Flashlights shone down on us. Slipping, my mom pulled me up the muddy hill. As I turned my head, I saw beams of light and the shadows of men. The dogs still barked.

My mom ran faster because she knew they had a clear shot at us. We got to the top and then dashed into the dark woods before us. Black shadows reached for us, trying to hold us back. My mom was tangled in branches that held her like barbed wire. I looked back again; the flashlights shone through the trees. "Mom, they are coming," I whispered. I pulled on her, but instead of pulling her out, I ended up getting pulled in. I thought my eyes were closed, it was so dark. Finally, struggling blindly, we got out and started forward again, hoping we were going the right way. We moved quickly, but not too quickly. Then it was dark.

We looked around. What had happened? The flashlights. The flashlights had disappeared. Were the men going to sneak up on us? We had to be careful, moving quickly but quietly, so they wouldn't find us. Was it a trick? Were we supposed to think that they were gone, that we could slow down or stop, and then they would catch us? We hurried to get away. My dad's voice called out to us in the forest. We followed it.

After walking for some time, we made it to the edge of the forest, where we found my dad and brother. We were in some kind of field. My mom laid down the sleeping bag for Peter and me. We stood, frozen, wet, and very tired, waiting for mom to get the sleeping bag ready. It turned out that the yelling was my dad falling down into the creek. "I think the creek was the border," he said. My brother and I got out of our wet clothes and climbed into the sleeping bag. As I drifted off to sleep, I thought about what we had just been through, and I knew that I would never forget it.

Later that morning, my parents woke us. We walked over to some nearby houses. We were now in Austria. My brother and I were still wet. We had no dry clothing because my dad had dropped the bag. My dad ended up going back over the border to get the bag with the clothes. This was dangerous, because it was light now and he could have easily been caught.

We waited for my dad's friends, who had escaped before us, to come pick us up and take us away from the border of the world we had left behind. Sitting in the morning sun, we heard a noise that we had never heard before. It was a moose. The moose was looking out from the forest, screaming, as if it were telling us we were free. I remember this well-it was the first thing I saw after we were free.

While we were waiting for my dad to come back and our friends to pick us up, an old lady from across the street saw us. She called us into her house. She spoke only German, so we didn't really understand her. She gave us food and let us play with toys. We waited for about two hours in her garden until our friends finally came.

After staying at our friends' house for a while, we went to a Gasthof house. There, my dad got a job as a logger so we could get money to fly to America. The Gasthof gave us a room, three meals a day and money for fruit. We also met new friends who now live only half an hour away from us.

When we got enough money together, we came to Beach, North Dakota. People in the town sponsored us-and the rest is another story.

APPENDIX B

Victims of Communism 1948-1989

A memorial to the victims of Communism in Czechoslovakia, erected in 2002 in Prague, Czech Republic, on the foothills of the area called Petřín.

Victims of Communism 1948-1989. As stated on the plaque below: 205,486 citizens were sentenced to prison or labor camps, 248 were executed, 4,500 died in prisons, 327 were killed while trying to cross the border, 170,938 defected successfully. These numbers still continue to grow as more documents and archives are becoming accessible. The exact number of victims will probably never be known, as the STB destroyed many documents during the fall of Communism.

The memorial to the victims of Communism is dedicated to all victims, not only those who were jailed or executed, but also those whose lives were ruined by totalitarian despotism.

Listed below are various occurrences of people killed while attempting to cross the border, from the most to the least common cause:

*Shot
*Killed by electric fences
*Drowned
*Committed suicide before being arrested
*Flying contraptions that were shot down or destroyed by border planes
*Died crashing vehicles while trying to break through border barriers
*Killed by mine explosions
*Mauled to death by border guard dogs
*Died from a heart attack after being arrested

APPENDIX C

History of STB

The STB was a political tool created only 1½ months after WWII, on June 30, 1945, by the Communist party. It was a non-uniformed force used for liquidation of members from opposing political parties and other individuals. After 1948, the STB became the strong-arm of Communist terror.

As early as the years of 1945-1948, the STB was performing illegal actions benefitting the Communist party, such as installing listening devices in opposing party leader's homes and places of business. They were also manufacturing false accusations and "proof" of illegal activities against the country, including assassinations, to clear a Communist's path.

The STB used methods like torture, blackmail, kidnappings, and drugs, to achieve confessions. After 1948, those actions became part of the everyday operations, strongly encouraged and supported by the Russian advisors, who were members of the NKVD,[*] which was the predecessor of the KGB.[**] These methods were commonly used during the major processes, for example Milada Horáková, Rudolf Slanský, and many others. Cases of accused people dying or becoming crippled as a result of torture while being interrogated were not only tolerated, but even preferred, as in the case of the Priest Josef Toufar, philosopher Jan Patočka, etc…

---

[*] NKVD: Narodnyj Komissariat Vnutrennikh Del (Peoples Ministry of Internal Affairs) was the secret police of Soviet Russia. Its main function was to protect the state security of the Soviet Union, which was successfully accomplished through massive political repressions, Gulags, torture, and mass murders.
[**] KGB: Komitet Gosudarstvennoy Bezopasnosti (Committee for State Security) was the official name of the umbrella organization serving as the Soviet Union's premiere security agency, secret police, and intelligence agency from 1954-1991.

The STB, with the utmost probability, also carried out the assassinations and murders, such as Minister Jan Masaryk, Přemysl Coufal, Pavel Švanda, and others whose names never came to public view.

The STB built, operated, and overseen labor concentration camps filled with political prisoners, where STB members often carried out unimaginable acts of cruelty, terror, and killings.

The STB created and operated a spy network all over the world, with the strongest presence in Austria, Germany, England, and America. Kidnappings, like in the case of Bohumil Laušman, murder and blackmail was a common part of their operations.

After the fall of Communism in 1989, investigations of the STB organization revealed, that many of their interrogators were primitive individuals, with little or no education, no experience, and no knowledge of the basic laws, especially during the years of the 1950's - reign of Communist's greatest terror. Their only authority was the party and its wishes. The lack of abilities and proof of fictional crimes were compensated for, by executing inhumane and horrific methods during interrogations.

The STB was dismissed on Feb 1, 1990, by the Minister of Interior, Richard Sacher.

APPENDIX D

"Thank You America" Monument

A monument in the town of Pilsen, dedicated to the United States Army as a thank you for liberation from the German occupying forces in 1945, was erected after the fall of Communism.

APPENDIX E

Pionýr Promise:

I (name) solemnly swear before my comrades to work, learn, and live in accordance with the Pionýr laws, to be a good citizen to my loved country the Czechoslovakian Socialistic Republic, and protect the honor of the Pionýr organization under SSM (Union of Socialistic Youth), by my actions!

Pionýr Laws:

1. Pionýr is dedicated to its Socialistic country and the Communist party of Czechoslovakia.
2. Pionýr is a friend of the Soviet Union and the defender of advancement and peace across the entire world.
3. Pionýr admires heroism, hard work, and a battle.
4. Pionýr does his part in advancing Socialistic lands by his own actions, by learning, and doing hard work.
5. Pionýr is proud of its Pionýr organization of SSM.
6. Pionýr is preparing to enter the Union of Socialistic Youth.